REPRESENTING THE PEOPLE

COMPARATIVE POLITICS

Comparative Politics is a series for students, teachers, and researchers of political science that deals with contemporary government and politics. Global in scope, books in the series are characterized by a stress on comparative analysis and strong methodological rigour. The series is published in association with the European Consortium for Political Research. For more information visit <http://www.ecprnet.eu>.

The Comparative Politics series is edited by Ferdinand Müller-Rommel, Director of the Center for the Study of Democracy, Leuphana University; Emilie van Haute, Professor of Political Science, Université Libre de Bruxelles; and Kenneth Carty, Professor of Political Science, University of British Columbia.

OTHER TITLES IN THIS SERIES

Representing the People

*A Survey among Members of Statewide and
Sub-state Parliaments*

Edited by

KRIS DESCHOUWER AND SAM DEPAUW

UNIVERSITY PRESS

Great Clarendon Street, Oxford, OX2 6DP,
United Kingdom

Oxford University Press is a department of the University of Oxford.
It furthers the University's objective of excellence in research, scholarship,
and education by publishing worldwide. Oxford is a registered trade mark of
Oxford University Press in the UK and in certain other countries

Published in the United States of America by Oxford University Press
198 Madison Avenue, New York, NY 10016, United States of America

British Library Cataloguing in Publication Data
Data available

Library of Congress Control Number: 2013958252

ISBN 978–0–19–968453–3

Printed and bound by
Clays Ltd, St Ives plc

Links to third party websites are provided by Oxford in good faith and
for information only. Oxford disclaims any responsibility for the materials
contained in any third party website referenced in this work.

Acknowledgements

This book is the result of a large comparative project. It reports the results of a survey among members of both statewide and sub-state parliaments in fifteen countries. Legislators of seventy-three assemblies were invited to answer our questions and 2,326 responses could be used for the analysis. Bringing these data together was a huge enterprise to which many people contributed. In each of the fifteen countries addresses had to be gathered, invitations and reminders had to be sent out, party leaders and group leaders of the different parliaments had to be convinced, and in some places face-to-face interviews had to be conducted. This was a collective enterprise and that shows in the way in which the book has been put together. All the chapters are co-authored—there are thirty-three authors in total—and all the names appearing in the book are names of colleagues who have contributed to the preparation of the survey, its fieldwork, and the analysis of the data.

We have been able to prepare the survey and the book very carefully. The group met four times in Brussels, first to discuss possible themes to be covered in the questionnaire, the operationalization of concepts and methodological choices to be made, and a second time to discuss the draft questionnaire. A third meeting was devoted to the research questions for each of the chapters of the book and at a fourth and final meeting we discussed the draft chapters of the book. That was all made possible thanks to the financial support of the Belgian Federal Science Policy. The research scheme on Inter-university Attraction Poles has funded the PARTIREP project on participation and representation in modern democracies, of which the MP survey was an important part. We are very grateful for this support.

Most of the people who participated in the planning of the project also appear as co-authors of one or more chapters. We would, however, also like to thank the colleagues who did not contribute as authors to this book, but whose input was very important for setting up and for executing the project. We have very much appreciated the help and input of Marc Hooghe, Sofie Marien, Petra Meier, Lieven De Winter, Heinrich Best, Michael Edinger, Jacek Wasilewski, José Manuel Leite Viegas, Mónica Méndez Lago, Isabelle Guinaudeau, Tinette Schnatterer, Patrick Lengg, Oliver Strijbis, Emilie van Haute, Jonas Lefever, Teun Pauwels, and Michael Saward.

Our heartfelt thanks also go to all the members of parliament who agreed to answer our questions. We were a large group with many different research interests that all had to find a place somewhere in the questionnaire. Filling it in took roughly forty minutes. Many legislators did however take the time to do so, and that has resulted in a very rich set of data on the way in which members of parliament represent the people.

The headquarters of the project was the Political Science Department of the Vrije Universiteit Brussel. Time, financial support, and colleagues willing to help were always available. We would in particular like to thank Audrey André for the active and invaluable role that she played in supervising the fieldwork in fifteen countries and in seventy-three parliaments, and for her tremendous help in putting together a nice and clean database.

Kris Deschouwer
Sam Depauw

Contents

Contents

List of Figures

List of Tables

List of Contributors

Rudy B. Andeweg is a professor in the Department of Political Science at the University of Leiden

Audrey André is a post-doctoral researcher at the Department of Political Science of the Vrije Universiteit Brussel

Jonathan Bradbury is Reader in Politics and Head of the Department of Political and Cultural Studies at Swansea University

Didier Caluwaerts is a post-doctoral researcher at the Department of Political Science of the Vrije Universiteit Brussel

Daniele Caramani is Professor of Comparative Politics at the University of St Gallen

Karen Celis is Research Professor at the Department of Political Science of the Vrije Universiteit Brussel

Dag Arne Christensen is a researcher at the Stein Rokkan Centre for Social Studies at the University of Bergen

Olivier Costa is Senior Research Fellow at CNRS (Centre national de la recherche scientifique), Centre Emile Durkheim, Institut d'Etudes Politiques de Bordeaux, University of Bordeaux

Sam Depauw is Assistant Professor and Postdoctoral Researcher at the Vrije Universiteit Brussel. His research concentrates on political representation, on legislative and electoral studies.

Kris Deschouwer is Research Professor of Politics at the Vrije Universiteit Brussel. He is the central coordinator of the PARTIREP research project on Political Participation and Representation in Modern Democracies (<http://www.partirep.eu>)

Agnieszka Dudzińska is Assistant Professor at the Institute of Political Studies of the Polish Academy of Sciences in Warsaw.

Nikolaus Eder is a researcher in the Department of Government of the University of Vienna

Silvia Erzeel is an F.R.S.-FNRS post-doctoral researcher at the Institut de sciences politiques Louvain-Europe (ISPOLE) of the Université catholique de Louvain

André Freire is Professor at the Centre for Research and Studies in Sociology at the Instituto Universitário de Lisboa (ISCTE-IUL)

Michael Gallagher is Professor at the Department of Political Science of Trinity College, Dublin

Reuven Y. Hazan is Professor in the Political Science Department of the Hebrew University in Jerusalem

Gabriella Ilonszki is Professor of Political Science at Corvinus University in Budapest

Marcelo Jenny is a post-doctoral researcher at the Department of Government of the University of Vienna

Reut Itzkovitch Malka is a researcher in the Political Science Department of the Hebrew University in Jerusalem

Tor Midtbø is Professor in the Department of Comparative Politics of the University of Bergen

Wolfgang C. Müller is Professor of Political Science in the Department of Government, University of Vienna

Pablo Oñate is Professor of Political Science at the University of Valencia

Zsófia Papp is a research fellow in the Department of Political Behaviour, Hungarian Academy of Science

Jean-Benoit Pilet is Director of Cevipol research centre and professor in political science at the Université Libre de Bruxelles (ULB)

Corentin Poyet is research assistant at CNRS (Centre national de la recherche scientifique), Centre Emile Durkheim, Institut d'Etudes Politiques de Bordeaux, University of Bordeaux

Giulia Sandri is Assistant Professor of Political Science at the European School of Political Science of the Catholic University of Lille

Filippo Tronconi is Assistant Professor of Political Science at the University of Bologna

Peter Van Aelst is Professor of Political Science at the University of Antwerp

Luca Verzichelli is Professor of Political Science at the University of Siena

Cynthia M. C. van Vonno is a researcher in the Department of Political Science of the University of Leiden

Stefaan Walgrave is Professor of Political Science at the University of Antwerp

Bram Wauters is Professor in the Department of Political Science of Ghent University

Bernhard Weßels is Deputy Director of the research unit 'Democracy: Structures, Performance, Challenges' at the Social Science Research Centre, Berlin (WZB)

1

Representing the People in Parliaments

Kris Deschouwer, Sam Depauw, and Audrey André

1.1 REPRESENTATION AND DEMOCRACY

Modern democracy is basically organized through representation. Governing by taking into account the wishes and demands of the people is indeed put into practice by allowing the people to elect those who govern in their name. Elected assemblies are meant to make society present and to let it deliberate about its future policies. That does not mean that representation is the only way in which democracy can be organized. And it does not mean that all forms of representation are democratic. Democracy and representation are two different things. Yet these twin concepts have become deeply connected to each other since representation became the dominant form to organize democracy (Manin 1997; Ankersmit 2008; Keane 2009; Alonso, Keane, and Merkel 2011).

This representative democracy comes in many different ways. Within the family of representative democracies there is indeed a wide variety of procedures and institutions. Electoral systems—to state the most obvious—display many differences. And the different electoral formulae, district sizes, and thresholds can be seen in endless combinations. The literature on electoral systems has not only illustrated this variety but has also pointed at the influences of the electoral rules on the functioning of party systems (e.g. Duverger 1951; Lijphart 1994). The way in which members of representative assemblies are elected also strongly influences the way in which they perceive and fulfill their task. The size of the parliaments, the number of houses, and the length of the term are a few other elements of the institutional context that can shape the process and practice of political representation.

Yet what all representative democracies have in common is the very obvious fact that members of parliamentary assemblies are elected. There are some exceptions to that rule in countries where a (second) house of the parliament is not or not fully elected, but these do not even nuance the statement that representative democracy is organized today as *elected democracy*. Elections are the basic procedure by which the members of a society give the political elite the right to govern in the name of the people. Candidates for elected positions are now furthermore very seldom running on their own. Another obvious feature of the current organization of representative democracy is the central role played by *political parties*. Although individuals are elected, the process of representation is collective. Candidates and elected members of parliament belong to political parties and behave as such. Political parties select the candidates for elections. Political parties compete with each other by referring to their identity, to party ideology, to the party platform, and partisan proposals to convince the voters that their ideas, interests, and identities will be better represented by them than by another party. This allows the citizens to make a meaningful choice and to send out representatives whose actions and attitudes in parliament will be to a certain extent predictable. Elected members of parliament behave indeed mostly in a coherent way, by defending the same ideas as their fellow partisans and by voting in the same way. The ideological and programmatic banner and the implicit and explicit policy pledges that are related to them offer citizens the tools and mental shortcuts with which they can judge the degree in which the representatives and their parties have indeed kept their promises and can be given another term in power. Parties thus offer voters, candidates, and elected representatives easy shortcuts for organizing the dialogue between citizens and decision-making, for understanding what they want and what they do and for finding each other both on election day and between election days. Modern representative democracy is both elected democracy and party democracy (Ranney 1962; Castles and Wildemann 1986; Katz 1987; Manin 1997; Mansbridge 2003).

There is one other important yet obvious and therefore most often implicit characteristic of elected democratic representation: it happens within the territorial limits of the national state. The current form of democratic government did indeed develop with and within the boundaries of national states. The mobilization of citizens, the granting and expansion of voting rights and of the related democratic liberties, and the development of political parties as central actors in the organization of elections occurred in national states. The process of state formation itself deeply influenced the way in which and the degree in which societal cleavages, political parties, and voter alignments could develop (Lipset and Rokkan 1967; Flora, Kuhnle and Urwin 1999; Bartolini 2005).

1.2 DEMOCRATIC REPRESENTATION UNDER STRESS

This model of state-bound, elected, and partisan representative democracy appears today to be under stress. Modern democracy is widely believed to be in a state of crisis. Whether representative democracy can survive in its current form is a matter of concern, debate, and scientific research (e.g. Alonso, Keane, and Merkel, 2011). Part of that debate is not at all new, and reflects the fact that democracy and representation have empirically been connected to each other but are not identical. Quite crucial in this respect is the question whether representation can be a form of democracy at all. Representation makes the people present in an elected assembly, but at the same time takes the power of decision-making and deliberation away from them and endows it to an elite that is different from the people. Representation installs an elected aristocracy (Manin 1997; Urbinati 2011; Ankersmit 2008). The line between the representatives and those being represented will therefore always be in some way disturbed. All forms of representation imply misrepresentation. And therefore the normative question to what extent and even whether the representation is good or can be good (e.g. Dovi 2007) cannot be avoided. Discussions about descriptive representation or substantive representation search for ways in which the built-in gap between elected representatives and those represented can be kept as limited as possible. The classic distinction between delegates who receive a clear mandate from their constituency and trustees who can fill in their role more freely also searches for the best way to organize the linkage between the elected agent and the represented principal (Eulau et al. 1959; Pitkin 1967; McCrone and Kuklinski 1979).

Some recent debates do tap into that issue of the compatibility between representation and democracy. The populist critique questions the decent functioning of representation. Populism points at misrepresentation, at elites that do not truly represent, at political institutions and rules and checks and balances in which the people are hard to find and in which the people are not speaking the last word. Populism is indeed a vision of democracy in which the people themselves and not representatives at the end of a disturbed and crooked line should be the main point of reference (Taggart 2004; Mény and Surel 2002; Canovan 1999). Defenders of the 'deliberative turn' search for alternative ways to represent society. Deliberative assemblies can be put together by using random sampling, which guarantees every member of society an equal chance of being part of the representative assembly. And in the functioning of these assemblies the importance of debate and discussion for finding common solutions is stressed and contrasted with the sterile aggregation of preferences in the elected and partisan representation (Bächtiger 2005; Bohman 1996; Dryzek 2000).

Yet if in the course of the last decades the viability of representative democracy is being questioned, this is done with reference to recent empirical developments rather than to the broader debate about the democratic value of representation. These empirical developments involve very much the role of political parties and the territorial organization of the state, two of the cornerstones of the practice of representative democracy. As said above, the political parties are the main actors of representative democracy. They structure the electorate and the political competition, but also the political decision-making and the functioning of the parliament. Yet political parties appear to be in trouble. The indicators for supporting this statement are by now well known. Opinion polls have shown repeatedly that political parties are among the least trusted actors of modern democracy. The relevance of this is not to be underestimated. It means that the organizations that select candidates for elections, that organize the activities of those that have been elected, that form and support governments and that at the end of the term ask permission to do that again, are not at all seen as organizations that can be trusted. Yet it is exactly the electoral process that should give them the legitimate right to govern (Mair 2009).

Another well-documented indicator is the decline of party membership (Van Biezen, Mair, and Poguntke 2012). There are some nuances and there are some parties that are able to increase their membership numbers, but the general trend leaves no doubt about what is happening. The decline of membership numbers reflects, on the one hand, a gradual withering away of the party on the ground, of the party as an organization rooted in society and connected to other organizations. It reflects on the other hand the strengthening of the party in public office, of the party as an organization that governs (Katz and Mair 1995).

The loosening of the ties with the societal roots is being reflected in voting behaviour. Here also the story is well known and well documented. The erosion of group interests and group identities based on class and religion has broken the solid and obvious link between societal groups and the parties historically belonging to them and representing their identity and interests in the policymaking process. Voters therefore easily switch between parties and are attracted—often only temporarily—by new parties mobilizing on new issues or trying to challenge existing parties on their position (Lucardie 2000). The result is a volatile electorate, of many voters in search of a party that might be able to represent them. The result is parties trying to reposition themselves, to redefine and adapt their ideological appeal to a secularized and post-industrial society. The result is parties trying to identify who their voters are and how they might be able to recreate solid bonds with them (Dalton, Flanagan, and Beck 1984; Evans 1999; Franklin, Mackie, and Valen 1992; Kriesi 1998).

One of the indicators of this lower capacity of parties to organize and to mobilize the electorate is the 'personalization' of politics (Karvonen 2010; Colomer 2011; McAllister 2007). The notion is still fairly vague and refers to different evolutions, but most authors using the term and trying to assess the importance of personalization do stress the fact that a shift is taking place from the use of a partisan frame to a personal frame in the dialogue between voters and their elected representatives. Persons, personal characteristics, and personal actions that can differentiate politicians from their party (and from the other candidates) are becoming more important. And in this sense the process of personalization—even if the empirical evidence for it is so far quite mixed—also points at changing patterns of political representation and of legitimation of decision-making.

Changes in society, erosion of the boundaries between social groups and thus in the ideological language of partisan competition are very important evolutions that oblige parties to rethink and reshape their organizations and strategies. These are thus changes that thoroughly affect the way in which political representation can be organized. Yet the evolutions on the input side of political systems are not the only elements putting pressure on the traditional forms of partisan electoral representation. Parties are confronting distrust and volatile voters while simultaneously a number of important elements of the broader institutional context are subject to change. Among these is the fragmentation of the centres of power. Several European countries have recently gone through a territorial reorganization granting power in varying ways to sub-national entities. Political representation in these multilevel systems is a complex and 'compounded' affair (Tuschhoff 1999), with all but straight and clear lines between population and those representing it. In multilevel systems all levels have limited powers, share competencies with other levels, and have conflicts amongst them and sometimes inside the parties governing at different levels. Governments in multilevel systems can shift the blame because it is never easy to trace exactly where demands have been voiced and to which demands the policies are responding.

The gradual and slow but in the end quite substantial growth of the importance of the European Union level of decision-making also has important effects on the way in which parties can represent their voters. Parties are indeed increasingly torn between responsiveness and accountability to the voters on the one hand and demands to be 'responsible', that is, to act and to conduct policies that abide by rules and principles that are put forward by the institutions of the European Union and of other international organizations or agencies. There are very extreme examples of that in countries like Greece and Portugal that have been obliged to seek external financial help and whose policies are now closely monitored by a 'troika' of European Commission, European Central Bank, and International Monetary Fund. But the very existence of the European Union to which many crucial policy instruments have been transferred has added a new and quite complex locus of power to that of the sovereign national state. Especially governing parties need to be the agents of many principals and not only of their constituents. They have problems legitimizing their policies in terms of representation, in terms of responses to the principal that is the most important one in democracy—the people. For non-governing parties it is then easy to demonstrate that the elected elite does not truly represent but misrepresents the population (Mair, 2009; Mair and Thomassen 2010).

This is—in a nutshell—the inspirational background for the research on which we report in this book. While political representation is at the core of modern democracy, the debates about the crisis of democracy point at difficulties for creating a meaningful linkage between the population and the elites representing them. An interesting and crucial question is then how the representatives themselves perceive their role and task. The best way to assess that is by asking them.

1.3 SURVEYING MEMBERS OF PARLIAMENT

1.3.1 Case Selection

The chapters in this book are all based on new data that were gathered among members of parliament. The project was initiated by the research programme PARTIREP, an inter-university network financed by the Belgian Federal Science Policy (<http://www.partirep.eu>). The network is engaged in several research projects on the changing patterns of participation and representation in modern democracies. One of these projects was a cross-national survey among MPs, to which researchers from Belgium and from fourteen other countries were associated.

Fifteen countries have indeed been selected for the fieldwork, allowing for a wide variation of state structures, electoral systems, and party systems. Since the territorial (re)organization of the state was identified as one of the possible elements that affects the functioning of democratic representation, we have included the most important multilevel countries. These are the classic federal states, but also the more hybrid decentralized states and states with directly elected parliaments for special status territories. The multilevel countries—nine in total—covered are Austria, Belgium, France, Germany, Italy, Portugal, Spain, Switzerland, and the United Kingdom. The six other—unitary—countries are Hungary, Ireland, Israel, Norway, Poland, and the Netherlands.

In the nine multilevel democracies the PARTIREP project further surveyed a number of regional parliaments. In Austria, Belgium, and Switzerland all regional parliaments were included (except for Appenzell-Innerrhoden). In other countries a selection was made, observing a balance from the east and the west in Germany (i.e. Brandenburg, Lower Saxony, Rhineland-Palatinate, and Thuringia), from the north and the south in Italy (Calabria, Campania, Lazio, Lombardy, Tuscany, and Aosta Valley), and in Spain between autonomous regions with stronger and weaker regionalist traditions (Andalusia, Catalonia, the Basque Country, and Valencia).

The selection further takes into account variation in size, electoral institutions, and party control of the regional government. In France it proved feasible only to survey Poitou-Charentes and Aquitaine. In the cases of Portugal and the United Kingdom there are marked asymmetries in terms of regional representation. The autonomous regions of Madeira and the Azores (both included) have elected representatives at both the state-wide and sub-national levels, whereas mainland Portugal does not. Scotland and Wales (both included) have regional parliaments, whereas England does not. The selection of sub-state parliaments thus ranges from the lowest regional authority (in Portugal and the United Kingdom) to the highest (Belgium, Germany, and Switzerland) as captured by Hooghe et al.'s (2008) index, combining the self-rule and shared rule dimensions first identified by Elazar (1987). The self-rule dimension measures the scope of devolved policies, fiscal autonomy, and administrative decentralization at the sub-national level; whereas the shared-rule dimension taps into sub-national participation in the state-wide legislative and executive arena, with regard to fiscal control and constitutional reform. The total number of parliaments in which the survey was conducted is seventy-three.

The elected representatives in this selection are elected using a wide variety of electoral institutions. Some are elected using plurality or majoritarian electoral formulae; some under proportional representation; and others in hybrid mixed-member systems combining a nominal tier and a proportional tier. Some are elected in preferential systems where voters have the option to indicate a preference among co-partisans running under the same party label; others in non-preferential systems where voters do not have that option. In addition, they represent districts of various magnitudes, ranging from single-seat districts to at-large nation-wide constituencies in Israel and the Netherlands.

Of course electoral institutions are installed by parties, mirroring party systems, and in turn shape party systems (Colomer 2005; Duverger 1951). Third, the selection therefore represents various party systems, ranging from two-party systems to extreme multi-party systems. Many are mainstream parties; others are niche parties putting forward issues that were previously outside the scope of party competition (Ezrow 2010; Meguid 2010). Several countries include strong regional and regionalist parties, challenging the polity that they are part of. By including countries that differ widely in state structure, electoral institutions, and party systems the PARTIREP survey further observes a geographical variety that ranges from Norway in the north to Israel in the south; and from Ireland in the west to Hungary and Poland in Central and Eastern Europe. It includes long-standing democracies and new democracies like Hungary, Poland, Portugal, and Spain. Represented are populations as large as Germany's and as small as Norway's; ethnically homogeneous societies such as Poland and divided societies like Belgium and Israel. All fifteen countries are—except for Switzerland—systems of *parliamentary government* in that the cabinet can be voted out of office by any majority in the legislature by means of a (constructive) motion of no confidence (Strøm 2000).

1.3.2 Description of the Data

For each parliament in the selection, macro data has been collected on the level of the political system, the party, and the district. The electoral rules, legislative organization, and the balance of powers between the national and regional levels of government constitute the most important system-level variables. Party characteristics include the party's ideology, size of the parliamentary group, and candidate selection procedures. District characteristics focus on geographical location, population size, and surface. Gathering data on the level of the individual legislator further required a two-pronged approach. First, information on a legislator's socio-demographic background and career trajectory is publicly available and has been collected from official sources such as the parliamentary websites and 'who's who' guides. Background variables include age, education, previous occupation, previous political career, and leadership positions they hold in the party and in parliament.

Second, the PARTIREP survey examined legislators' attitudes and characteristic behaviours. Conceptions of representation were explored through questions on the democratic system, role orientations, and constituency definition. Self-reported behaviour includes their actions in parliament, in the parliamentary party group, and in the constituency. Particular attention was given to the extent and nature of contact between legislators within and across parliaments. The questionnaire also captured the campaign strategies they pursue and how vulnerable they estimate they are to electoral defeat. The study examines prominent election issues, including attitudes to economic issues and opinions on felony, gender equality, and immigration. General attitudes on the left–right dimensions of the policy space, devolution, and Europeanization were also sought. The study investigates how legislators go about their duties representing the people and how they see their political future.

The survey was designed with a closed-ended question format either presenting legislators with a scale or a limited number of options to choose from. Occasionally they were asked to fill out a number estimate or to specify what they think of when ticking the box 'other'. To develop the questionnaire input was received from a wide circle of legislative scholars and extensive pilot interviews with former politicians. To guarantee cross-national comparability the survey was kept rigorously constant in content. If required, the question wording was adapted slightly to better reflect countries' or parliaments' institutional peculiarities. In Israel and the Netherlands or Brussels and Geneva, for instance, reference is made to the local area instead of the district as legislators are elected in a single constituency. Teams of researchers in each of the participating countries continuously worked in close contact to translate the questionnaire into fourteen languages (including some regional languages). Teams from Belgium, France, and Switzerland collaborated on the French version; teams from Austria, Belgium, Germany, and Switzerland on the German version; teams from Italy and Switzerland on the Italian version; and teams from Belgium and the Netherlands on the Dutch version. Translations were compared within a broader language group, moreover.

Between spring 2009 and winter 2012 all members of the selected parliaments were contacted, employing a variety of methods. The fieldwork was done at different moments in the electoral cycle in different countries (Table 1.1). In Austria, Belgium, and Switzerland for instance the study took place mid-term, the general elections a distant horizon. In the Netherlands, Norway, and Spain, by contrast, data collection ended with the start of the election campaign. Significant rescheduling ensued following sudden crises in government prompting early elections in Ireland and the Netherlands, a breaking scandal in the United Kingdom, a natural disaster in Madeira, and the 10 April 2010 plane crash in Poland which killed ninety-six, among them the president and fifteen members of parliament.

In most countries a combination of web-based and print questionnaires were used. Legislators typically received a personalized introduction letter and email presenting the project and inviting them to participate by web-based survey. Postal and email addresses were sourced from the public domain, in particular the parliamentary websites. The introduction letter emphasized the cross-national comparative design and detailed our anonymity policy. In the United Kingdom endorsements were added from party leaders and senior members of the party. They further received at least two online reminders (excluding 'hard' refusals) and the option was offered to them to fill out a print questionnaire. A final invitation was frequently by telephone—in order to boost response rates. In Austria, however, only print questionnaires were sent. In Hungary, Israel, and the Netherlands legislators were interviewed.

The PARTIREP cross-national survey netted 2,326 responses (having answered at least 25 per cent of the questionnaire)—that is, about one in four elected representatives filled out the questionnaire. The number is similar to other projects of comparable scope. It is lower than we dared hope for but better than some. Parliamentary elites are notoriously pressed for time and increasingly suffer from survey fatigue. Finally, 2,096 completed the questionnaire, taking them thirty minutes on average to respond to all forty-six questions. Dropout, moreover, cannot be traced back to particular questions deemed incomprehensible, confidential, or vexing by respondents. No

TABLE 1.1 *The PARTIREP MP survey: fieldwork period, method, return rates, and representativeness*

	Number of regional parliaments in the selection	Fieldwork period	Method				Number of responses	Return rate	Duncan index of dissimilarity regarding			
			online	hard copy	interview	telephone			National vs. regional level	Government vs. opposition	Party	Sex
Austria	9	2011		x			227	36.0	5	0	5	4
Belgium	4	2009	x	x			163	35.2	11	3	10	2
France	2	2011	x	x			90	12.6	25	8	21	8
Germany	4	2009–10	x	x			279	26.5	11	6	8	2
Hungary	—	2009			x		99	25.8	—	1	2	1
Ireland	—	2009–10	x	x			34	22.4	—	5	8	4
Israel	—	2009			x		39	32.5	—	13	18	3
Italy	6	2010–11	x	x	x	x	128	12.9	28	6	16	3
Netherlands	—	2010–11		x	x		65	43.3	—	6	18	1
Norway	—	2009	x	x			46	27.2	—	5	9	2
Poland	—	2009–10	x	x			55	12.0	—	4	14	6
Portugal	2	2010	x	x			118	35.3	4	1	7	1
Spain	4	2011	x	x			272	35.4	7	7	16	4
Switzerland	25	2010	x	x			604	21.8	1	5	13	3
United Kingdom	2	2010	x	x	x	x	107	12.9	19	5	14	0

Note: The Duncan index of dissimilarity measures the percentage differences between the distribution in the population and the sample. The index ranges from 0 (no difference) to 100 (maximum difference).

particular questions stand out with larger numbers of 'no answer'. Table 1.1 reports response rates per country.

Cross-national differences in response rate make the question of representativeness of critical importance. Table 1.1 further reports representativeness tests for the level of government, for government-opposition, and for party. The Duncan index of dissimilarity measures differences between the sample and the population distributions. The selection closely resembles the population in most respects: the deviation in the level of government in the samples from the populations is 8 per cent; it is 3 per cent for the balance between parties supporting the government and opposition parties; and 4 per cent for the balance between the sexes. For individual countries the Duncan index is below 15 per cent in most cases. In Austria, Belgium, Germany, Portugal, Spain, and Switzerland differences in response rates are small between national and regional legislators—about 10 per cent at most. In some of the larger countries, France, Italy, and the United Kingdom, the differences are higher, regional legislators participating more often than national legislators. It has been our experience that securing legislators' participation by personally contacting representatives is labour- and time-intensive. High return rates are harder to obtain in this manner in the larger parliaments.

Differences regarding government and opposition parties are below 10 per cent in most cases. Only in Israel is the balance more skewed against government parties. As a result of the high fractionalization of the Israeli party system a considerable number of members of the Knesset on the government side are members of the cabinet, who as a rule participate less in surveys. With regard to party composition, differences between the samples and populations are below 15 per cent in most cases. Larger discrepancies are often situated in the more fragmented party systems. In Israel government parties, but in particular Likud, are underrepresented. In the Netherlands the survey has focused on the mainstream government and opposition parties, excluding smaller right-wing and religious formations, PVV and SGP. In Italy Partito Democratico is slightly overrepresented and Berlusconi's Popolo della Libertá slightly underrepresented. In France and Spain the balance favours the Socialist Party at the cost of the Conservative Party. But in each of these cases deviations among the main parties account for about 10 per cent; the remainder is due to the accumulation of deviations among a large number of minor parties. Differences in the sex balance in the individual countries are low and exceed 5 per cent only in France and Poland, with women participating more than men in these cases. More caution might be advisable for those countries with low return rates. For this reason the data are first weighted by parliamentary party in each parliament and then a corrective weight is applied to correct overrepresentation of the Swiss cantonal parliaments. In any case comparative analyses focusing on relations between variables should be less subject to this potential problem.

1.4 PLAN OF THE BOOK

To what extent can political representation (still) be understood as an activity that is driven by belonging to a political party? To what extent is the responsible party model the frame that gives meaning to political representation and that guides the actions and strategic choices of members of parliament? Or do MPs to the contrary search for more personal and individual strategies to respond to their voters and to seek election and re-election? Does it matter whether the representative role is played in a statewide parliament or in the parliament of a sub-state? Is representation different in strong and powerful sub-states than in weaker sub-states? Can we confirm that the electoral system affects the way in which members of parliament opt for particular roles and strategies? Can members of parliament be free and creative or is their choice rather limited by the institutional context in which they have to function?

The PARTIREP MP survey covers a wide variety of institutional contexts, and the data thus do allow us to answer these questions. Each of the chapters of the book looks at a different aspect of parliamentary representation, and always from a comparative perspective. All chapters use all the countries and all the parliaments, except for chapter 10 that only looks at the MPs in multilevel states.

Chapter 2 looks at the classic notion of representational roles. Agnieszka Dudzińska, Corentin Poyet, Olivier Costa, and Bernhard Weßels look at the two dimensions of these roles: the focus and the style of representation. The focus of representation defines whom MPs represent or should represent: the electorate as a whole or a part of it, like specific categories and subgroups of the electorate. The style of representation on the other hand describes the way in which an MP comes to his or her decisions: by following his or her own judgment (acting as a trustee) or by following others' instructions (acting as a delegate). For both dimensions of the role, Dudzińska et al. assume that institutional factors can help explain the choices made by MPs. The decision to represent the whole nation or the interests of specific groups and the decision to act as a trustee or as a delegate appears indeed not to be a matter of personal choice or personal background. In particular the level of government at which MPs have been elected appears to be very important for both the focus and the style of representation.

In chapter 3 Daniele Caramani, Karen Celis, and Bram Wauters analyse the extent to which MPs claim to represent specific groups in society. The traditional partisan representation assumes a clear link between societal cleavages and political parties. The group-based politics with parties representing specific groups like the working class or members of religious denominations is now believed to have become less important. Secularization, tertialization, mediatization, and individualization have led to a decline of structural and ideological voting and to increased electoral volatility. This might have led to a greater choice for individual MPs, that is, to a shift from parties to individual politicians as channels of representation. The findings of this chapter do, however, point towards a strong partisanship effect. Old groups—like class—are still seen as the core constituency of parties that have emerged from them, and leftist parties clearly pay more attention to groups than rightist parties. That is also true for new groups like age groups and gender. The chapter also finds the level of government to be of significant effect: regional MPs pay more attention to groups than MPs of statewide parliaments.

In chapter 4 Silvia Erzeel, Didier Caluwaerts, and Karen Celis zoom in on one of the new groups—women—who have been asking for a better descriptive and substantive representation. The territorial and the partisan logic of electoral representation has indeed no formal space for guaranteeing the presence of (enough) women in parliamentary assemblies and for making sure that their interests are being defended. Using the frequency of self-reported speaking during meetings of the parliamentary groups for signalling situations in society that are disadvantageous for women, the chapter seeks to identify the institutional factors that directly influence this behaviour. The effect of the electoral system is quite clear: MPs elected under proportional rule are more likely to promote women's interests and they are also more likely to do so when the lists are open and allowing voters to cast a preferential vote. And here also the difference between MPs elected at the statewide and at the regional level is striking. Regional parliaments are more important venues for women's substantive representation than national or federal parliaments.

Audrey André, André Freire, and Zsófia Papp analyse in chapter 5 the relation between electoral systems and the personal vote-seeking of members of parliament. Assuming that members of parliament want to be re-elected, it is commonly argued that the electoral institutions affect what legislators do in parliament and beyond. Electoral institutions more in particular affect the degree in which MPs opt for a partisan or for a more personal strategy, the latter being aimed at distinguishing himself or herself from the party and from the party image and reputation. The wide range of electoral systems and rules available in the PARTIREP data have made it possible to describe this relation in detail and in a truly comparative way. The authors distinguish between four types of electoral systems: non-preferential, mixed-member, weak preferential, and strong preferential, offering a continuum in the degree in which the voters have the possibility to vote for persons within parties. And these electoral rules do have an impact: personal vote-seeking—measured as opting for individualized campaign strategies—is stronger in preferential systems. Over and above the effect of electoral rules, party-related factors have also an impact on the nature of a legislator's campaign. Representatives from leftist parties are more party-oriented, and representatives of governing parties have a higher likelihood of pursuing candidate-intensive campaigns. Personal vote-seekers furthermore behave in a different way when elected. They consider the promotion of constituency interest more important and they are more willing to desert the party line when voting in parliament.

One of the important characteristics (or consequences) of partisan representation is indeed the unity of a party's MPs when voting in parliament. Cynthia van Vonno, Reut Itzkovitch Malka, Sam Depauw, Reuven Hazan, and Rudy Andeweg explore in chapter 6 how this unity can be achieved. They suggest a sequential model that also creates a greater conceptual clarity. Party agreement is the situation in which MPs toe the party line because they simply agree with their party's position. Party loyalty comes about when MPs believe that party unity is important for parliamentary government. Party discipline means following a logic of consequentiality, that is, MPs vote with the party because they want to avoid the possible sanctions in case of dissent. Party agreement—so the authors show—is the most important pathway to party unity. Yet party unity is affected by the institutional context. Electoral systems, and in particular the incentives for personal vote-seeking shape the MPs' frequency of agreement with the party line. Legislators of a governing party cannot duck their responsibility for public policy as the opposition can. And party loyalty is also more frequent in sub-state parliaments.

In chapter 7 Marcelo Jenny, Wolfgang Müller, Jonathan Bradbury, Nikolaus Eder, and Gabriella Ilonszki also stress the fact that today's democracy is building on political parties, on their programmes and candidates, on their internal unity and cohesion, and on relations between them. The latter, the inter-party relations, are, however, seldom the object of research. This chapter therefore wants to explore the relations and interactions between members of parliament belonging to different parties. These relations can be of the 'non-party mode', when members of parliament collaborate to control the government. More important and more adapted to the age of the mass parties and of party government is the 'inter-party mode' in which MPs seek contacts with partners in the government or the opposition. In the 'cross-party mode' the MPs collaborate to fight for common causes across the government–opposition division line. In the survey the question was asked whether MPs had good contacts with colleagues of other parties and whether these contacts had been helpful politically. The first important finding is that there is a huge variation in the frequency of these contacts, with Switzerland, Norway, Portugal, Israel, and the Netherlands displaying high numbers of good contacts and France and Italy with only a minority of MPs reporting good cross-party contacts. System-level variables can therefore explain this variation. More or broader contacts appear to be a function of the presence of proportional representation, minority or coalition government, a higher share of female representatives—used here as a proxy for a more consensual parliamentary culture—and a higher number of parties.

Much research on representation focuses on policy congruence or descriptive representation. Yet whether a citizen feels represented by an MP might also depend on the degree in which and the way in which he or she is able to promote and defend the interests of the geographical constituency or of individual constituents. That is the topic of chapter 8, in which Audrey André, Michael Gallagher, and Giulia Sandri analyse the way in which and especially the degree in which MPs seek to connect with constituents. The 'constituency members' are the legislators who believe that casework or project work is the most important task they have to perform as elected representatives. These constituency members are more numerous in systems where the voters can cast a preference vote (see also chapter 5). The impact of these electoral incentives is, however, conditioned by the conception of political representation that the MPs hold. Constituency orientation comes with a bottom-up conception of representation. And the authors also find a clear effect of the level of government. MPs at the regional level prioritize casework and project work in the constituency, but less so when the degree of regional authority increases.

In chapter 9 Tor Midtbø, Stefaan Walgrave, Peter Van Aelst, and Dag Arne Christensen also look at the way in which the members of parliament try to interact with their voters. They do, however, focus on the way in which the media play a role in this, on how MPs give information to the media (media access) and how they use information from the media (media reaction). The relationship with the media is portrayed by the MPs as being asymmetric: according to them they get their actions more often in the media than the media inspire their own actions. There are however significant differences between the members of parliament. Generalist MPs interact more with the media than specialists, younger MPs more than the old, the experienced more than the inexperienced, and high profile MPs (like party leaders, speakers, or committee chairs) more than others. The data actually suggest the existence of two types of MPs: media-savvy MPs who interact intensely and MPs who are isolated from the media. There are also important party effects. There is a strong tendency for opposition MPs to rely more on information from the media than governmental MPs. And MPs from extreme right parties seem to struggle to get access to the media.

For understanding the opinions, actions, and strategies of members of parliaments, it is important to know where they are in the political institutions. That is also the strong message of chapter 10, in which Jean-Benoit Pilet, Filippo Tronconi, Pablo Oñate, and Luca Verzichelli look at career patterns of MPs. They have selected the multilevel countries in the database and focus in particular on career movements across levels of government. Three patterns have been distinguished in the literature: the unidirectional career where politicians climb the ladder to the highest level, the separate careers in which MPs specialize in one level, and the 'level-hopping' career moving back and forth between levels. Overall the second pattern seems to be the dominant one, with, however, some variation between countries. The authors also want to know whether different careers influence the attitudes of the MPs. There are two alternative models: one in which MPs are being socialized at one level and take their ideas and opinions with them to another level, and one in which their views are determined by the level at which they are at the moment of the survey. Preferences for the distribution of powers between levels and the focus of representation (the country versus the region) were used as indicators. The findings are quite straightforward: the level of government where an MP is currently serving is more important than the previous trajectory of his or her political career. And this is true for both senior and newly elected representatives. What matters is not where they come from, but where they are.

This conclusion is very much in line with what all the previous chapters have found. Members of parliament are to a large extent making choices and voicing opinions that can be explained by the institutional context in which they function. All chapters present statistics of the dependent variable per country, before proceeding with the analysis. The variation between countries is always quite large. Yet when institutional variables are entered into the models—like the type of political system, the electoral system, or the party to which MPs belong—the variation between countries appears to be a variation between institutions and not between national political cultures. In the final chapter Kris Deschouwer and Sam Depauw look back at these findings, and present three major conclusions of the book. The first is that democratic political representation is and remains partisan. Parties select candidates and parties govern, and therefore the party to which one belongs and the place that party has in the system and along the ideological spectrum matters for the way in which the representational roles are being played. The second major conclusion is that electoral systems matter a lot. This is not a new finding, but the very wide range of electoral systems that were included in the PARTIREP survey has allowed refining the insights on how the way in which one is elected affects the way in which one represents. And finally the level of government is crucial. The countries in the survey were deliberately selected to include a variety of federal and decentralized systems. That has allowed a comparison of political representation across levels and across types of sub-states. The assumption was that representation is not the same at the statewide and at the sub-state level. This book has produced ample evidence to prove that point.

REFERENCES

Alonso, S., J. Keane, and W. Merkel (2011), 'Rethinking the Future of Representative Democracy', in S. Alonso, J. Keane, and W. Merkel, *The Future of Representative Democracy*. Cambridge: Cambridge University Press, 1–22.

Ankersmit, F. (2008), 'On the Future of Representative Democracy (Comments on the Future of Representative Democracy Project), available at <http://ondemocracy.org/component/k2/item/139-on-the-future-of-representative-democracy> accessed 9 December 2013.

Bächtiger, A. (2005), *The Real World of Deliberation: A Comparative Study of Its Favorable Conditions in Legislatures.* Bern: Berner Studien zur Politikwissenschaft.

Bartolini, S. (2005), *Restructuring Europe: Centre Formation, System Building, and Political Structuring between the Nation State and the European Union.* Oxford: Oxford University Press.

Bohman, J. (1996), *Public Deliberation: Pluralism, Complexity and Democracy.* Cambridge, MA: MIT Press.

Canovan, M. (1999), 'Trust the People! Populism and the Two Faces of Democracy', *Political Studies*, 47 (1): 2–16.

Castles, F. G. and R. Wildenmann (1986), *Vision and Realities of Party Government.* New York, NY: De Gruyter.

Colomer, J. M. (2005), 'It's Parties that Choose Electoral Systems (or, Duverger's Laws Upside Down)', *Political Studies*, 53 (1): 1–21.

—— (ed.) (2011), *Personal Representation: The Neglected Dimension of Electoral Systems.* Colchester: ECPR Press.

Dalton, R., S. C. Flanagan, and P. A. Beck (eds.) (1984), *Electoral Changes in Advanced Industrial Democracies: Realignment or Dealignment?* Princeton, NJ: Princeton University Press.

Dovi, S. (2007), *The Good Representative.* Oxford: Blackwell.

Dryzek, J. S. (2000), *Deliberative Democracy and Beyond: Liberals, Critics, Contestations.* Oxford: Oxford University Press.

Duverger, M. (1951), *Les Partis politiques.* Paris: A. Colin.

Elazar, D. J. (1987), *Exploring Federalism.* Tuscaloosa, AL: University of Alabama Press.

Eulau, H., J. C. Wahlke, W. Buchanan et al. (1959), 'The Role of the Representative: Some Empirical Observations on the Theory of Edmund Burke', *American Political Science Review*, 53 (3): 742–56.

Evans, G. (ed.) (1999), *The End of Class Politics?* Oxford: Oxford University Press.

Ezrow, L. (2010), *Linking Citizens and Parties: How Electoral Systems Matter for Political Representation.* New York, NY: Oxford University Press.

Flora, P., S. Kuhnle, and D. Urwin (1999), *State Formation, Nation-building and Mass Politics in Europe: The Theory of Stein Rokkan.* Oxford: Oxford University Press.

Franklin, M. N., T. T. Mackie, and H. Valen (eds.) (1992), *Electoral Change: Responses to Evolving Social and Attitudinal Structures in Western Countries.* Cambridge: Cambridge University Press.

Hooghe, L., A. H. Schakel, and G. Marks (2008), 'Appendix B: Country and Regional Scores', *Regional & Federal Studies*, 18 (2–3): 259–74.

Karvonen, L. (2010), *The Personalization of Politics: A Study of Parliamentary Democracies.* London: ECPR Press.

Katz, R. (1987), *Party Governments: European and American Experiences.* Berlin: De Gruyter.

—— and P. Mair (1995), 'Changing Models of Party Organisation and Party Democracy: The Emergence of the Cartel Party', *Party Politics*, 1 (1): 5–28.

Keane, J. (2009), *The Life and Death of Democracy.* Sidney: Simon & Schuster.

Kriesi, H. (1998), 'The Transformation of Cleavage Politics: The 1997 Stein Rokkan Lecture', *European Journal of Political Research*, 33: 165–85.

Lijphart, A. (1994), *Electoral Systems and Party System: A Study of Twenty-seven Democracies, 1945–1990*. Oxford: Oxford University Press.

Lipset, S. M. and S. Rokkan (1967), *Party Systems and Voter Alignments: Cross-national Perspectives*. Toronto: The Free Press.

Lucardie, P. (2000), 'Prophets, Purifiers and Prolocutors: Towards a Theory on the Emergence of New Parties', *Party Politics*, 6 (2): 175–85.

Mair, P. (2009), 'Representative versus Responsible Government', working paper, Max-Planck Institute for the Study of Societies, Köln, available at <http://www.mpifg.de/pu/workpap/wp09-8.pdf> accessed 10 December 2013.

—— and J. Thomassen (2010), 'Political Representation and Government in the European Union', *Journal of European Public Policy*, 17 (1): 20–35.

McAllister, I. (2007), 'The Personalization of Politics', in R. Dalton and H. D. Klingemann (eds.), *Oxford Handbook of Political Behavior*. Oxford: Oxford University Press.

McCrone, D. and J. Kuklinski (1979), 'The Delegate Theory of Representation', *American Journal of Political Science*, 23: 278–300.

Manin, B. (1997), *The Principles of Representative Government*. Cambridge: Cambridge University Press.

Mansbridge, J. (2003), 'Rethinking Representation', *American Political Science Review*, 97: 515–28.

Meguid, B. M. (2010), *Party Competition Between Unequals: Strategies and Electoral Fortunes in Western Europe*. Cambridge: Cambridge University Press.

Mény Y. and Y. Surel (eds.) (2002), *Democracies and the Populist Challenge*. Houndmills: Palgrave

Pitkin, H. (1967), *The Concept of Representation*. Berkeley, CA: University of California Press.

Strøm, K. (2000), 'Delegation and Accountability in Parliamentary Democracies', *European Journal of Political Research*, 37 (3): 261–28.

Taggart, P. (2004), 'Populism and Representative Politics in Contemporary Europe', *Journal of Political Ideologies*, 9 (1): 269–88.

Tuschhoff, C. (1999), 'The Compounding Effect: The Impact of Federalism on the Concept of Representation', *West European Politics*, 22 (2): 16–33.

Urbinati, N. (2011), 'Representative Democracy and Its Critics', in S. Alonso, J. Keane, and W. Merkel (eds.), *The Future of Representative Democracy*. Cambridge: Cambridge University Press, 23–49.

van Biezen, I., P. Mair, and T. Poguntke (2012), 'Going, Going,… Gone? The Decline of Party Membership in Contemporary Europe', *European Journal of Political Research*, 51 (1): 24–56.

2

Representational Roles

Agnieszka Dudzińska, Corentin Poyet, Olivier Costa, and Bernhard Weßels

2.1 REPRESENTATIONAL ROLES: FOCUS AND STYLE

Political representation is generally defined as the activity of making citizens' voices, opinions, and perspectives 'present' in the public policymaking processes.[1] Starting from there, many different aspects and dimensions of representation have been identified. Pitkin (1967) differentiates between four different forms of representation: formalistic (institutional arrangements), symbolic (a symbol brings the symbolized/corresponding object to mind even if it is not similar to it), descriptive (reflecting the whole picture by its part, e.g. reflecting the socio-demographic profile of citizens or their opinions), and substantive (the activity of representing). Representation is thus a complex concept with several dimensions (see also Vieira and Runciman 2008). Politicians who are supposed to represent are facing different options on how to define their representation and how to behave according to it. For academics a wide variety of approaches are available. Which dimension of representation should be studied? Should representation be analysed from the perspective of citizens or from the perspective of MPs? The objective of this chapter is to do the latter. We have questioned MPs about their vision of their job and will attempt to explain the choices made by them. This is in line with the general political science approach towards legislative roles, which is more focused on MPs' self-perception and less on social expectations (Blomgren and Rozenberg 2012b: 9), These self-perceptions and considerations are numerous and can be difficult to reconcile (De Winter 1997), In this chapter we try to explain the inter-country differences in the representative role perceptions. We will therefore treat the roles as the independent variables, and look at institutional factors to explain the variation. These institutional factors include characteristics of the political system in which the MPs define their role and the political party for which they have been elected.

Many authors have shown that representatives are submitted to multiple sources of pressure and often have several principals. These include citizens in general, their constituencies, those who voted for them, their parties, their parliamentary groups, public opinion leaders, the media, or interest groups (see Bradbury 2007; Costa 2002; Farrell and Scully 2010; Kerrouche 2004; Weßels and Giebler 2011). These findings challenge the legal principle and the cultural norm that says that MPs are to represent all people in the country, as well as the legal and normative idea of the independent mandate, according to which MPs should follow their own opinions rather than someone else's instructions. MPs are also likely to face conflicting interests.

There is empirical evidence that MPs play different roles depending on the situation in which they find themselves and on the problem to be solved (Andeweg 2012: 81), The seminal study of Miller and Stokes shows, for example, that models of representation and thus role structures differ between issue areas (Miller and Stokes 1963), Costa and Kerrouche (2007, 2009) have highlighted a dual conception of the mandate in France: all MPs claim to represent the nation but, at the same time, a vast majority of them considers that it is also their duty to advocate for their constituency and constituents, and that there is no contradiction in these terms. This tension between the universal norm of representing all people and actual trade-offs between conflicting foci of representation has also been found at the regional and the local level in Poland (Dudzińska 2011, Dudzińska and Post 2009).

The way in which MPs perceive their role as representatives has received much attention in political science and is very much inspired by the famous speech of Edmund Burke to the Electors of Bristol in 1779.[2] His role definition was both universalistic (national interest) and independent (following one's own judgment). These two aspects of the representational role are labelled 'focus' and 'style' (Eulau et al. 1959). The focus of representation defines whom MPs represent or should represent: the electorate as a whole or a part of it. For the latter, Eulau and Karps (1977) distinguish between three categories: interests defined territorially (geographical representation), interests defined functionally (group representation), and interests defined individually (representation of their own voters).[3] The style of representation on the other hand describes the way in which the MP comes to his or her decisions: following his or her own judgment or following others' instructions. For the style of representation the categories are usually described by the labels of 'trustee' (own judgment) and 'delegate' (instructions of a principal).[4] Based on empirical evidence from France, Converse and Pierce (1986) further distinguished between a 'party's delegate' and a 'voters' delegate'. The research on representative roles has developed a set of standardized questions to measure MPs' preferences for a specific style (e.g. Gross 1978, Weßels and Giebler 2010).

Although the trustee/delegate model has been much challenged and discussed, it seems to remain useful (Blomgren and Rozenberg 2012a: 4). The strongest criticism has come from the responsible party model (Mair 2008; Thomassen and Schmitt 1997; Weßels 2007), in which the main actor in the process of representation is the party, and not the individual MP. In this regard, who exactly stands for an election is less important than what his or her party stands for, and parties are therefore central to explain MPs' behaviour, more than their own views and those of their constituents. Parties can also be incorporated into the delegation chain (Braun and Gilardi 2006; Müller 2000). Political parties in this approach help parliamentary democracies to deal with adverse selection (parties reduce the information problems of citizens), although they do not solve the problem of moral hazard which concerns elected representatives. Still another way of dealing with parties is to argue that instructions from voters also comprise those from political parties. In this view, elections are a multistage process and parties are important selectors: MPs feel obliged to be responsive to both the party structures and the party voters. This is also related to the electoral system, as we will discuss later. It has been demonstrated, however, that even if parties are playing a key role in elections and in parliamentary work, MPs can still influence public policy without their support and generally enjoy more autonomy than predicted by the responsible party model (Thomassen and Andeweg 2004).

Our analysis shares the view of Wahlke (1962), who argues that an MP's role influences his or her legislative activity. In other words, a delegate's activities differ from those of a trustee. We will explore how the members of national and regional parliaments perceive their role. Specifically, we asked MPs how important it is for them to promote the views and interests of certain groups of people (their perception of the focus of representation), and how MPs should decide in the face of conflicting opinions in voting situations (their perception of the norm concerning the style of representation). We then look for possible determinants of both focus and style.

The most recent studies on this topic stem from neo-institutionalist perspectives and emphasize the influence of the institutional context on representation (Müller and Saalfeld 1997; Searing 1994; Weßels 1999a; Strøm 2012). Since the seminal works by Miller and Stokes (1963), Mayhew (1974), and Fenno (1978), a large body of literature has studied especially the effect of electoral institutions on MPs' legislative activities. These authors have demonstrated how electoral institutions indeed affect the way in which MPs build their vision of representation. According to this literature, these institutions are thus more important than individual factors and background traits that only have little impact on them (Jewell 1970; Weßels 1999a). We will also show that institutions do matter. We will look at the political system and at the parties in which the MPs have to act. Here the power of parties over the selection and nomination of candidates will appear to be crucial.

2.2 STATE OF THE RESEARCH, APPROACHES, AND HYPOTHESES

In the field of representation studies, the majority of the research is country-specific (Bradbury 2007) and comparative studies are rather scarce (but see for example Pilet, Freire, and Costa 2012a; Miller et al. 1999; Schmitt and Thomassen 1999). Some works have a comparative ambition, but they often suffer from a lack of sufficiently standardized data to allow reliable comparisons or they rely only on a limited number of cases. In order to determine which factors impact on representational roles, it is necessary to adopt a comparative perspective and to use standardized data from a large number of countries presenting various institutional designs. The PARTIREP dataset is perfectly suited for this purpose.

We want to analyse the influence of three sets of factors on the perception of the representative role defined by its two dimensions, focus and style.[5] The factors that we expect to influence role perception are primarily the characteristics of the political system and a number of party variables. For the political system, we have selected the following elements: (1) multilevel versus unitary system, (2) regional versus national parliament, (3) electoral formula (4) type of the list, (5) preferential vote, (6) whether ballot papers mention candidates' names, (7) the influence of district magnitude. Several of these factors—and especially those related to the electoral system—have already been studied for some countries, with results that are, however, not consistent. In their analysis of the possible influence of ballot structure on MPs attitudes, Pilet, Freire, and Costa (2012b) have not found any relation between ballot structure and constituency representation. It is the district magnitude that appears to be more important than the ballot structure. Other studies have shown a positive effect of open-list systems on the MPs' focus on their constituency (Bowler and Farrell 1993; Carey and Shugart 1995). The literature has also highlighted the effect of electoral formula: according to Thomassen and Andeweg (2004) and Weßels (1999b), proportional systems have negative effects on the importance of the constituency. However, the effect of this factor must be put into perspective because it is hard to determine whether it is a result of the electoral formula or rather of the number of MPs by district (single- or multi-member district). More empirically, the majority system with single-member districts seems to encourage MPs' focus on the party (Pilet, Freire, and Costa 2012b).

The impact of district magnitude is emphasized by Mayhew (1974) and Fenno (1978). However, its effect has also been widely discussed. For Weßels (1999b: 222), large districts bring MPs to define their focus of representation less in terms of their district, because large districts are not, in Rehfeld's terms (2005), communities of interests. Empirically, this negative effect has been demonstrated by Pilet, Freire, and Costa (2012b), who compared the cases of Belgium, France, and Portugal. These results corroborate partially those of Carey and Shugart (1995): for them, the effect of district magnitude depends on electoral rules and particularly on the possibility for voters to modify the lists or not. They show that large district magnitude negatively affects the focus on constituency only in closed-lists systems.

Next to the characteristics of the political system, a specific set of institutional arrangements related to the MPs' representative roles stems from political parties. These party factors are: (1) government participation, (2) party ideology, (3) the degree of centralization of the nomination procedure, (4) nomination procedure by the party (party agency or primaries) or by party leaders, (5) change in the vote share for the party from the previous election, (6) position of a party on the left–right scale. Internal party selection rules have seldom been analysed directly in connection with representative roles. However, Weßels and Giebler (2010) have shown some limited effects of party selection rules. For example, they found a higher relevance of party representation as opposed to representation of people in a region if national party leaders have a high impact on candidates' nomination. Several other studies, which do not concern representation as such, hint at the impact of other aspects of nomination and selection on role orientations. According to Morgenstern (2004), selection procedures influence the level of party cohesion and, hence, MPs' attitudes and behaviours. Coppedge (1994) has shown that centralized candidate selection enhances party cohesion. Costa and Kerrouche (2007) have found similar results in France, where party leaders have considerable power over candidates' selection. Hence, we can expect MPs from parties with strong leaders and centralized selection procedures to be very focused on their party. However, in order to favour the personal vote and to maximize their chance of winning the election, MPs are also encouraged to take care of their reputation in the constituency and, thus, to pay much attention to this level of representation. This, obviously, only makes sense when a ballot paper mentions candidates and when the lists are open.

We will, in what follows, test across the variety of institutions that we have in the PARTIREP data the effects of the political system and of the political parties to which the MPs belong. In the analysis we will also add a few individual characteristics of the MPs, to check whether they have an effect after controlling for the institutional variables. The individual variables are (1) sex, (2) age, (3) education, (4) political experience at the local level, (5) holding a prominent position in the parliament (speaker, party group leader, chair of a permanent committee), and (6) parliamentary experience.

We expect that despite the normative assumption of promoting the universal interests of the political entity instead of more specific ones, MPs rather tend to choose a particularistic or a group approach to political representation (for a classification of group specificity and regional scope of representational foci see Weßels 1999b). We estimate institutional factors to have an effect on the way in which and the degree to which MPs tend to focus on their constituencies, on their parties, on their voters, or on specific groups. A focus on the party should be related to party factors, especially the internal selection rules. The more centralized and exclusive the nomination procedure, the stronger the focus on the party should be. A focus on voters should be stronger in single-member districts. And the focus on the geographical constituency should be stronger for regional MPs than for national ones.

The style of representation—so we expect—will depend mainly on party factors and on some institutional ones. The style of a party delegate will be enhanced by a centralized nomination procedure and a lack of inclusive primaries, as well as by closed lists under PR system. The style of a trustee should be connected with open lists, and a lower level of nomination. The style of a voters' delegate should be more frequent under majority/plurality formula and in small districts.

The mechanisms which produce different priorities in both style and focus of representation can be understood as incentives set out by the electoral system and the combination with rules of nomination. The argument for a fully proportional list system would be because candidates are running on lists (electoral system), parties decide who gets where on the list (nomination), and a candidate's success in getting a mandate is fully dependent on where the party places him or her. Parties as organizations have an inherent interest in coherence, demanding fit to the party. Thus, the appropriate role for a candidate to take in order to make it to a promising place on the list is to present himself or herself as a party representative, focusing on party voters. In contrast, the success of a candidate in a single-member district depends on his or her individual ability to mobilize votes. Every party in such a system would be well advised to nominate candidates according to this ability. In this case, the incentive comes from the constituency and demands the representation of its interests. Thus, in a majority or plurality system, the chances of a candidate's success are determined by the voters rather than by the party.

2.3 MEASURING STYLE AND FOCUS

For the measurement of the focus of representation, we have asked the MPs to indicate on a 7-point scale (1 = of no importance, 7 = of great importance), which group they represent: all people in the country (or all people in the region for regional MPs), the party, one's voters,[6] the constituency, and a specific group.[7] Table 2.1 presents the figures broken down by country. It reveals significant differences in the importance of the five foci among the countries under study. The mean importance of the universal focus of representation ranges from 4.8 in the United Kingdom to 6.5 in Israel. The party focus ranges from 4.8 in Ireland to 6.4 in Norway. The mean for the voters' focus varies between 4.9 in Ireland to 6.0 in Hungary. The importance of representing a specific group goes from 3.5 in France to 5.4 in Austria, and of the constituency focus ranges from 3.9 in Israel (where it was defined as 'area of residence') to 6.2 in Austria. These variations between countries suggest indeed that the political system shapes at least in part these representational foci.

Three styles of representation have been distinguished, based on the transitive patterns of the answers to three questions concerning decisions in case of certain pairs of conflicting opinions. MPs were asked whether they believed that—when these opinions are different—they should follow their own opinion or that of their party, their own opinion or that of their voters, their party's opinion or that of their voters.[8] The transitive styles are: 'trustee', 'party delegate', and 'voters' delegate'. Those who do not demonstrate any transitive pattern fall into the category of 'undecided'. Table 2.2 presents the frequency of each of the styles in the fifteen countries of our dataset. And here also it is quite clear that the variation between the countries is important. It ranges from 7 per cent (Norway) to 68 per cent (Switzerland) for the trustee style, from 14 per cent (Switzerland) to 86 per cent (Netherlands) for the party delegate, and from 5 per cent (Norway) to 26 per cent (Portugal) for

TABLE 2.1 *The mean importance of five foci of representation in fifteen countries*

	All people	Party	Voters	Specific group	Constituency
Austria	5.0	5.8	6.0	5.4	6.2
Belgium	4.9	5.3	5.2	4.4	5.1
France	5.9	5.1	5.3	3.5	5.5
Germany	5.2	5.5	5.7	4.6	6.1
Hungary	5.3	5.8	6.0	5.1	5.6
Ireland	5.1	4.8	4.9	4.0	5.5
Israel	6.5	5.6		5.3	3.9
Italy	5.4	5.1	5.3	4.0	5.3
Netherlands	5.2	5.8	4.9	5.2	4.1
Norway	5.8	6.4		3.7	5.5
Poland	5.7	4.9	5.1	3.8	5.3
Portugal	6.0	5.5		4.1	5.8
Spain	5.9	6.1		5.2	6.2
Switzerland	5.0	5.4	5.6	4.6	5.2
United Kingdom	4.8	5.4	5.1	3.8	5.9
In general	5.4	5.6	5.5	4.6	5.7

'Constituency' was replaced by 'area of residence' in Israel and the Netherlands.

TABLE 2.2 *The frequency of representational styles in fifteen countries (row percentages)*

	Trustee	Party delegate	Voters' delegate	Undecided
Austria	26	48	22	4
Belgium	26	52	13	9
France	47	43	10	0
Germany	34	55	6	5
Hungary	25	47	18	10
Ireland	10	77	10	3
Israel	20	53	17	10
Italy	38	28	22	12
Netherlands	8	86	6	0
Norway	7	81	5	7
Poland	39	45	12	4
Portugal	32	37	26	5
Spain	9	65	24	2
Switzerland	68	14	15	3
United Kingdom	40	44	10	6
In general	31	48	16	5

voters' delegate style. That suggests that here also a number of characteristics of the political system must play a role.

If we look at the mean importance of the five foci for the total population—see Table 2.3—we see that it is almost the same for each of them (a mean value of around 5.5), except for the focus on a specific group which is rated significantly lower than other foci. There is thus seemingly not much tension between different foci of representation. Table 2.3 also looks at the differences between parliaments: national in unitary systems, national in multilevel systems, and regional parliaments. The universal focus on 'all people' is the most important for regional MPs, then for MPs from national parliaments in unitary systems, and the least important (with still the high value of 5.2, however) for national MPs in multilevel systems. 'Constituency', although quite important for all three groups of MPs, is the least important at the national level in unitary systems (5.1 compared with 5.7 and 5.9 for national MPs in multilevel systems and for regional MPs, respectively). This suggests a relative acceptance for the principle of a unitary system, not only in terms of governance, but also in terms of political culture. The nation as a whole is considered more important than the constituency.

When we look at the style dimension—see Table 2.4, we can observe the dominance of the party delegate model (48 per cent) and the trustee model (31 per cent) over the minority of MPs who opt for the style of voters' delegate (16 per cent). The figures for regional MPs do not differ much from those for national MPs, although the voters' delegate is slightly more frequent for them and the trustee less frequent. This result is important when we compare it with citizens' expectations: in the cases of Finland and the United

TABLE 2.3 *The mean importance of five foci of representation per type of parliament*

| Parliament | All people | Party | Foci | | |
			Voters	Specific group	Constituency
National, unitary system	5.5	5.7	5.3	4.6	5.1
National/federal, multilevel system	5.2	5.4	5.5	4.3	5.7
National in general	*5.3*	*5.5*	*5.4*	*4.4*	*5.5*
Regional	5.6	5.7	5.6	4.8	5.9
In general	5.4	5.6	5.5	4.6	5.7

TABLE 2.4 *The distribution of styles of representation over types of parliament*

Parliament	Trustee	Party delegate	Voters' delegate	Undecided
National, unitary system	20	61	12	7
National/federal, multilevel system	40	42	14	5
National in general	*33*	*48*	*13*	*6*
Regional	28	48	18	5
In general	31	48	16	5

Kingdom, voters do not expect an MP to be a party delegate (Bengtsson and Wass 2011; Carman 2006). Hence, there is some indication of a gap between citizens' expectations and the choices made by the MPs.

Some striking differences are found between MPs from national parliaments, depending on the unitary or multilevel system of governance. The unitary system, with a figure of 61 per cent, seems to promote the style of a party delegate the most. This is obviously at the cost of the role of a trustee which is twice less appealing among national MPs from unitary countries than among those from multilevel countries. Some institutional arrangements may be partly responsible for these differences. We will explore these later in the multivariate analysis.

To determine if the two role orientations are empirically interrelated, we can compare the mean values on the scale of importance of the foci for different styles. This is done in Table 2.5. Although most of the differences seem small, they are statistically significant for every focus except the universal one. These results are in line with the traditional view of two interrelated dimensions. The most noticeable one is the positive relationship between being a party delegate and having higher scores for the focus on the party.[9] Also, for voters' delegates, voters are, as expected, a much more important focus than for the other style orientations. Another category that receives its highest score in this group is the constituency. Voters' delegates also find it more important to promote specific groups than others do.

TABLE 2.5 *The relation between focus and style of representation (mean score for focus per style)*

	All people	Party	Voters	Specific group	Constituency
Trustee	3.2	5.2	5.5	4.4	5.6
Party delegate	5.4	5.8	5.4	4.6	5.7
Voters' delegate	5.5	5.5	6.1	4.9	6.0
In general	5.4	5.6	5.5	4.6	5.7

2.4 THE DETERMINANTS OF THE FOCUS OF REPRESENTATION

We have used a multiple regression to identify the determinants (i.e. political system, party-related, or individual characteristics) of the importance of each focus. Our results as presented in Table 2.6 show that the explaining variables slightly differ for each of the foci. In general, a comparison of the R^2 values computed separately for each set of explaining variables reveals that political-system factors best explain the importance of promoting the interests of the constituency.[10] Individual factors, in turn, best explain the importance of specific groups and the party. Surprisingly, party factors turn out to be the weakest group of predictors of the focus. The influence of the three sets of factors on the importance of the universalistic focus (all people) is quite balanced. The focus on voters depends less on the political system factors than on the party and individual ones. However, all the three groups are pretty balanced for the focus on voters as well.

Universal focus: Members of regional parliaments and members of national parliaments in unitary systems are more inclined to focus on 'all people' than national MPs from multilevel systems. In addition, if there is the opportunity for citizens to vote for a candidate within a list, MPs tend to increase their concentration on the universal focus. Finally, the importance of the universal focus is disfavoured by the visibility of the candidates' names on the ballot papers and also by closed lists rather than open ones. Party factors lead to less clear results: although the coefficient is not statistically significant, as theoretically expected, the procedure of candidates' nomination in party primaries works against the universal focus of representation. Party's ideological heritage also matters: the more the party is positioned to the left, the more its MPs value the universal focus. However, belonging to a green/ecologist party decreases its importance. A low level of nomination, namely a decentralized nomination procedure, also decreases the importance of the universal focus. These results are largely in accord with the expectations. Rehfled's (2005) considerations about the size of the district and the influence of the existence of communities of interest find support. MPs elected in large districts and at the national level are less interested in the representation of

TABLE 2.6 *The determinants of representational foci (multiple linear regression—all coefficients are beta)*

	All people	Party	Constituency	Voters	Specific group
	B	B	B	B	B
Political system factors					
Multilevel system of governance	−0.186***	−0.076*	0.080**	0.073	0.008
Regional level of governance	0.187***	0.074*	0.131***	−0.021	−0.085**
Paper mentions candidates	−0.095**	0.093**	0.060*	−0.085	0.061*
Voters can vote for (a) candidate(s)	−0.150***	−0.021	−0.144***		−0.036
Open list	0.034	−0.160***	−0.129***	0.016	−0.129***
Majority system	−0.012	0.033	0.053*		−0.001
District magnitude (logged)	−0.041	−0.035	−0.247***	−0.116*	−0.020
R^2	0.054	0.033	0.144	0.036	
Party factors					
Governing party	−0.003	−0.004	−0.047	−0.059	−0.019
Socialists	−0.057	−0.057	−0.094	0.020	−0.041
Christian democrats	−0.036	−0.117*	0.158***	0.078	0.040
Conservatives	0.081	0.043	0.172***	0.137	0.020
Liberals	−0.040	−0.050	0.036	0.057	−0.057
Green	−0.125***	0.004	−0.090*	−0.001	0.049
Far right party	−0.053	0.041	0.089*	0.083	−0.007
Low level of nomination	−0.066	0.055	0.196***	0.136***	−0.024
Selection by party leaders	0.027	0.041	0.088**	−0.008	0.018
Index of volatility of party voters (continuous)	0.022	−0.069*	−0.007	0.096*	−0.020
Position of the party on a L–R scale (from 0 left to 10 right)	−0.017	−0.034	−0.100*	0.024	−0.138***
R^2	0.044	0.026	0.056	0.047	0.025
Individual factors					
Woman	−0.015	0.134***	−0.008	−0.027	0.132***
Age (in years)	−0.059	−0.043	−0.016	−0.032	−0.111***
University education	0.015	0.058*	0.005	−0.022	−0.050
Local political experience	0.057	0.047	0.016	0.024	−0.019
Prominent functions	0.069*	0.003	0.010	0.024	−0.029
Parliamentary experience (in years from the first entrance)	−0.033	−0.061	−0.089**	−0.106*	−0.019
R^2	0.013	0.036	0.009	0.016	0.042

*** $P < .001$; ** $P < .01$; * $P < .05$.

'all people'. Ballot structure appears as one of the most important factors to explain the importance of the universal focus. This result is in line with the conclusions of Pilet, Freire, and Costa (2012b) concerning the relative impact of electoral formula and ballot structure.

Individual characteristics of MPs also have an impact: promoting the interests of all people is more important for men and for younger MPs. Having a local political experience now or in the past is another source of attaching more importance to the universal focus of representation, whereas parliamentary experience has a negative effect. Prominent parliamentary functions also favour the universal focus, namely being a speaker or deputy speaker of the chamber or being a leader of a parliamentary party group.

Focus on party: Turning to the focus on the party, our results show that four out of the seven examined political-system factors have a significant impact on it. The first two are the type of list and the presence of candidates' name on the ballot (although the possibility of voting for a specific candidate does not have any effect). The positive effect of closed lists can be explained by MPs' wanting to be selected as the head of the list in order to have the greatest chance of being elected. The second result indicates that the focus on party is enhanced by the presence of candidates' names on the ballot. Other significant results concern the level of governance and the structure of the state. First, being elected in a regional parliament favours the focus on the party. In addition, MPs in a multilevel state focus less on their party than MPs in unitary states. Regarding party, our analysis reveals that two factors are significant. First, the higher the index of volatility, the lower the importance for MPs of promoting the interests of the party. When it comes to party families, we see that Christian democratic MPs are less party-oriented. It is interesting to note that party structure cannot be considered as useful to predict party focus—MPs are therefore not prisoners of their party. A centralized nomination or/and a selection by party leaders have only little impact, although we could expect strong effects, especially about the nomination procedure. Two individual factors further affect the importance of the party: promoting party interests is more important for women and for MPs with a university degree.

Constituency representation: The idea of promoting the constituency's interests is strongly affected by all of the selected political-system factors. Both a multilevel system and being a member of a regional parliament increase MPs' interest in the constituency. Small districts and closed lists have the same effect as voters cannot opt for a specific candidate. In other words, MPs give more importance to the constituency when citizens cannot vote for them personally but only for a closed party list. Some of the party-related characteristics also play a role: the nomination of candidates by party leaders—and not through primaries or an agency—increases the importance of the focus on constituency. MPs value the interest of their constituency less when belonging to green parties, and more when belonging to conservatives and Christian democratic parties. Although multi-collinearity may be responsible for this, the position of the party on a left–right scale confirms this result. In addition, as expected, a low level of nomination increases the importance given to the constituency. As for the individual factors, the interest in constituency is negatively related to MPs' parliamentary experience measured in years.

Representation of voters: The voter-focus is only weakly related to political-system factors. Only one of them shows a clear positive effect, namely small districts. In addition, only one party characteristic has an effect, too: MPs pay more attention to voters when they were selected at a lower level. Having increased a party's share of votes in the last election has a similar effect. On the contrary a procedure of selection led by party leaders works against the focus on voters. Also, MPs pay more attention to the interest of voters when their party is located more to the left. When it comes to individual characteristics, the longer MPs' political experience, the less they are inclined to choose a voter focus.

Specific groups: The focus on some specific groups is influenced by most of the institutional factors. The interests of such groups are especially important for regional MPs. Other political system characteristics which have a positive effect are the visibility of candidates' names on the ballot paper and closed lists. Furthermore, the smaller the district, the greater the importance given to specific groups. Regarding party-related factors, only one factor is significant: the position of the party on a left–right scale. The figures indicate that MPs belonging to a left party have a greater probability of representing specific groups than others have. The same applies to female MPs and to the youngest MPs.

To summarize the impact of institutional factors, according to the theory of communities of interest (Rehfeld 2005), small districts favour the importance of particularistic foci (constituency and voters) but not at the cost of the interests of all people. Similarly, closed lists account for the greater importance of particularistic foci (party, constituency, and specific groups). The universal focus is the only dependent factor which has a strong negative link with a multivariate system of governance. This means that especially MPs elected in a unitary system assign more importance to the representation of all people.

2.5 THE DETERMINANTS OF THE STYLE OF REPRESENTATION

We also investigated the determinants of the style of representation, concentrating on the aspects that are theoretically the most interesting ones: institutional and nomination factors which were highlighted by previous literature on styles of representation (Weßels and Giebler 2010). Here we have used multiple binomial logit regressions.

Table 2.7 shows that each level of governance corresponds to a specific style. Being elected at the national level in a unitary state enhances the probability of operating as a party delegate. Being a regional MP favours the probability of acting as a voters' delegate, while the probability of being a trustee increases when an MP is elected at the national level in a multilevel state. The visibility of candidates' name on the ballot paper increases the probability of being a party delegate while the likelihood of choosing the style of trustee or voters' delegate decreases at the same time. The possibility for citizens to vote for a candidate follows the same pattern.

Let us turn to the effect of the electoral system: in comparison with a PR closed list, being elected in a majority system decreases the probability of being a party delegate and also a voters' delegate. On the contrary, majority systems favour the style of trustee. Still, compared to PR closed lists, MPs elected on open lists follow the same pattern as MPs elected in a majority system. The effect of district magnitude is not significant for the variable measuring the party delegate style. However, this factor is significant for the voters' delegate and the trustee style. A larger district does not favour the voters' delegate style but increases the probability of being a trustee. These results are in accord with the theory of communities of interest (Rehfeld 2005): MPs from small districts are able to listen to their voters' demands and to take them into account when a conflict between two sources of representation appears. The presence of primaries enhances the probability of being a trustee and a party

TABLE 2.7 *The determinants of the style of representation (binomial logistic regression)*

		Party delegate	Voters' delegate	Trustee
Level of governance[1]	National/ unitary	0.407 (0.182)*	–0.534 (0.245)*	–0.045 (0.207)
	National/ multilevel	–0.342 (0.144)*	–0.557 (0.198)**	0.772 (0.160)***
Paper mentions candidates		0.733 (0.162)***	–0.509 (0.196)**	–0.551 (0.179)**
Voters can vote for (a) candidate(s)		0.490 (0.187)	–0.388 (0.254)	–0.335 (0.213)
Electoral system[2]	PR open lists	–1.689 (0.195)***	–0.014 (0.254)	1.930 (0.209)***
	Majority	–0.400 (0.271)	–1.392 (0.401)***	1.264 (0.298)***
District magnitude		0.078 (0.071)	–0.362 (0.091***	0.162 (0.077)**
Primaries		0.162 (0.180)	–0.710 (0.281)**	0.255 (0.200)
Level of nomination		–0.176 (0.157)	–0.495 (0.205)**	0.562 (0.169)***
R^2		0.116	0.092	0.158

Source: PARTIREP MPs survey *** P<.001; ** P<.01; * P<.05; all coefficient are Beta. S.E. are in parenthesis.
Notes: [1]Regional level; [2]PR closed list.

TABLE 2.8 *The determinants of representational styles (multinomial logistic regression)*

		Party delegate[1]	Voters' delegate[1]
Level of governance[2]	National/unitary	0.141 (0.213)	−0.461 (0.288)
	National/multilevel	−0.732 (0.167)***	−1.026 (0.228)***
Paper mentions candidates		0.769 (0.191)***	0.014 (0.230)
Voters can vote for (a) candidate(s)		0.461 (0.219)*	−0.114 (0.296)
Electoral system[3]	PR closed list	0.981 (0.309)**	2.023 (0.447)***
	PR open list	−1.187 (0.327)***	0.703 (0.455)
District magnitude		−0.060 (0.082)	−0.394 (0.105)***
Primaries		−0.145 (0.204)	−0.830 (0.316)**
Level of nomination		−0.503 (0.177)**	−0.789 (0.229)***
R^2		0.172	

*** P < .001; ** P < .01; * P < .05; all coefficient are Beta. S.E. are in parenthesis.
Notes: [1]Trustee; [2]Regional level; [3]Majority.

delegate but decreases the likelihood of selecting the style of voters' delegate. Finally, the higher the level of nomination, the lower the probability to select the style of a party or voters' delegate. On the other hand, a high level of nomination favours the style of trustee.

These analyses produce interesting results, but also lead to quite complex conclusions. Many factors have the same effect on different styles. In addition, the low coefficients of determination indicate that our models are not completely efficient. In order to overcome these difficulties, we computed a multinomial logistic regression indicating which factors explain the choice of one style over another. The results are displayed in Table 2.8 with trustee as the category of reference for the dependent variable.

The effect of the level of governance is then clearly confirmed by this multinomial regression. For each category there is a corresponding style (regional level for voters' delegate, unitary state for party delegate, and multilevel state for trustee). The reference of candidates' names does not favour the trustee style but enhances the probability of being a party delegate. The effect of the electoral system is clearer in the multinomial regression. Proportional closed lists decrease the probability of choosing the style of trustee instead of the two other styles. MPs elected in a majority system have lower chances of choosing the style of a voters' delegate than proportionally elected MPs. Other factors confirm the results provided by the last table: a high district magnitude works against the style of voters' delegate. MPs selected through primaries are more likely to be trustees than party or voters' delegates. The effect of the level of nomination follows the same pattern: a high level of nomination favours the style of trustee rather than the two other styles.

2.6 CONCLUSIONS

Which conclusions on the distribution and determinants of role orienta-tions can be drawn from our findings? One is certainly that the analysis and explanation of representational roles is a complex task, because the phenom-enon is multifaceted. Two important points do however stand out. The first is the impact of institutional choices: institutions induce the type of roles they are built for. The second conclusion refers to the parties: the way in which they function does affect the way in which their elected MPs fulfil their representational role.

Both for the focus and for the style of representation the institutions have the effects that could be expected. Especially, the level of government mat-ters. In unitary systems, MPs have a more universal focus of representation, whereas regional MPs rather choose a more local one through constituency or voters' focus. Electoral systems also work in the theoretically expected direction: the more an electoral system promotes personal representation, the more the representational focus is localized. The more an electoral system promotes party representation, the more MPs tend to focus on party or on 'all people'.

And together with the institutional context, the party organization mat-ters. The stronger the organizational power of the party organization over the selection and nomination process, the more parties are able to push MPs towards a party focus. If parties define the list order and if the voting rules do not allow voters to choose a particular person, a partisan focus of representa-tion is much more likely.

For the style of representation, results are similarly straightforward. The more the fate of MPs in terms of their past and future nomination for elec-tion depends on the party, the more they are likely to choose a trustee role. On the contrary, when candidates as persons matter, that is, the more personal-ized the electoral system and the nomination, the more a voters' delegate role is probable.

NOTES

1. Stanford Encyclopedia of Philosophy available online at <http://plato.stanford.edu/entries/political-representation/> accessed 9 November 2013.
2. 'Your Representative owes you, not his industry only, but his judgment; and he betrays, instead of serving you, if he sacrifices it to your opinion. . . . Parliament is not a Congress of Ambassadors from different and hostile interests; which inter-ests each must maintain, as an Agent and Advocate, against other Agents and

Advocates; but Parliament is a deliberative Assembly of one Nation, with one Interest, that of the whole; where, not local Purposes, not local Prejudices ought to guide, but the general Good, resulting from the general Reason of the whole. You chose a Member indeed; but when you have chosen him, he is not Member of Bristol, but he is a Member of Parliament.' (Burke, 'Speech to the Electors of Bristol', available at The Online Library of Liberty: <http://oll.libertyfund.org/index. php?option=com_staticxt&staticfile=show.php%3Ftitle=659&layout=html> accessed 9 November 2013.)

3. Esaiasson (2001) points to the lack of party interests in this approach, but it seems legitimate to count them as group interest (a functional representation).
4. Eulau (1986: 187) distinguished also a third style, called 'politico', an MP who takes the role of a trustee or a delegate depending on the situation. However, the politico style has not found much response among later analysts of the representative role.
5. There are also other typologies of representative roles. Many of them develop the typology of Searing (1994). For their review and comparison see Andeweg (2012).
6. Asked only where the electoral system allowed for candidate preference.
7. We decided to drop party voters from our foci because of the strong correlation between one's own voters ($r = 0.643$) and the party ($r = 0.642$).
8. The distribution of answers for each single question was: 61 per cent the party's opinion rather than own opinion (39 per cent), 67 per cent one's own opinion rather than voters' opinion (33 per cent), and 65 per cent party's opinion rather than voters' opinion (35 per cent).
9. This result is confirmed by an additional analysis of the importance of representing one's own party in relation to other foci of representation, i.e. by comparing the scores for party with all other foci in pairs. Party is always more or equally important than other foci for 19 per cent of all MPs, out of which it is more important than any other foci for 3 per cent. The respective figures for party delegates are higher: 21 per cent and 5 per cent, while the lowest scores are among voters' delegates (12 per cent and 1 per cent).
10. We are aware of the problem of comparing R square across different samples. The problem is minimized, however, by the use of adjusted R square. For those who want to be fully on the safe side, comparison of R square within each focus across different set of variables is unproblematic; comparison across foci should be done with care.

REFERENCES

Andeweg, R. (2012), 'The Consequences of Representatives' Role Orientations: Attitudes, Behavior, Perceptions', in M. Blomgren and O. Rozenberg (eds.), *Parliamentary Roles in Modern Legislatures*. London: Routledge/ECPR, 66–84.

Bengtsson, Å. and H. Wass (2011), 'The Representative Roles of MPs: A Citizen Perspective', *Scandinavian Political Studies*, 34: 143–67.

Blomgren, M. and O. Rozenberg (2012a), 'Introduction', in M. Blomgren and O. Rozenberg (eds.), *Parliamentary Roles in Modern Legislatures*. London: Routlegde/ECPR.

—— (2012b), 'Legislative Roles and Legislative Studies: The Neo-institutionalist Turning Point?' in M. Blomgren and O. Rozenberg (eds.), *Parliamentary Roles in Modern Legislatures*. London: Routlegde/ECPR.

Bowler, S. and D. Farrell (1993), 'Legislator Shirking and Voter Monitoring: Impacts of European Parliament Electoral Systems upon Legislator-voter Relationships', *Journal of Common Market Studies*, 31: 45–70.

Bradbury, J. (2007), 'Introduction', *Regional and Federal Studies*, 17 (1): 3–22.

Braun, D. and F. Gilardi (2006), 'Taking "Galton's Problem" seriously towards a Theory of Policy Diffusion', *Journal of Theoretical Politics*, 18 (3): 298–322.

Burke, E. (1774), Speech to the Electors of Bristol, available in The Online Library of Liberty: <http://oll.libertyfund.org/index.php?option=com_staticxt&staticfile=show.php%3Ftitle=659&layout=html> accessed 8 November 2013.

Carey, J. M. and M. S. Shugart (1995), 'Incentives to Cultivate a Personal Vote: A Rank Ordering of Electoral Formulas', *Electoral Studies*, 14 (4): 417–39.

Carman, C. J. (2006), 'Public Preferences for Parliamentary Representation in the UK: An Overlooked Link?' *Political Studies*, 54 (1): 103–22.

Converse P. E. and R. Pierce (1986), *Political Representation in France*. Cambridge, MA: Belknap Press.

Coppedge, M. J. (1994), *Strong Parties and Lame Ducks: Presidential Partyarchy and Fractionalism in Venezuela*. Stanford: Stanford University Press.

Costa, O. (2002), 'Les députés européens entre allégeances multiples et logique d'institution', *Journal of European Integration*, 24 (2): 91–112.

—— and E. Kerrouche (2007), *Qui sont les députés français? Enquête sur des élites inconnues*. Paris: Presses de Sciences Po.

—— (2009), 'Representative Roles in the French National Assembly: The Case for a Dual Typology?' *French Politics*, 7: 219–42.

De Winter, L. (1997), 'Intra- and Extra-Parliamentary Role Attitudes and Behaviour of Belgian MPs', *Journal of Legislative Studies*, 3 (1): 128–54.

Dudziṅska, A. (2011), 'Radni wojewódzcy o roli reprezentanta', in E. Nalewajko (ed.), *Radni sejmików wojewódzkich*. Warsaw: ISP PAN, 79–96.

—— and B. Post (2009), 'Political Representation at the Local Level', in J. Wasilewski (ed.), *Political Leadership in Polish Counties*. Warsaw: ISP PAN, 151–77.

Esaiasson, P. (2001), 'Political Representation—A Discussion on Concepts, Measurement, and Selected Empirical Findings', a manuscript presented at the General Conference of ECPR, 6–8 September 2001 in Canterbury (Great Britain).

Eulau, H. (1986), *Politics, Self, and Society: A Theme and Variations*. Cambridge, MA: Harvard University Press.

—— and P. D. Karps (1977), 'The Puzzle of Representation: Specifying Components of Responsiveness', *Legislative Studies Quarterly*, 2: 233–54.

—— J. Wahlke, W. Buchanan et al. (1959), 'The Role of the Representative: Some Empirical Observation on the Theory of Edmund Burke', *American Political Science Review*, 53: 742–56.

Farrell, D. and R. Scully (2010), 'The European Parliament: One Parliament, Several Modes of Political Representation on the Ground?' *Journal of European Public Policy*, 17 (1): 36–54.

Fenno, R. (1978), *Home Style: House Members in Their Districts.* Boston: Little Brown.

Gross, D. (1978), 'Representative Styles and Legislative Behavior', *Western Political Quarterly*, 31, 3 (Sept.): 359–71.

Jewell, M. (1970), 'Attitudinal Determinants of Legislative Behavior: The Utility of Role Analysis', in A. Kornberg and L. Musolf (eds.), *Legislature in Developmental Perspective.* Durham: Duke University Press, 460–500.

Kerrouche, E. (2004), 'Appréhender le rôle des parlementaires: étude comparative des recherches menées et perspective', in O. Costa, E. Kerrouche, and P. Magnette (eds.), *Vers un renouveau du parlementarisme en Europe?* Brussels: Editions de l'Université de Bruxelles, 35–55.

Mair, P. (2008), 'The Challenge to Party Government', *West European Politics*, 31 (1–2): 211–34.

Mayhew, D. (1974), *Congress: The Electoral Connection.* New Haven: Yale University Press.

Miller, W. and D. E. Stokes (1963), 'Constituency Influence in Congress', *American Political Science Review*, 57 (1): 45–56.

—— R. Pierce, J. Thomassen, et al. (1999), *Policy Representation in Western Democracies.* Oxford: Oxford University Press.

Morgenstern, S. (2004), *Patterns of Legislative Politics: Roll-Call Voting in Latin America and the United States.* Cambridge: Cambridge University Press.

Müller, W. C. (2000), 'Political Parties in Parliamentary Democracies: Making Delegation and Accountability Work', *European Journal of Political Research*, 37 (3): 309–33.

—— and T. Saalfeld (eds.) (1997), *Members of Parliament in Western Europe: Roles and Behaviour.* London: Frank Cass.

Pilet, J.-B., A. Freire, and O. Costa (eds.) (2012a), 'Political Representation in France, Belgium, and Portugal', *Representation*, 48: 4.

—— (2012b), 'Ballot Structure, District Magnitude and Constituency-orientation of MPs in Proportional Representation and Majority Electoral Systems', *Representation*, 48: 4.

Pitkin, H. (1967), *The Concept of Representation.* Berkeley: University of California Press.

Rehfeld, A. (2005), *The Concept of Constituency: Political Representation, Democratic Legitimacy, and Institutional Design.* Cambridge: Cambridge University Press.

Schmitt, H. and J. Thomassen (eds.) (1999), *Political Representation and Legitimacy in the European Union.* Oxford: Oxford University Press.

Searing, D. (1994), *Westminster's World.* Cambridge, MA: Harvard University Press.

Strøm, K. (2012), 'Roles as Strategies: Towards a Logic of Legislative Behavior', in M. Blomgren and O. Rozenberg (eds.), *Parliamentary Roles in Modern Legislatures.* London: Routledge/ECPR.

Thomassen, J. and R. B. Andeweg (2004), 'Beyond Collective Representation: Individual Members of Parliament and Interest Representation in the Netherlands', *Journal of Legislative Studies*, 10 (4): 47–69.

—— and H. Schmitt (1997), 'Policy Representation', *European Journal of Political Research*, 32 (2): 165–84.

Viera, M. and D. Runciman (2008), *Representation*. Cambridge: Polity Press.

Wahlke, J. (1962), *The Legislative System*. Chichester: John Wiley & Sons.

Weßels, B. (1999a), 'Whom to Represent? Role Orientations of Legislators in Europe', in H. Schmitt and J. Thomassen (eds.), *Political Representation and Legitimacy in the European Union*. Oxford: Oxford University Press.

—— (1999b), 'System Characteristics Matter: Empirical Evidence from Ten Representation Studies', in W. Miller, R. Pierce, J. Thomassen et al. (eds.), *Policy Representation in Western Democracies*. Oxford: Oxford University Press, 137–61.

—— (2007), 'Political Representation and Democracy', in R. J. Dalton and H. D. Klingemann (eds.), *The Oxford Handbook of Political Behavior*. New York: Oxford University Press, 833–49.

—— and H. Giebler (2010), 'Focus and Style—An Old Debate Revived', paper presented at the Annual Meeting of the American Political Science Association, Washington, 2–5 September 2010, Washington DC.

—— (2011), 'Choosing a Style of Representation: The Role of Institutional and Organizational Incentives' paper presented at the 6th ECPR General Conference, 25–7 August, Reykjavík.

The Representation of Old and New Groups

Daniele Caramani, Karen Celis, and Bram Wauters

3.1 INTRODUCTION

This chapter addresses the question of changing group representation in Europe. It investigates comparatively whether individual representatives (MPs) at national and regional level represent and mobilize in terms of groups as cleavage theory has maintained for a long time, or if in more recent times this form of representation and mobilization is no longer predominant.[1] While a comparison with the past is not possible due to the lack of similar data for earlier periods of time, the chapter attempts to identifying changes in the way in which MPs think about the representation of socio-economic and cultural segments of the society and if social cleavages are still relevant in their mobilization strategies.

Two qualifications should be made from the outset of this chapter. The first one concerns the unit of analysis. The chapter focuses on individual MPs, their goals, motivations, social environments, and preferences rather than political parties as the main actors of mobilization and representation. While the chapter also includes comparisons between parties, one of the main goals is to capture changes in representation in an age of the declining role of parties, the weakening of organizational ties, and the blurring of ideological differences. We assume that in a context in which parties play a lesser role, the role of individual MPs increases and gains scope. The second qualification concerns the type of data the chapter relies on. Data are responses of individual MPs about their preferences, choices, and perceptions about how to best perform mobilization and representation of groups. It is a 'subjective' type of data and not 'objective' information on the relevance of cleavages and social stratification. The data shed light on how much cleavages and stratification matter to individual MPs in their strategies.[2]

The chapter thus looks at the role of group mobilization and representation from the perspective of individual MP's strategies and how this translates into practices of electoral mobilization but also into meaning-construction of their democratic role. We look at changes in groups (the *represented*) from social- to value-based, as well as changes in the actors (the *representatives*) from party- to MP-based. In addition, available data allows us not only to focus on substantive representation but also to distinguish between *substantive and descriptive* (numerical) *representation* and to analyse the extent to which these different representation modes overlap with specific party families.

The next section analyses some shifts that the literature has identified in group representation, namely from social- to value-based, from bottom-up to top-down mobilization and from the aforementioned change from party- to MP-centred. A substantial descriptive section follows in which major strategies of group representation are depicted along cross-country, cross-family, and cross-level (regional vs. national) dimensions: the 'what' and the 'how' of representation. The last section provides explanatory models to account for variations in strategies of group representation among MPs. In the conclusion we address the implications of our empirical findings.

3.2 CHANGING CLEAVAGE STRUCTURES: FROM OLD TO NEW GROUPS

3.2.1 The Decline of Old Cleavages

Party politics of a large part of the twentieth century has been marked by the cleavages described in the seminal work by Stein Rokkan (1999): church versus state; working class versus bourgeoisie, centre versus periphery, and urban versus rural.[3] Cleavage politics implies a strong and stable fusion of party and group identity (Bartolini and Mair 1999; Knutsen and Scarbrough 1995). It is defined by a fixed connection between social structure (i.e. social groups and their interests) on the one hand, and political agency (i.e. political parties giving coherence and political expression to the beliefs, values, and interests of those social groups) on the other hand. Structural social divisions are transformed into cleavages if political actors give ideological coherence and organizational expression to beliefs, values, and experiences among the members of social groups.

For some this type of group-based politics with political parties representing specific groups in society, for instance, socialist parties representing the working class, has come to an end (Dalton et al. 1984; Franklin et al. 1992). The reasons fuelling this evolution in post-industrial society are multiple, and include tertialization, mediatization, affluence, cognitive mobilization, individualization, and secularization (Enyedi 2008: 289). These developments influence first of all the very existence of social units in society, and also lessen group closure. Citizens stop living in closed and homogeneous socio-political 'pillars'. The result of the process of de-structuring of the traditional cleavages, or the de-alignment of traditional links between social groups and parties, is a decline of structural and ideological voting, as noted for Western and Central Europe (van der Brug 2010). Electoral behaviour becomes volatile and 'floating' on the waves of short-term issues, popularity of party leaders, and the retrospective evaluation of government performance (Enyedi 2008; Enyedi and Deegan-Krause 2010). This leads, for instance, to the (perceived) decline of class voting (Clark and Lipset 1991). At the same time, political parties no longer appeal to these traditional social groups like blue-collar workers and turn to a catch-all strategy free from social structural anchors (Kirchheimer 1966; Katz and Mair 1995; Przeworski and Sprague 1988).

Some scholars, however, nuance the picture of de-structuring and de-alignment. Enyedi (2008) and Kriesi (2010) draw attention to significant counter-tendencies that point to the continuous relevance of group-based politics. First, although blue-collar workers increasingly vote for radical right populist parties and left parties win votes from the middle class, class patterns in voting behaviour do not lose all relevance. It has been shown that class divisions still matter for policy positions of voters on socio-economic issues (role of trade unions, organization of social security, and so on). These issues are however increasingly trumped as vote determinants by socio-cultural or left-libertarian topics (attitudes towards ethnic minorities, and so on). On these topics, workers often take a more authoritarian stance, which drives them to (extreme) right parties (Van der Waal et al. 2007). Yet the appeal of rightist parties does not mean that their class position no longer determines points of view on socio-economic topics.

Second, the de-alignment thesis suffers from conceptualization problems and heavily depends on the use of class categories that no longer adequate characterize contemporary social structures. When social status is captured by employer relations, working environment, task structure, the autonomy of the job, life styles, consumption patterns, or the ability to change residence, some studies show that it still informs voting behaviour (Evans 1999; Oesch 2008).

Third, other social structures like religion, territory and ethnicity still define political behaviour in large parts of Europe. Furthermore, gender also structures contemporary mass politics (Inglehart and Norris 2000) and age groups (retired people versus people in the labour market) might increasingly do so in the near future (Enyedi 2008).[4]

3.2.2 The Rise of a New Value-based Cleavage

Another important debate concerns not so much the irrelevance of the old cleavages, but the relevance of a new cleavage based on value orientations.

Controversy exists about whether this division based on values is indeed a cleavage that meets the definitional requirement of socio-structural origins and well-defined socio-structural bases.[5] One must be willing, as Kriesi (2010) and Enyedi (2008) suggest, to stretch the concept to the extent that it includes group-specific party appeals, group-specific behaviour, and polarized political systems, regardless of whether they are caused by social categories or values. Indeed, the value-based cleavage does not neatly fit social categories or identities. Yet, it has roots in the socio-structural categories of class, occupation, education, generation, and nation (Kriesi 2010; Stubager 2009).

Furthermore, groups defined on value orientation might not feature the same type of closure, social control, and sanctioning as was the case with traditional cleavages. But the highly diverse and specialized new media do allow for high level in-group orientation—what Blumler and Kavanagh (1999) call the 'electronic equivalents of gated communities'. Present-day media techniques also feed into cleavage politics in another important way: parties can tailor their strategies to specific groups, of whom they have more detailed information than ever before (Enyedi 2008: 297). This allows for cleavage-centred strategies, at the same time as catch-all-strategies to cater for the median voter as well as for specific groups.

3.2.3 From Redistribution to Recognition

The literature on political cleavages sketched in the above paragraphs suggests that traditional cleavages have blurred and consequently that the relevance of representing class and religious interests has diminished. At the same time, however, the representation of new groups in society has gained interest. Especially the under-representation of women and ethnic minorities is questioned (Phillips 1995), and efforts are made to enhance their representation. This shift from class and religion to other groups occurred simultaneously with a new conception of equality.

According to Fraser (1997) the retreat from economic egalitarianism has been assisted by new ways of thinking about political equality. The old politics of redistribution with a firm focus on class was replaced by a new politics of recognition focusing on identity groups like women and ethnic minorities. In her seminal work *Which Equalities Matter?* (1999) Anne Phillips elaborates on the fact that through much of the twentieth century inequality was understood as primarily a class phenomenon, something to do with the distribution of income and wealth and the effects of private property (Phillips 1999: 21). Today equality is thought to be foremost a political or cultural matter implying a recognition of the different identities based on, for instance, race and gender. The new concept of political equality links equality with acknowledgement of difference, which radically differs from the economic equality that was very much about erasing (class) differences. Indeed, Phillips contends that ignoring the different nature of these identity groups, and instead holding on to race or gender neutrality, results predominantly in expecting ethnic minorities and women to conform to norms and institutions that were not developed by them or for them. This is the opposite of equal treatment and, hence, equality can only be reached 'through difference' (Phillips 1999: 25).

Furthermore, the recognition approach or identity politics is different from the 'live-and-let-live' strategy of tolerance because the latter does not imply that difference and equality are thought of together (Phillips 1999: 28). Nevertheless, Phillips stresses, the turn towards political equality need not lead people away from matters of social and economic concern (Phillips 1999: 15). Quite the contrary: 'commitment to political equality gives new urgency and importance to the case for economic equality, and this is particularly so because of what is implied in recognizing other citizens as one's equals' (Phillips 1999: 19).

3.2.4 New Concepts of Political Representation

As mentioned above, group-based politics have not withered away with the decline of class-based strategies. The latter might not have completely disappeared (yet) and new groups have come to the fore. Being rational actors political parties develop strategies to connect to these groups and win their votes. Overall, political parties apply two types of strategies in that respect, one related to descriptive representation, the other related to substantive representation. The descriptive representation strategy concerns the inclusion of blue-collar workers, women, ethnic minorities, age groups, and so forth on the electoral lists, and the increased presence of these groups in elected assemblies and governments.[6] The substantive representation strategy is about parties and politicians making claims to represent the interests, views, and needs of specific groups. In order to do that parties count on descriptive representatives of the group, but they also forge alliances with civil society organizations or establish women's or ethnic minority wings within the party structure in order to feed electoral and party programmes with group interests (Celis, Eelbode, and Wauters 2013).

Concerning the substantive representation of group interests and how this relates to society, recent developments in representation theory importantly stress the aesthetic and cultural dimension of representation. According to Saward a representative should be regarded as an 'artist', a 'maker of representations', a 'portrayer of the represented' (Saward 2010: 16). In the process of making claims to represent someone (or a group) the representative creates the represented and their interests. This approach differs fundamentally from earlier theories on representation that consider substantive representation only in terms of a principal–agent relationship in which the representative 'brings in' already existing interests. The claims-making approach to representation, in contrast, conceives responsiveness as more dynamic, as a 'two-way street' (Severs 2010, 2011).

In other words, representatives can echo the claims of groups, but can also construct groups through the process of making claims for them and what is in their interests. Similarly, Enyedi (2008: 3) points at the role of agency in cleavage politics. Parties are able to define the identity of social coalitions, to create new relations among social-background variables, and parties can intensify group consciousness and group specific voting. In his words: 'whether new conflicts can institutionalize into cleavages depends to a large extent on the elite's support of the old order, they can have group specific appeals' (Enyedi 2008: 296).

3.2.5 The Chapter's Goals and Research Design

This chapter investigates the relevance of traditional and new social divisions in contemporary European parliaments: are old cleavages still relevant for the representation and mobilization strategies of MPs? Have they been complemented or replaced by new groups? Our aim is to map which groups are represented by MPs, and the parties they belong to. The latter enables us to answer the question whether class is still represented, or whether it is indeed true that social democratic parties have abandoned blue-collar workers in favour of the middle classes, and that extreme-right populist parties have the working class in their sights. It also allows us to see to what extent parties are focused on one specific group (as was the case in cleavage politics) or whether parties apply a catch-all strategy and address a plurality of groups.

The chapter adds insights to the cleavage scholarship in that it investigates whether or not MPs today see the need to represent 'old groups' like class and religious groups, and whether or not 'new groups' are addressed. Regarding the latter we leave it open if these groups are addressed as part of the new value-based 'cleavage', for instance, the representation of minority rights as an expression of progressivity or democratic values like inclusion. As mentioned, we also ignore the matter of whether these old or new groups (still) form a 'real' cleavage or not, thereby meeting all the definitional requirements to claim such a label. Nevertheless, taking new views on representation and the agency role of parties in cleavage politics into account, it is, first, reasonable to assume that when the representation of old groups occurs, it is a stronger indication that this cleavage is still or again relevant, than the contrary. Second, it is also reasonable to assume that in the case where new groups are represented this is a stronger indication that cleavage building is occurring, or might occur, than the opposite.

In order to tap the representational strategies of MPs, questions about both their attitudes and their behaviour were incorporated in the questionnaire. Research has shown that MPs who are aware of the problems of the social group they belong to and attach importance to these problems, do not always succeed in translating these attitudes into behaviour due to constraints such as party discipline (e.g. Cowley and Childs 2003). Therefore, it is important to make a distinction between attitudes and behaviour in our analysis. The first attitudinal question asks MPs about how important it is for them personally to promote the views and interests of various groups in society. Substantive representation of social groups can be stimulated in two ways: either by descriptive representatives, who can bring in their experience in the representational process, or by additional resources, such as contacts with relevant organizations, who can feed MPs with their experiences and expertise and can point them to possible topics that are relevant for their social group. A second question measures the attitude towards the former element, namely the necessity to have a balanced descriptive representation of specific social groups in parliament. A third question relates to the latter aspect, namely, contacts with organizations. This question no longer examines attitudes, but behaviour. MPs are asked how often in the last year they had contact with organizations defending the interests of particular social groups. Our analysis is largely based on these three indicators.

3.3 PARTY FAMILIES AND REPRESENTATION STRATEGIES

The empirical analysis is divided into two subsections: a descriptive part, in which we describe the results in general terms, and an explanatory part, in which we try to find explanations for the variation in the attention given to the representation of social groups. After that we describe the 'what' and the 'how' of group representation.

3.3.1 The Importance of Group Representation

The first step is to establish how important MPs perceive the representation and mobilization of groups to be, before moving to the question of which groups their representation strategies focus on. Basic figures by country appear in Table 3.1. The first column in the table gives the average value of the 1–7 scale along which MPs stated the relevance for them of representing social groups.[7]

TABLE 3.1   *The importance of representing social groups by country*

Country	Mean	Standard deviation	Percentages (categories 5–7)	N
Austria	5.38	1.49	67.00	212
Israel	5.34	2.01	71.80	38
Netherland	5.2	1.63	50.80	48
Spain	5.17	1.51	65.40	264
Hungary	5.08	1.54	62.60	93
Germany	4.63	1.60	53.80	266
Switzerland	4.57	1.52	52.30	144
Belgium	4.38	1.42	46.60	159
Portugal	4.12	1.62	39.80	109
Italy	4.05	1.71	40.60	121
Ireland	4.01	1.62	38.20	34
Poland	3.8	1.98	32.70	52
United Kingdom	3.77	1.61	33.60	102
Norway	3.65	1.57	30.40	46
France	3.45	1.75	23.30	81
Total	4.59	1.69	51.20	1,770

Note: Countries ordered by mean level of importance (1–7 scale).

As it appears from the total line, the average for all MPs is 4.59. This points to a persistence in the view of MPs that it is important to represent specific social groups, or at least that this is part of what they think of as being one of their core activities. The third column in the table gives the percentages of MPs that have responded 5, 6, or 7 to the question, that is, the upper portion of the scale. More than 50 per cent of MPs either at regional or national level state that representing specific social groups is important. Both aspects therefore seem to confirm that in several countries in Europe group representation is relevant for individual MPs. A next question is then which groups and cleavages these MPs represent, whether there is a change in the type of groups that are targeted by MPs' strategies, and whether differences in the ways MPs realize group representation can be explained by particular party or country characteristics. Are the 'old' groups identified by the classical literature on cleavage structures and party systems relevant in today's landscape or have they been complemented or even replaced by 'new' ones? These questions are tackled in this chapter. Basic figures broken down by party family appear in Table 3.2.[8]

The two indicators (i.e. the average on the 1–7 scale and the percentages of MPs responding in the range 5–7) are consistent and the rank-order of the families goes from more to less importance. MPs attaching the most importance to group representation are those of the green and the regionalist parties (even if, for the latter, the figure is strongly influenced by Spanish and British MPs) for which the relationship to specific groups (women and territorially-based populations) is quite obvious. The score is on the other

TABLE 3.2 *The importance of representing social groups by party family*

Party family	Mean	Standard deviation	Percentages (categories 5–7)	N
Greens	5.07	1.49	64.6	77
Regionalists	4.75	1.60	61.2	85
Religious parties	4.68	1.67	54.5	314
Socialists	4.67	1.66	51.8	636
Conservatives	4.59	1.71	51.3	324
Extreme-right parties	4.31	1.77	40.2	76
Liberals	3.99	1.63	35.7	189
Total	4.59	1.69	51.2	1,770

Note: Party families ordered by mean level of importance (1–7 scale).

hand particularly low for liberals and extreme-right parties. This may be consistent with the traditional liberal view of society based on individuals rather than social groups, but also with the traditional nationalist view of society (in the case of extreme-right parties) based on the ideology of the unitary nation. Looking at the overall distribution of party families, it seems possible to detect a *left–right pattern* with MPs from left-wing families attaching more importance to group representation than MPs from right-wing families

3.3.2 'What': Substantive Representation

The next step is to look in more detail at which groups MPs consider important to represent. When addressing the question about which groups MPs relate to mostly, the analysis has been limited to those MPs who on the previous questions ticked 5, 6, or 7 on the 1–7 scale of importance of representing specific groups. MPs who see it as their duty to represent all people and which give therefore a maximum score of 7 to all separate items referring to a particular group (but gave a low score on the question about representing specific groups in general), cannot be considered as group representatives, and were consequently excluded from the analysis.[9] The indicator used in this part of analysis is again a 1–7 scale on which MPs could indicate to what extent they find it important to raise the interests of a number of particular social groups.[10]

Table 3.3 reports the results by party family. The table includes two indicators: first, the average score of importance to represent a specific group on the 1–7 scale; second, percentages of MPs who responded either 6 or 7 on the scale. The reason for using the second indicator is that MPs may all have a tendency to respond towards the higher end of the scale (it is important to represent all the listed social groups) and therefore to have an indicator with low variation. As before it should be recalled that this indicator allows us to assess the degree to which MPs think that it is important to

TABLE 3.3 *The importance of promoting the views and interests of specific groups in society by party family*

Party family	Young people		Elderly		Employees		Employers		Women		Farmers and fishermen		Ethnic minorities		Church or religious group	
	Mean	% (6–7)	Mean	% (6–7)	Mean	% (6–7)	Mean	% (6–7)	Mean	% (6–7)	Mean	% (6–7)	Mean	% (6–7)	Mean	% (6–7)
Greens	6.10	79.5	5.52	55.1	5.73	59.0	4.75	30.8	5.95	67.9	4.12	21.8	5.58	57.7	2.69	12.8
Socialists	6.17	72.9	5.93	64.4	6.17	74.1	4.90	33.4	5.95	63.7	4.52	30.3	5.37	49.3	3.26	13.1
Religious parties	6.03	70.7	5.82	62.6	5.46	49.4	5.51	49.5	5.35	45.0	4.93	37.7	4.56	26.2	4.69	31.4
Regionalists	6.15	74.4	5.92	67.1	6.02	70.7	5.90	64.6	5.99	68.3	5.82	62.2	5.68	56.1	4.37	29.3
Conservatives	6.07	70.9	5.95	64.9	5.67	56.6	5.75	58.9	5.67	54.9	5.44	54.0	4.88	36.3	4.68	30.1
Liberals	5.73	56.8	5.45	50.0	5.18	38.4	5.60	52.6	5.22	42.6	4.48	30.5	4.54	26.7	3.39	14.2
Extreme-right	5.99	69.2	5.97	66.7	5.56	55.1	5.31	48.7	5.35	47.4	4.85	37.2	3.51	12.8	3.49	11.5
Total	6.07	70.5	5.85	62.5	5.78	60.2	5.28	44.8	5.68	56.0	4.84	37.9	5.00	39.5	3.85	20.5

Note: N = 1,601.

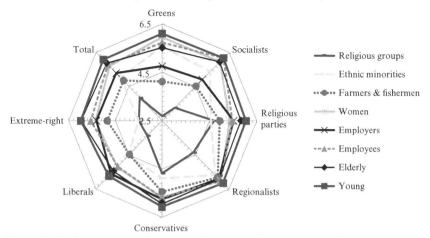

FIGURE 3.1 The importance of promoting the views and interests of specific groups in society by party family (mean scores)

represent certain groups. This is extremely valuable information as it indicates to what extent representation in terms of the substantive representation of specific groups is currently present in Europe or if, on the contrary, it is a mode of representation of the past and no longer relevant for the strategy of MPs today.

Looking at the table confirms the persistence of the importance of representing specific groups in relation to which parties MPs come from. Results therefore seem to attest to the link between party families and specific groups, that is given party families tend to mobilize—and consider it important to represent—some groups more than others. In other words, this table confirms what the classical literature on cleavages and substantive representation has found for earlier phases: that there is a clear correlation between party families and groups mentioned as being important to be represented.[11] But before coming to a more detailed discussion of the relationship between party families and social groups, it is interesting to note which groups in general are mentioned as being important to be represented. The group that clearly stands out is that of the younger generation with an average score of 6.07 and more than 70 per cent of the MPs ticking categories 6 or 7 on the 1–7 scale of importance. Also scoring generally highly on both indicators are the elderly. 'Age' or 'generation' seems therefore to be a specific dimension along which most MPs agree in saying it is important that groups are represented. On the lower end of the scale one finds religious groups (scores of 3.85 and 20.5 per cent on the two indicators respectively) and farmers and fishermen, in both cases a reflection of socio-economic and cultural changes such as industrialization and secularization.

Turning now to the question of 'if', and if yes, 'which' groups parties represent, the results point to the persistence of old party–group relationships, such as those of workers'[12] mobilization by left parties and employers' mobilization by right-wing parties, or that of religious groups by Christian democratic, Catholic or Protestant parties.[13] As mentioned, the classical literature on cleavages does not include the representation of some groups: women and younger generations in particular. In this chapter we identify the groups that were already mobilized in the early phases of mass democratic mobilization as 'old' groups, including *economic groups* (employees, employers, farmers and fishermen) as well as *cultural groups* (religious groups and ethnic minorities). On the other hand, we identify the groups that were not mobilized by established parties as 'new' groups, including mostly the 'demographics' dimension, namely, *age groups* (the younger generation and the elderly) and *women*.[14]

Let us start with the representation of 'old' groups and with what perhaps is the most typical party–group relationship, the one between socialist (social democratic) parties and employees. This relationship appears very clearly: current socialist MPs think it is important that they represent employees (average score of 6.17 on the 1–7 scale and almost 75 per cent of MPs ticking levels 6 or 7). No other party family attaches so much importance to the representation of this social group, with the limited exception of regionalist parties which—in many countries—lean toward progressive positions. As far as the mirror-relationship between economically right-wing parties (liberals and conservatives) and employers is concerned, one notices that the relationship is present for both party families although with lesser intensity if compared to the relationship between socialists and employees. Among the 'old' groups one of the most interesting cases is the low level of linkage between MPs of religious parties and religious groups (scores of 4.69 and 31.4 per cent on the two indicators respectively). MPs from religious parties do not seem to attach a preferential role to the representation of religious people. This may have several explanations among which is the role of Christian democratic parties as inter-confessional organizations beyond specific religious groups, as well as their role as functional equivalent of (centre-) right-wing parties in countries such as Belgium, Germany, and Austria among others, in which they are the conservative party. Finally, there is the representation of ethnic minorities which, according to the classical literature on cleavages, gave rise to regionalist and ethnic parties during the standardizing and centralizing National Revolution in the nineteenth and early twentieth century. Here one notices the role of regionalist parties in mobilizing these minorities which are, however, also mobilized by the green MPs. Most probably the ethnic minorities represented by the regionalist parties are the ethnic minorities already present at the moment of nation-building and state formation (such as the Basque, the

South Tyrolian, and the Scots), whereas the ethnic minorities resulting from immigration (such as the Turks in Germany, former-Yugoslavs in Switzerland, and Pakistanis in Britain) are most probably mobilized by left-wing and more specifically 'new left' (green) parties.[15]

If we now turn to the representation of 'new' groups, one sees that they are represented by a combination of 'new' parties, such as the greens, and established parties that were able to incorporate their claims in their programmes and policies—or, more precisely, say it is important to do so. MPs from all parties mention the very large importance of representing women, but the greens really stand out in this respect.[16] Women are mentioned as a very important group also by the main left-wing family which are the socialists. Much less attention is given to elderly by the greens, whereas the socialist MPs mention them as an important group to be represented. This mirrors the generational element of the post-material value system at the root of green parties which is less present in the case of socialists MPs who have stronger links to trade unionism and the protection of pensioners' rights.

If one looks at how important the representation of new groups is for right-wing families, it appears quite clearly from Table 3.3 that the scores are significantly lower than for left-wing families. This points to a *left–right pattern* in the representation of new groups (young people, women, immigrant groups) which are mentioned as important in the representation circuit more often by MPs of the left than of the right.

Finally, there is the interesting case of MPs from one specific 'new' party family, namely extreme-right populist parties that have appeared and gained support in the recent decades as a consequence of the opening up of national borders, and mobilize on cultural and economic threats from the outside. As already seen before, it appears also from Table 3.3 that the type of representation appearing here is not one of groups but one of the 'whole' with very little attention paid, in comparison to other party families, to specific groups (with the exception of age groups such as young people and the elderly). This is in line with the role of these parties in their function of 'embodying'—rather than 'representing'—the nation. The low scores of attention to specific groups of the populists is surprisingly similar to that of the liberals. As mentioned, also in this case the view of representation is not one based on specific groups. Nor is it one of embodying the 'whole', however, being based on a more individualistic and maybe atomized view of society.

3.3.3 'How': Strategies of Representation

How do these privileged relationships between certain party families and specific social groups (be it new or old ones) translate into the concrete activity

TABLE 3.4 *Contacts with social organizations by party family*

Party family	Youth organizations	Elderly organizations	Workers' organizations and unions	Employers' organizations	Women's organizations	Farmers' organizations	Ethnic minorities' organizations	Religious organizations
Greens	35.0	18.8	45.0	12.5	35.4	15.2	25.0	7.5
Socialists	46.5	43.4	52.5	24.4	31.9	12.8	18.0	11.5
Religious parties	52.5	53.9	33.6	33.8	25.8	29.1	9.8	35.6
Regionalists	30.2	22.4	40.7	37.6	14.1	21.2	21.2	12.9
Conservatives	46.1	38.6	36.3	41.9	21.9	27.4	11.5	25.1
Liberals	33.0	26.6	20.5	29.0	16.1	17.1	10.1	14.0
Extreme-right parties	50.6	42.0	17.1	17.3	18.3	14.6	3.7	7.3
Total	44.7	40.0	40.2	29.2	26.0	19.9	14.5	18.5

Note: Figures are percentages of MPs responding they had contact at least once a week or a month.

of MPs in their mobilizing strategies? This section turns to the question of the behaviour of MPs after having seen what they consider important. To answer this question the analysis relies on MPs who have responded with a score of 5 or more on the 1–7 scale to the question of how important group representation is.[17]

Strategies of representation confirm the previous section regarding the great attention devoted to the younger generation. Table 3.4 indicates that a considerable number of MPs have contact once a month or even once a week with relevant social organizations. Two social categories receive comparable levels of attention from MPs: elderly and workers' organizations (mostly trade unions) each receive about 40 per cent of mentions. In this respect contact with the new groups of 'age' are more frequent than with older socio-economic and cultural groups such as professional and cultural associations (employers, specific professional categories, and religious associations). Interestingly, contacts with women's associations are very rare (26.1 per cent of MPs state that they have contacts as frequent as monthly). Also rare is contact with organizations of ethnic minorities. This again may hide the ambiguity between native ethnic groups and immigrant ethnic groups with the members of the latter groups (immigrants) rarely having the right to vote and therefore do not appear as an interesting pool of votes.

How are such contacts distributed across party families? The contacts with the 'traditional' organizations seem again to be confirmed for the various party families. Workers' organizations (trade unions) have most frequent contacts with socialist parties. Also for MPs from socialist parties, trade unions are the type of organization with which they have the most frequent contact. On the other hand, only very few liberal and conservative MPs have contacts with workers' organizations. Conservative MPs have the most frequent contact with employers' associations who, in turn, have most of their contacts with conservatives as opposed to MPs from other party families. While this pattern confirms the traditional link between parties and socio-economic groups, religious parties have a much looser contact with religious organizations.[18] Their most frequent contacts are with organizations of age groups, such as organizations for young people and for the elderly. On the other hand, however, from the perspective of religious organization, MPs from religious parties are the primary partner among all party families. As far as the mobilization of 'age' is concerned (young people and the elderly), one sees that it is the resort of the main mass parties such as socialists, Christian democrats, and conservatives, as well as the extreme-right populist parties. On the contrary, 'gender' seems to be the resort of new politics parties such as the green family (as well as the socialists).[19]

The party family comparison appearing in the last column of Table 3.4 reveals once more a left–right pattern in the way in which MPs keep contacts with organizations of their core socio-economic and cultural constituencies.

MPs from left-wing party families such as greens and socialists display much more frequent contacts with the core organizations than MPs from right-wing party families. The greens clearly stand out with 28.5 per cent of MPs stating that they have contacts with organizations and associations once a month if not more, followed by the socialists with a percentage of 18.3. The contrast is strong with party families of the right such as conservatives and liberals for which the percentages are 8.3 and 9.9 respectively, but also for religious parties (12.7 per cent).

3.3.4 Descriptive Representation

We now turn to the question of descriptive representation, that is, the extent to which MPs attach importance to the fact that representatives reproduce the social composition of parliaments given social dimensions, such as gender balance, age, social origin, and so forth. Table 3.5 displays the information by party family.[20] Before looking at differences between party families, it is interesting to note that, overall, two dimensions seem important for MPs across Europe—namely, gender balance and regional origin. For 30.5 per cent of MPs it is very important that the proportion of women in parliament mirrors the proportion of women in society. The percentage of MPs who think similarly about regional origin is 23.4. On the contrary, only very few MPs think that the proportion of religions in parliament should match that in society. The percentage is a mere 2.6. Figures for age, class, ethnicity, and language are roughly between 8 and 15 per cent.

Concerning variations in regard to the importance attached to descriptive representation across party families, Table 3.5 shows that it is mostly green MPs (28.5 per cent) and socialist MPs (18.3 per cent) who attach most importance to it. As opposed to these high figures one finds the lowest figures for liberal and conservative MPs. There seems to be a left–right divide in terms of how important descriptive representation is considered. Green and socialist MPs attach most importance to the proportional presence in parliament compared to society for women (78.3 and 46.8 per cent of green and socialist MPs respectively) but also for social class and age. On all three dimensions (gender, age, class) the percentages are lowest for liberals and conservatives. Green MPs, but much less other MPs, attach importance to the presence in parliament of MPs mirroring the ethnic diversity in society (24.4 per cent for green MPs). The descriptive representation of regional and linguistic diversity is important for MPs of regionalist parties, as one might expect.

To conclude this section one should point out the high degree of overlap between the main strategies for group representation across parties. MPs from parties that value the substantive representation of certain groups as important also cultivate contacts with the corresponding organizations and

TABLE 3.5 *Importance of descriptive representation of social dimensions by party family*

Party family	Age	Class	Gender	Ethnicity	Religion	Language/Culture	Region
Greens	20.3	32.5	68.8	22.5	1.3	10.0	21.5
Socialists	16.0	19.8	42.9	9.8	2.4	5.1	20.1
Religious parties	10.1	10.4	17.6	3.3	2.4	8.9	28.8
Regionalists	11.8	15.3	27.1	11.8	4.7	14.1	25.9
Conservatives	8.7	3.5	10.7	3.5	1.4	4.3	19.7
Liberals	8.5	9.5	14.5	3.5	2.0	5.5	16.1
Extreme-right parties	8.5	8.5	9.8	8.5	1.2	24.4	20.7
Total	12.3	13.8	27.7	7.3	2.3	7.4	21.2

Note: Figures are percentages of MPs responding 'fairly' or 'very important'.

think that MPs should reflect the balance between groups as it appears in society.[21] There are nonetheless some discrepancies which indicate different strategies according to party families. First, there is the strong importance attached to descriptive representation, as opposed to the maintenance of contacts, by green MPs. Second, there is the opposite pattern for liberal and conservative MPs who seem to devote more time and effort to contacts with the relevant organizations than to representing social groups through descriptive representation. In this aspect, liberal and conservative MPs are joined by MPs from the other large historical party organization, namely socialist, for which contacts with civil society associations is very important. This is true for most social groups with the exception of women, for which socialists MPs think that descriptive representation is at least as important as representation through contacts with women's associations.

Overall, the previous tables show that differences across party families are significant pointing to a persistent role for party affiliation and ideology in the preferences expressed by MPs and their mobilization and representation strategies. Data presented here do not attest to a true shift from parties to individual MPs as channels of representation.

3.4 REPRESENTATION STRATEGIES AND NEW/OLD GROUPS

The final analysis of group representation concerns the degree to which the three indicators about the relevance of group representation, and the strategies used (either contacts or descriptive representation) are related to one another in terms of 'new' and 'old' groups. Does the representation of some cleavages follow a different strategy with respect to other cleavages?

The output of the factor analysis appearing in Table 3.6 provides an answer to this question. Because of the different formulations of the questions in the questionnaire, the variables of the factor analysis for each of the three questions do not entirely overlap. It is nonetheless possible to compare results across the three variables on 'importance', 'contacts', and 'descriptive representation'.[22] From the first factor analysis in Table 3.6 on which specific groups are perceived as important to be represented, one sees that the first factor loads more strongly on variables about the representation of age groups (both young and old people), class (workers), and gender (women): all above 0.700 in the table. This correlation between age, class, and gender appears to be the constituency to which left parties mainly appeal and is constituted by a combination of old and new cleavages. What is remarkable is the absence from the groups of variables with the highest scores in this dimension of ethnic minorities. As mentioned above, this group is ambiguous in its inclusion of both national and immigrant minorities, the former not being one of the main social constituencies of the left, the latter not having the right to vote in most countries and therefore not representing a conspicuous electoral basin. The second factor appearing from the analysis of which groups are perceived as important to be represented is less clear-cut. It includes, on the one hand, a strong loading on the variable concerning religious groups and, on the other hand, factors with some weight on the employers' groups, and farmers and fishermen.

This latter group of various employers and self-employed point to a more typical 'old' liberal-conservative and Christian democrat electoral constituency, but also to a typical constituency identified as 'losing out' from the opening up of labour markets and globalization, which today is mobilized to a large extent by extreme-right wing populists. Apparently, MPs who estimate the representation of these groups highly relevant, also attach importance to the representation of the interests of religious groups. Combined, the two dimensions reveal once again a left–right pattern.

The other two factor analyses appearing in Table 3.6 both focus on variables addressing the strategies of representation (making contacts with organizations and social associations, and through descriptive representation). The basic pattern detected above is confirmed. We find a first factor combining strategies of representation through contacts with age groups, class (mainly through the contact with trade unions), and women to which corresponds a desire to see these groups represented in parliament through descriptive representation. Interestingly, and somewhat contradictorily with what was found earlier, in this latter strategy one finds the representation of ethnic diversity also loading heavily on the first dimension, that is, the 'typical' left constituency combining old and new groups.

This last factor analysis is interesting also for the fact that it includes an explicit reference to the representation of 'territory' or 'region' which is absent

TABLE 3.6 *Factor analysis of the mentioning of different societal groups*

	Variables						
	Importance of representation		Contacts with organizations		Representation in parliament		
	Component		Component		Component		
Social groups	1	2	1	2	1	2	3
Young people	0.743	–.0306	0.670	–0.073	0.720[a]	–0.404[a]	0.008[a]
Elderly	0.775	–0.120	0.690	–0.049			
Employees	0.772	–0.209	0.655	0.018	0.743[b]	–0.065[b]	–0.098[b]
Employers	0.615	0.438	0.576	0.562			
Women	0.806	–0.261	0.659	–0.350	0.672	–0.512	–0.201
Farmers and fishermen	0.671	0.463	0.481	0.617	–	–	–
Ethnic minorities	0.683	–0.149	0.584	–0.492	0.773	0.086	–0.336
Religious groups	0.408	0.676	0.562	–0.056	0.579	0.605	0.036
Region	–	–	–	–	0.573	–0.119	0.782
Language or culture	–	–	–	–	0.630	0.531	–0.012

Note: Extraction method: principal component analysis.

[a] Young people and elderly together as 'age'.

[b] Employees and employers together as 'social class'.

in the first two sets of variables on relevance and contacts. The factor 'region' appears here clearly as a distinct dimension in addition to the first two dimensions, which are similar to what came out of the previous factor analyses. On the second dimension one finds again the contacts with employers and professional groups. This dimension is however absent in the factor analysis on descriptive representation. Descriptive representation therefore does not seem to be a strategy considered relevant for the representation of economic groups such as employers, farmers and fishermen for which contacts are more important in the representation circuit. Descriptive representation, thus, seems to be a strategy for the representation of 'socio-cultural' groups, such as age, gender, and even class, for which 'identity' elements are more important than 'interest' factors. While the representation of 'territory' is clearly a separate factor, the representation of religion has a weak correlation with other cultural cleavages such as region and language.

To confirm this analysis a correlation matrix has been produced for each question. Although there are differences in the strengths of correlations between different groups in all three questions there is a generally high correlation between the stated importance and the strategy used to represent the various groups, be it class, gender, age, and so forth.[23] Again, however, it appears that the differences in the strength of correlations reveal groups that are typically privileged by leftist MPs (such as women, class, and immigrant minorities) or by rightist MPs such as employers in general (both liberal and conservatives MPs) but also religious groups and young people (in the case of Christian democrats).

Table 3.7 provides insights into how to account for differences between MPs in their perception of the importance of group representation with the aid of a number of contextual variables.[24] As far as sociological variables are concerned, women are more likely than men to regard group representation as important by more than half a point on the 1–7 scale (the result is also statistically significant). Also young MPs tend to attach more importance to group representation. The year of birth exhibits a clear positive effect. On the other hand, seniority does not seem to affect the view of relevance of group representation to a significant extent. The year of first election (used as an indicator of seniority) does not display strong results. The fact that both women MPs and young MPs themselves belong to a group that strives to attain (more) political representation, could be an explanation here.

Next, the size of the district in which MPs are active shows that the larger the district in terms of inhabitants and voters, the more importance MPs attach to group representation. This effect can partially be explained by the effect of the electoral formula: PR systems have in general a larger district magnitude than majoritarian systems, and tend to be more supportive for group representation. But this effect also captures another element, as the effect is larger than that of a dummy variable 'PR' (not displayed in the table). The larger the district in which an MP is elected, the more MPs are elected, the more room for a division of labour between MPs which lessens the need to represent the district as a whole and which creates opportunities for group representation. In sum, district magnitude is important, and also when comparing between PR systems.

The regression table confirms some of the insights gained in the previous descriptive analysis, and particularly that rightist party families perceive group representation as less relevant than leftist party families. This appears through the dummy variable 'rightist party' in Table 3.7 which displays a significant and negative impact on the perception of the importance of group representation. The table does not display the positive effect of the dummy variable 'leftist party'. The negative effect of being right-wing (namely from conservative, liberal, and extreme-right parties) is, however, stronger than the positive effect of being left-wing (namely, from social-democratic and green parties).

Finally, there is the effect of being elected to a regional parliament. MPs of regional parliaments attach more importance to group interests than MPs in national parliaments (both in unitary and federal states). As the size of the district tends to be smaller for regional parliaments, one might suspect that there is an intervening effect between regional parliaments and district size. In order to test this, we included an interaction term (regional parliament*district size) to the model. This interaction term did, however, not show a significant effect nor did the coefficients or the significance levels of the two separate variables change much. In sum, the effect of regional parliament does not

TABLE 3.7 *Explaining variation in the perception of importance of group representation (multiple regression)*

	OLS		OLS with interaction term	
	Unstandardized coefficients (Standard error)	Standardized coefficients Beta	Unstandardized coefficients (Standard error)	Standardized coefficients Beta
Gender	0.535*** (0.089)	0.146	0.539*** (0.089)	0.147
Year of birth (age)	0.014*** (0.005)	0.085	0.014*** (0.005)	0.084
Year of first election (seniority)	0.004 (0.007)	0.15	0.004 (0.007)	0.014
Size of district (number of inhabitants)	0.042*** (0.010)	0.102	0.046*** (0.011)	0.110
Unitary state	0.218 (0.118)	0.050	0.210 (0.118)	0.048
Regional parliament	0.453*** (0.092)	0.133	0.505*** (0.102)	0.148
Either speaker or leader of parliamentary party	0.042 (0.167)	0.006	0.032 (0.167)	0.005
Dummy right-wing party	−0.260** (0.086)	−0.073	−0.260** (0.086)	−0.073
Interaction term regional parliament*size of district			−0.045 (0.039)	−0.032
Constant	−31,311 (12,479)		−31,081 (12,479)	
Adj. R²	0.064		0.064	
N	1,663		1,663	

Notes: The dependent variable is 'How important is it to you, personally, to promote the views and interests of a specific group in society?' (Q12.5) with a 1–7 response scale in which 1 stands for 'of no importance' and 7 'of great importance'. Collinearity: VIF for all variables between 1.0 and 1.6. Estimation: OLS. Statistical significance: *** ($p < 0.001$), ** ($p < 0.01$), * ($p < 0.05$).

interfere with district size. Other explanations for the effect of regional parliaments might include the fact that they are less path-dependent and thus more open to new groups and new groups' claims (Mackay 2006); are closer to the groups' grass-root organizations (Ortbals 2008); and are less marked by the strong antagonism between subdivisions within a federal or decentralized state thus leaving more space for groups and concerns that cross-cut these subdivisions (Rebouché and Fearon 2005; see also the chapter by Erzeel, Caluwaerts, and Celis in this volume).

3.5 CONCLUSION

In his 1997 Stein Rokkan lecture 'The Transformation of Cleavage Politics' Hanspeter Kriesi concluded: 'The crux is to identify theoretically and empirically the relevant social divisions of a world in flux, and to study their political formation' (Kriesi 1998: 181). This chapter testifies to the salience of social divisions in today's representative politics and to the persistence of group politics following party lines. In other words, group-based strategies are still of major importance in political parties' endeavours for establishing responsiveness to societal concerns. This is the case notwithstanding the massive party de-alignment, the de-structuring of traditional cleavages, and the emergence of the volatile voter. Group representation is of importance to the majority of the MPs in European representative democracies. Group-based politics has thus not withered away. It has, quite on the contrary, expanded its reach in terms of groups (including, for example, age groups) and parties involved (including the greens). The 'old' groups are still the focus of representatives (especially class) and 'new' groups (especially age groups and women) have gained political territory.

Group-based politics is furthermore not a matter of individual MPs. It is still, as in the classic cleavage era, party politics. There is a persistent distinction between the parties involved in group politics and those who are not, and the patterns in the groups the parties represent as well as the strategies for group representation they prefer. The left–right divide is strong. Leftist parties are more inclined to represent groups, and, more precisely, they represent old groups like class and newer ones like age groups, women, and (but to a lesser extent) ethnic minorities. The concern for these groups also translates into contacts with these groups and the wish that these groups are descriptively represented (although the latter is foremost the case for women).

Given that these groups are the focus of parties that attach greater importance to group representation, groups represented by the right seem to have a weaker substantive and descriptive linkage with representative politics. These groups include religious groups (no longer of major importance to religious parties) and employers (not of central concern to liberal and right-wing parties).

These findings, firstly, beg questions about the substantive and the descriptive representation of the groups and their interests. For instance, if women are foremost represented by leftist parties, what about the representation of conservative women (see also Celis and Childs 2012)? Secondly, the broader implication of our findings concerns the importance of group-based politics that this chapter has revealed. This underlines the importance of the questions raised in the literature regarding the nature of the old and new cleavages, the shift in meaning of equality, and the constitutive aspect of representation. What exactly are the differences, similarities, and specificities about today's group-based party politics compared with the old cleavage politics? As the literature on representation points at, group representation might have different aims in terms of socio-economic interest representation or recognition of identities. They might echo structural-societal and/or value-based divisions in society, and at the same time constitute them. Hence, next to showing that group-based politics is still salient, and that all in all there is more continuity than a drastic break with group-based politics, this chapter points at a vast future research area.

NOTES

1. Reference is made here first and foremost to representation along the cleavages that genetic models have shown to be the main elements of the structuration of European party systems, resulting from the transformations of the nineteenth and early twentieth century, and their stabilization in subsequent decades (Bartolini and Mair 1990), but also to the incorporation of new cleavages as those resulting from post-industrial transformation, materialism vs. post-materialism as well as the globalization cleavage (Inglehart 1977; Kriesi et al. 2008).
2. The cross-party analysis allows us to address the question of who represents the 'new' groups (new parties or individual MPs within established parties which were able to incorporate new concerns) and whether 'old' groups or cleavages are still the preserve of established parties.
3. For convenience and scientific accuracy we use the edited volume *State Formation, Nation-Building and Mass Democracy* (Rokkan 1999) as a reference to all of Rokkan's work.
4. When electoral participation is added to the mix, the picture becomes even more nuanced. Some scholars contend that the decreasing weight of traditional class position is due to the fact that immigrants tend to vote less (Enyedi 2008). Class is still important but no longer appears in electoral data. Also Tóka and Gosselin (2010) point to the possibility that electoral alignments are in fact stable, in spite of cleavage decline. However, the group of voters with such clear voting predispositions constitutes a decreasing share of the population. In the same vein, van der Brug's research (2010) concludes that structural voting is still present, but it is strongest in the oldest age groups and, hence, 'phases out'.
5. This value cleavage has been given different names: 'authoritarian/libertarian' (Flanagan 1987; Kitschelt 1994; Dolezal 2010); 'libertarian-universalistic/ traditionalist-communitarian' (Bornschier 2010); 'materialist/post-materialist' (Inglehart 1977); 'self-expression/survival' (Inglehart and Baker 2000).
6. On ethnic minorities see Bird (2004); on women see Krook (2009); on blue-collar workers see Wauters (2012).
7. Table 3.1 is based on Question 12 in the questionnaire. The phrasing of the question is 'How important is it to you, personally, to promote the views and interests of a specific group in society?' with a 1–7 response scale in which 1 stands for 'of no importance' and 7 'of great importance'.
8. In tables the following shortcuts for party families have been used: greens (for ecological or environmental parties), socialists (also applicable to labour, workers and social democratic parties), regionalists (this categories includes ethnic parties as well), religious parties (Christian democrats, Catholics, Protestants, etc.), conservatives, liberals, and extreme-right parties (including nationalists and populist parties).
9. In total forty-eight observations have been excluded, corresponding to about 3 per cent of the sample.
10. Table 3.3 is based on Question 13 in the questionnaire. The phrasing of the question is 'Thinking about various groups in society, how important is it to you, personally, to promote their views and interests?' with a 1–7 response scale in which 1 stands for 'of no importance' and 7 'of great importance'. The various groups are those appearing in the headings of the columns of Table 3.3.

11. The Chi-square between the two variables in the table (party family and specific group) indicates that the relationship is significant.
12. Note that in the questionnaire, the term 'employees' was used, which involves the working class, but also (parts of) the middle class.
13. MPs were able to tick multiple responses and therefore percentages do not add up to 100 per cent. Percentages appearing in the table are 'row percentages'.
14. This latter category is particularly relevant as the classical literature has always stressed how little female enfranchisement has modified the electoral balance because of factors of family socialization and roles within the family. In most European countries women have been granted the right to vote after men.
15. Unfortunately the data do not allow us to distinguish between these two types of ethnic minorities.
16. In the case of the greens this also includes ethnic minorities, more likely to be a 'new' group such as immigrant minorities.
17. Table 3.4 is based on Question 22 in the questionnaire. The phrasing of the question is 'In your role as a Member of Parliament, how often in the last year have you had contact with the following groups, persons, or organizations?' with 1 = at least once a week, 2 = at least once a month, 3 = at least every three months, 4 = at least once a year, and 5 = (almost) no contact. The various social organizations are those appearing in the headings of the columns of Table 3.4.
18. It is interesting to note that this is not the case for parties classified as liberals. This category, however, also includes social liberal parties which do not have economic and business claims at the core of their agendas.
19. The same analysis has been performed without selecting MPs who say representing specific groups is important. Results follow more or less the same pattern, with attenuated differences between party families. For this reason results have not been presented in the tables.
20. Table 3.5 is based on Question 36 in the questionnaire. The phrasing of the question is 'For each of the following divisions in society, how important is it that the various groups corresponding with them are present in Parliament in proportion to their number in the population?' with values being 1 = not at all important, 2 = not very important, 3 = fairly important, and 4 = very important. The various divisions in society are those appearing in the headings of the columns of Table 3.5.
21. Because of the different operationalization of the variables a direct comparison between strategies cannot take place. The following remarks are based on the rank order of categories rather than on quantitative differences.
22. Cases have been selected as follows: only those respondents who had responded between 5 and 7 on the 1–7 scale on Question 12, concerning the importance of representing specific social groups, have been included in the factor analysis. The extraction mode is the principal component before rotation.
23. In this regard one should account for a high degree of social desirability in the answers, meaning that the representation of all social groups is important. This is the reason why the analysis focuses on differences in the strength of correlations (responses on the scales concentrate on the higher values). One should also bear in mind that the question about 'relevance' is formulated to capture what personally are considered important groups, which does not necessarily reflect the view of the party to which MPs belong.

24. Here we used the responses on the general question about group representation. We also did some tests with questions about the representation of specific groups (women, ethnic minorities, etc.), but as these yielded more or less the same results as the general variable, these analyses are not presented here.

REFERENCES

Bartolini, S. and P. Mair (1990), *Identity, Competition and Electoral Availability: The Stabilization of European Electorates, 1885–1985*. Cambridge: Cambridge University Press.

Bird, K. (2004), 'Obstacles to Ethnic Minority Representation in Local Government in Canada', in C. Andrew (ed.), *Our Diverse Cities*. Ottowa: Metropolis and the Federation of Canadian Municipalities, 182–6.

Blumler, J. G. and D. Kavanagh (1999), 'The Third Age of Political Communication: Influences and Features', *Political Communication*, 16: 209–30.

Bornschier, S. (2010), 'The New Cultural Divide and the Two-dimensional Political Space in Western Europe', *West European Politics*, 33: 419–44.

Celis, K. and S. Childs (2012), 'The Substantive Representation of Women: What to Do with Conservative's Claims?' *Political Studies*, 60 (1): 213–25.

—— F. Eelbode, and B. Wauters (2011), 'Ethnic Minorities in Local Political Parties: A Case Study of Three Belgian Cities (Antwerp, Ghent and Leuven)', *Politics*, 33 (3):160–71.

Clark, T. N. and S. M. Lipset (1991), 'Are Social Classes Dying?' *International Sociology*, 6: 397–410.

Cowley, P. and S. Childs (2003), 'Too Spineless to Rebel? New Labour's Women MPs', *British Journal of Political Science*, 33: 345–65.

Dalton, R., S. C. Flanagan, and P. A. Beck (eds.) (1984), *Electoral Changes in Advanced Industrial Democracies: Realignment or Dealignment?* Princeton, NJ: Princeton University Press.

Dolezal, M. (2010), 'Exploring the Stabilization of a Political Force: The Social and Attitudinal Basis of Green Parties in the Age of Globalization', *West European Politics*, 33: 534–52.

Enyedi, Z. (2008), 'The Social and Attitudinal Basis of Political Parties: Cleavage Politics Revisited', *European Review*, 16: 287–304.

—— and K. Deegan-Krause (2010), *The Structure of Political Competition in Western Europe*. London: Routledge.

Evans, G. (ed.) (1999), *The End of Class Politics?* Oxford: Oxford University Press.

Flanagan, S. C. (1987), 'Value Change in Industrial Societies', *American Political Science Review*, 81: 1303–19.

Franklin, M. N., T. T. Mackie, and H. Valen (eds.) (1992), *Electoral Change: Responses to Evolving Social and Attitudinal Structures in Western Countries*. Cambridge: Cambridge University Press.

Fraser, N. (1997), *Justice Interruptus: Critical Reflexions on the 'Postsocialist' Condition*. London: Routledge.

Inglehart, R. and Norris, P. (2000), 'The Developmental Theory of the Gender Gap: Women's and Men's Voting Behavior in Global Perspective', *International Political Science Review*, 21: 441–63.

—— and W. E. Baker (2000), 'Modernization, Cultural Change, and the Persistence of Traditional Values', *American Sociological Review* 65: 19–51.

Katz, R. and P. Mair (1995), 'Changing Models of Party Organization and Party Democracy: The Emergence of the Cartel Party', *Party Politics*, 1: 5–28.

Kirchheimer, O. (1966), 'The Transformation of West European Party Systems', in J. Palombara and M. Weiner (eds.), *Political Parties and Political Development*. Princeton, NJ: Princeton University Press, 177–200.

Kitschelt, H. (1994), *The Transformation of European Social Democracy*. Cambridge: Cambridge University Press.

Kriesi, H. (1998), 'The Transformation of Cleavage Politics: The 1997 Stein Rokkan Lecture', *European Journal of Political Research*, 33: 165–85.

—— (2010), 'Restructuration of Partisan Politics and the Emergence of a New Cleavage Based on Values', *West European Politics*, 33: 673–85.

Krook, M. L. (2009), *Quotas for Women in Politics: Gender and Candidate Selection Reform Worldwide.* New York: Oxford University Press.

Mackay, F. (2006), 'Descriptive and Substantive Representation in New Parliamentary Spaces: The Case of Scotland', in M. Sawer, M. Tremblay, and L. Trimble (eds.), *Representing Women in Parliaments: A Comparative Study*. London: Routledge, 171–87.

Oesch, D. (2008), 'The Changing Shape of Class Voting: An Individual-level Analysis of Party Support in Britain, Germany, and Switzerland', *European Societies*, 10: 329–55.

Ortbals, C. D. (2008) 'Subnational Politics in Spain: New Avenues for Feminist Policymaking and Activism', *Politics & Gender*, 4: 93–119.

Phillips, A. (1995), *The Politics of Presence*. Oxford: Clarendon Press.

—— (1999), *Which Equalities Matter?* London: Polity.

Przeworski, A. and J. Sprague (1988), *Paper Stones: A History of Electoral Socialism*. Chicago, IL: University of Chicago Press.

Rebouché, R. and K. Fearon (2005), 'Overlapping Identities: Power Sharing and Women's Rights', in I. O'Flynn and D. Russell (eds.) *Power Sharing: New Challenges for Divided Societies.* London: Pluto Press, 155–71.

Saward, M. (2010), *The Representative Claim*. Oxford: Oxford University Press.

Severs, E. (2010), Representation as Claim-making: Quid Responsiveness? *Representation*, 46: 411–23.

—— (2011), 'Bringing "The People" Back In: Representative Democracy and the Potentiality of Responsiveness', paper presented at the ECPR Joint Sessions, April, St Gallen.

Stubager, R. (2009), 'Education-based Group Identity and Consciousness in the Authoritarian–Libertarian Value Conflict', *European Journal of Political Research*, 48: 204–33.

Tóka, G. and T. Gosselin (2010), 'Persistent Political Divides, Electoral Volatility and Citizen Involvement: The Freezing Hypothesis in the 2004 European Election', *West European Politics*, 33: 608–33.

Van der Brug, W. (2010), 'Structural and Ideological Voting in Age Cohorts', *West European Politics*, 33: 586–607.

Van der Waal, J., P. Achterberg, and D. Houtman (2007), 'Class Is not Dead—It Has Been Buried Alive: Class Voting and Cultural Voting in Postwar Western Societies (1956–1990)', *Politics and Society*, 35: 403–26.

Wauters, B. (2012), 'Blue Collars Striking the Red Flag: Formal and Descriptive Representation of the Working Class in the Belgian House of Representatives 1946–2007', *Labor History*, 53: 225–43.

4

From Agency to Institutions and Back: Comparing Legislators' Acting on Behalf of Women in Parliamentary Democracies

Silvia Erzeel, Didier Caluwaerts, and Karen Celis

4.1 INTRODUCTION

In its most elementary form, our system of democratic representation is one of interest representation. In the words of Hanna Pitkin (1972: 209): substantive representation takes place when representatives 'act in the interest of the represented, in a manner responsive to them'. Representation thus requires that the concerns and interests of citizens are adequately made present in the political decision-making process. But citizens' concerns and interests do not translate automatically into political decisions. Representation has an important institutional dimension: representative institutions and processes impact upon how constituencies are defined and consequently influence how interests are formulated (Williams 1998; Mezey 2008). Decision-making in the US, for instance, is characterized by strong territorial politics. This is not the result of the fact that all politics is local, Rehfeld (2005) argues. Rather, it is the nature of the electoral system, and the fact that electoral constituencies are typically confined by territorial boundaries, that encourage representatives to define interests in territorial terms. In European democracies, interests are often aggregated at the party level (Mezey 2008). Interests are then typically packaged along traditional left–right party cleavages and these alternative packages of ideas are presented to citizens.

A recurring problem with this notion of representation is that it does not fully account for interests that are not defined strictly in territorial or partisan terms (Urbinati and Warren 2008). This is problematic if we accept that party and territory never fully capture all relevant interests at stake (Phillips 1995; Williams 1998). In this light, the (under)representation of women's interests in decision-making processes has recently moved centre stage. Scholars of women's substantive representation argue that women as a social group have particular interests and needs that originate from their experiences and their position in society (Sapiro 1981; Diamond and Hartsock 1981; Jónasdóttir 1988). These interests need to be taken into account in the representational process because ignoring them would jeopardize the legitimacy and democratic value of policy outputs and legislation (Young 2002). But women's interests are not geographically concentrated and they tend to be transversal interests that cut across different party lines. How, then, do we guarantee that these interests are put forward in the representational process?

At this point, there is some disagreement on the *conditions* under which the representation of women's interests, that is, their substantive representation, takes place. For a long time, scholars have hypothesized that women's substantive representation depends on the *agency* of female legislators in parliament. Because female representatives are able to rely upon their own experiences 'as women', they are arguably more likely than their male colleagues to pay attention to women's interests and to actively promote these interests in parliament (Phillips 1995; Mansbridge 1999). Other studies go even further and emphasize the importance of the numerical presence of women in parliament: especially when the percentage of women reaches a 'critical mass' of more or less 30 per cent, are female representatives able to weigh on the political agenda and to guarantee women-friendly policy outcomes (Thomas 1991; Mateo Diaz 2005; Dahlerup 1988).

In more recent studies, however, the focus on the agency of female representatives as *'the sole or primary vehicle of women's substantive representation'* (Mackay 2008: 125) has come under scrutiny, not the least because empirical studies provide mixed results. Sex differences in legislative behaviour are sometimes small and simply increasing the number of women is often not enough to guarantee women-friendly policy outcomes. As a result, many scholars have broadened their analytical focus. They accept that women's (numerical) presence in parliament constitutes *one of many* roads to women's substantive representation and they consequently explore various additional roads to the same goal (Celis et al. 2008).

Furthermore, studies document that *institutions* mediate the complicated relationship between women's presence in parliament and the representation of women's interests (Dahlerup 1988; Kathlene 1995; Rosenthal 1998; Tremblay 2006; Reingold 2000). These studies emphasize that acting on behalf of women is sometimes a difficult undertaking for female representatives operating in 'male-dominated' institutions because these institutions tend to marginalize women (Kanter 1977; Kathlene 1995; Rosenthal 1998; Heath, Schwindt-Bayer, and Taylor-Robinson 2005). They also demonstrate that some institutions provide opportunities for women to make a difference because they provide incentives to female representatives to promote women's interests (Swers 2002; Reingold 2000; Celis and Wauters 2010).

In many of the above-mentioned studies institutions are hypothesized to impact *indirectly* on women's substantive representation: institutions help to explain when and why women's numerical presence in parliament 'makes a difference' for women's substantive representation. In this contribution, however, it is our aim to study whether or not institutions also have significant *direct* effects on the substantive representation of women (see also Waylen 2008; Weldon 2002; Beckwith and Cowell-Meyers 2007). The institutions we study are mostly macro-level institutions relating to the parliamentary, electoral, and political system. More specifically, our central hypotheses are that (1) the presence of a gender equality committee in parliament, (2) the fact whether the representative acts take place in a national or regional parliament, and (3) the electoral system all play a role in explaining legislators' acting on behalf of women. Studying these institutions will provide insights into how women's substantive representation takes place regardless of the presence of a 'critical mass' in parliament. Moreover, we shift our attention from women to *men and women* acting within the institutional setting. It is a significant shortcoming in the current literature on women's substantive representation that scholars focus almost exclusively on female legislators (Celis et al. 2008; but see Kathlene 1995). A focus on the direct effects of institutions then transcends the male–female legislator dichotomy since it considers the favourable or unfavourable conditions that institutions create for both female and male legislators' acting on behalf of women. At a more general level, the focus on the direct effects of institutions speaks to the broader question of whether institutions can be modified or 'engineered' to ensure the political inclusion of groups that are not strictly defined in territorial or partisan terms and that are at risk of being underrepresented.

In the following parts of this chapter, we first formulate our hypotheses regarding the impact of several institutions. We then elaborate on our methodological choices. Next, we present the results of the explanatory analysis. We finally conclude by discussing our results and formulating directions for future research.

4.2 THE ROLE OF INSTITUTIONS: HYPOTHESES

The new institutionalist turn has encouraged politics and gender scholars to devote attention to institutions when explaining the occurrence of women's substantive representation (see Weldon 2002; Waylen 2010; Chappell 2006). New institutionalism defines institutions as creating regularities in the behaviour of individuals, either through rules, routines, practices, or norms (Peters

1999; March and Olsen 1989). As such, institutions play an important role in shaping political outcomes (Peters 1999; Hall and Taylor 1996). They shape legistlators' acting (on behalf of women) by providing a 'relatively systematic and stable set of opportunities and constraints' (Lowndes and Leach 2004: 560). Institutions thus set the scene against which legislators decide whether or not to act for women. They offer incentives or disincentives within formal decision-making structures to advance the interests of women. They do so by fostering what is generally considered to be appropriate behaviour and by discouraging inappropriate behaviour (March and Olsen 1989; Chappell 2006). Tied back to debates on the substantive representation of women, institutions only rarely impose a formal obligation for legislators to act (or not) for women, but rather create a favourable or less favourable context for women's substantive representation.

One such incentive structure relates to legislative organization. In order to sustain and guarantee the representation of women's issues, parliaments have often called into existence specific legislative bodies dealing with matters of gender equality and women's affairs. Studies of the US Congress and of the Canadian parliament, for instance, demonstrate that women's caucuses play an important role in supporting female legislators and stimulating gender-related policies (Thomas 1994; Steele 2002). They solve collective-action problems by providing knowledge and resources to legislators so that they can act for women (Kanthak and Krause 2010).

Because our aim in this chapter is to study the activities of female *as well as* male legislators and because caucuses in general play a less important role in policymaking in European parliaments, we focus on a second type of legislative organizations, namely *parliamentary committees*. Contrary to caucuses, committees constitute more formal organizational structures in parliament. They also bring together members of different parties. Committees are important because they encourage policy specialization and promote 'informational efficiency' in parliament (Gilligan and Krehbiel 1990; Krehbiel 1991). Especially when issues on the agenda are new—which will arguably be the case for many women's issues—legislators find it difficult to predict the relationship between policy instruments, policy legislation, and policy outcomes (Gilligan and Krehbiel 1990). Relevant policy information and expertise is then provided by members of committees or subcommittees who serve as 'information specializers' in policymaking (Krehbiel 1991; Gilligan and Krehbiel 1990; Diermeier and Myerson 1999). The presence of a committee on women's issues or gender equality in parliament shows that members are able to pool information regarding women's issues, which should benefit the formulation of women's interests in parliament. We therefore hypothesize that *members of parliaments with a committee that considers legislation of importance to women—more precisely, gender equality, equal opportunities, or women's issues—will be more likely to take women's interests into account than members in parliaments without such a committee.*

A second hypothesis is that the substantive representation of women depends on whether legislators' acting on behalf of women do so in *regional parliaments* or not. We assume that *members of regional parliaments will be more likely to promote women's issues than members of national/federal parliaments* for three reasons. First of all, regional parliaments are relatively 'new' parliaments and in some way distinct or innovative compared to the federal/national parliament. Usually national parliaments and their institutional characteristics suffer from path dependency in that they always reflect and reproduce earlier institutional choices. Regional parliaments, in contrast, offer new opportunities for promoting a different political culture, for establishing new power relations within the newly formed institutions, and for including the interests of previously marginalized groups (Mackay 2006; Mackay et al. 2002; Chaney 2006; Celis and Woodward 2003).

A second reason why women's substantive representation might benefit from federalism is that feminist movements are more likely to gain access to regional parliaments because the latter exist at the meso-level of governance and are 'closer' to the workings of grass root organizations (Ortbals 2008).

Thirdly, we argue that linking the substantive representation of women to the difference between national and regional parliaments also involves looking at the nature of federalism. The choice to resort to federal arrangements usually indicates there is strong antagonism within the country (Lijphart 1999). The granting of self-rule and the creation of regional levels of government is thus a means of containing conflicts. At the federal level, these conflicts continue to dominate the political agenda. At the regional level, there is usually more room for the representation of interests that transcend the traditional cleavages, for instance the representation of social groups (Rebouché and Fearon 2005).

As a third variable, the *electoral system* sets the scene in which representative acts take place. Electoral systems have entered research on women's representation primarily through descriptive representation, namely through the finding that certain electoral rules provide more opportunities for increasing the number of female legislators than other systems (Matland 1998; Rule 1987; Leyenaar 2004). From this point of view, electoral system design influences women's substantive representation *indirectly*: it affects women's numerical presence in parliament, which in itself might influence the occurrence of women's substantive representation. Here, however, we hypothesize that electoral system design also has a *direct* effect on women's substantive representation. After all, electoral rules determine how the representative understands representation and defines his or her constituency (Norris 2004; Mezey 2008). An electoral system holds cues for legislators on how their electorate is composed, and which legislative and representative strategies they have to use.

Traditionally, scholars make a distinction between plurality/majority electoral systems on the one hand and proportional (PR) electoral systems on the other hand. Representatives in the first group tend to be elected in small single member districts and are likely to define interests in geographical terms (Rehfeld 2005; Mezey 2008). In PR systems, electoral districts are usually larger and more heterogeneous than in majority systems. Interest representation is therefore more likely to surpass 'geographical boundaries' (Sawer 1998) and to leave room for the representation of non-territorial constituencies in PR systems (Tremblay 2003, 2006). A PR system emphasizes the importance of representing social diversity, and women are part of this diversity. As a result, we hypothesize that *representatives under PR systems are more likely to act on behalf of women than representatives under plurality/majority systems.*

A second feature of the electoral system that might affect representatives' acting on behalf of women relates to the type of electoral list in PR systems. In closed-list systems, the party determines the order on the list and the allocation of seats is based solely on this list order. In open-list systems, candidates are able to obtain preferential votes and the allocation of seats takes into consideration the number of preferential votes received by a candidate. Especially in closed-list systems, the partisan focus is strong and representatives will likely define their constituency in partisan terms (Mezey 2008). In open-list systems, the partisan focus of representatives will be less strong. Parties are less likely to dominate the reselection process and candidates receive more incentives to cultivate a personal vote (Carey and Shugart 1995). Especially *female* legislators might seize this opportunity to develop a personal vote and solicit the support of female voters (Tremblay 2006). We hypothesize that *female legislators elected under closed-list rules will be less likely to act on behalf of women than female legislators elected under open-list rules.*

4.3 METHODOLOGY

The need to determine the institutional antecedents of women's substantive representation requires more than case-study research. Establishing causality necessitates a broad and rigorous *comparative design* with uniform indicators in all cases. Previous research often used datasets with different indicators (e.g. Mateo Diaz 2005). This is a methodological pitfall the PARTIREP study circumvents. After all, based on a large-scale survey conducted in fifteen countries, we can offer systematic cross-country comparisons. Together, these countries and parliaments represent a variety of political systems in terms of parliamentary organization, multilevel governance, electoral systems, and women's descriptive representation.

4.3.1 Dependent Variable

We study the occurrence of women's substantive representation as a dependent variable. Legislators substantively represent women when they '*act in the interest of the represented [i.e. women], in a manner responsive to them*' (see Pitkin 1972: 209). Substantive representation is an active form of representation and requires that legislators act for—rather than merely stand for— women (Pitkin 1972). Substantive representation can be conceptualized as an outcome-variable as well as a process-variable (Franceschet and Piscopo 2008). Many scholars who study the impact of institutions analyse policy outcomes (Weldon 2002; McBride and Mazur 2010). A contribution we make in this chapter is that our data analysis relies on measures for legislators' acting on behalf of women during the *process of representation*.

Studying individual members' acting in favour of a specific (sub)constituency in parliamentary democracies, however, is potentially problematic. After all, parties function as central mechanisms in the process of representation, and not so much individual legislators (see Müller 2000). However, as Thomassen and Andeweg (2004) and Esaiasson (2000) argue, the role of individual legislators should not entirely be ignored. Party positions result from internal debates and individual members have various opportunities to shape party positions *before* they are presented in parliament. As such, individual legislators do participate in interest representation: they make efforts to realize specific benefits for individual citizens or for a particular group in their constituency (Esaiasson 2000; Thomassen and Andeweg 2004).

Such interest representation does not require a formal act in parliament, but follows from behaviour in 'informal' arenas of representation, such as the parliamentary party group (PPG) (Thomassen and Andeweg 2004). The PPG plays a crucial role in the workings of parliament. It is in the PPG that a party's legislative work is launched and prepared. The PPG also constitutes the nexus of a party's work in parliament. The PPG is the place where individual legislators can influence their party's standpoints. Because of its role as a central node in the parliamentary workings, we will analyse legislators' behaviour in the parliamentary party group.

What constitutes acting 'in the interest of women' is often the topic of much debate (see Schwindt-Bayer and Taylor-Robinson 2011). Women as a social group have a similar positioning in the social field but they do not necessarily share the same interests (Young 2002; Phillips 1995). This is especially the case in cross-national comparative research where women's issues that occur on the political agenda in one country differ from those that appear on the political agenda in another country (Celis 2009). The result is that scholars are unable to make a priori assumptions about the exact content and direction of women's interests. In order to measure women's interests, we therefore do not specify in advance policy issues that are considered relevant for women. Rather, we use a 'formal' or 'open' definition (Celis 2009) asking legislators to indicate how often they 'speak during meetings with your parliamentary party group to signal a situation in society that you consider disadvantageous for women'?[1] Legislators were able to indicate whether they do this at (almost) every meeting, monthly, tri-monthly, yearly, or almost never.[2]

Based on legislators' answers to the survey question, we are able to single out a group of 'non actors' and a group of 'actors'. The group of 'actors' is composed of those legislators who act *at least once every three months or more often for women*. We use a dummy variable because the original variable is not normally distributed and because the data did not meet the 'parallel lines' assumption necessary for conducting an ordinal regression analysis, namely that the regression equation is similar for each category (Long 1997). The threshold for action might seem rather high, but we are especially interested in identifying 'frequent' actors in women's substantive representation. Because of the frequency of their actions, we can consider these actors as central actors in women's substantive representation. They intervene on a regular basis on behalf of women and as such increase the general level of attention paid to women's interests in the PPG. They are more actively involved with women's substantive representation than other actors and are as a result 'critical' for women's substantive representation to occur (Childs and Krook 2009).

4.3.2 Independent Variables

Following our hypotheses, we distinguish between three independent variables. First of all, we have argued that legislators' membership of regional parliaments plays a role. We distinguish between members of national/federal parliaments (coded 0) and members of regional parliaments (coded 1). The dataset included several multilevel countries, namely Austria, Belgium, France, Germany, Italy, Portugal, Spain, Switzerland, and the United Kingdom. This selection brings together federal states (such as Austria, Germany, Belgium, and Switzerland) and decentralized states (such as Spain, Italy, and the United Kingdom). In each of the countries, the selection of regional parliaments reflects a geographical diversity. In Germany, eastern and western regions were included. In Italy, northern and southern regions are present.

In addition, we assumed that women's substantive representation might benefit from the presence and membership of gender-related (sub)committees. We define 'gender-related' (sub)committees as those (sub)committees that explicitly mention women's affairs, gender equality, or equal opportunities in the title or in the description of the competencies. We translated this into a binary variable that distinguishes between parliaments without relevant women's affairs, gender equality, or equal opportunities (sub)committees (coded 0) and parliaments with such a (sub)committee (coded 1).[3]

Finally, with regard to the electoral system, we make use of two separate variables. A first dummy variable refers to the electoral formulae under which legislators are elected. This variable distinguishes between majority systems (including plurality and two-rounds majority systems, coded 0) and proportional systems (including PR-list systems and PR-single transferable vote, coded 1).[4] A second variable relates to the list type in PR systems. Two categories are used: (1) 'closed-list systems' where the party determines the list order and the allocation of seats is based solely on this list order (coded 1), and (2) 'open-list systems' where the allocation of seats takes into consideration the number of preferential votes (coded 0).[5] In this light, it is important to mention that we identify list types as being 'open' when preferential voting *significantly* influences the allocation of seats to candidates (see André, Depauw, and Deschouwer 2011: 4). This means that Norway and the Netherlands, although they allow for preferential voting, were coded as 'closed-list' systems. The impact of preferential voting in these countries is all in all very small (André, Depauw, and Deschouwer 2011).

4.4 EMPIRICAL RESULTS

4.4.1 Descriptive Results

Despite the fact that parliamentary party groups are important venues for interest representation in Europe, they are not often the topic of academic research (but see Heidar and Koole 2000). The PARTIREP survey has gathered new background information on the frequency of PPG meetings and legislators' activity level in the PPG in each of the countries under study. The results show that PPGs in many countries are quite active: in a large majority of parliaments, PPGs meet at least once a week. Several parties meet less frequently but still gather once a fortnight: this is the case for the German parties in the Bundestag, some parties in the Austrian regional parliaments, the Polish parties, and some Hungarian parties. Swiss PPGs and some Austrian regional PPGs finally meet only once a month (or less). Despite these differences in the frequency of PPG meetings, we find that legislators claim to be rather active participants in these meetings. Legislators in the PARTIREP survey were asked to indicate how often they speak at the meetings of their parliamentary party. Sixty per cent of the legislators say that they speak at (almost) every meeting whereas only 8 per cent indicates that they speak irregularly ('at least once a month' or '(almost) never') (see Table 4.1).

TABLE 4.1 *Legislators' frequency of speaking during PPG meetings*

(Almost) every meeting	Once a month	Every three months	Once a year	(Almost) never	Total
1,278 (60.3%)	443 (20.9%)	229 (10.8%)	88 (4.2%)	81 (3.8%)	2,119 (100%)

TABLE 4.2 *Number and percentage of legislators acting for women in the PPG, by country*

Country	Non-actors	Actors
Austria (N = 207)	97 (46.9%)	110 (53.1%)
Belgium (N = 143)	89 (62.2%)	54 (37.8%)
France (N = 78)	56 (71.8%)	22 (28.2%)
Germany (N = 247)	167 (67.6%)	80 (32.4%)
Hungary (N = 95)	77 (81.1%)	18 (18.9%)
Ireland (N = 33)	16 (48.5%)	17 (51.5%)
Israel (N = 34)	17 (50%)	17 (50%)
Italy (N = 120)	58 (48.3%)	62 (51.7%)
Netherlands (N = 61)	44 (72.1%)	17 (27.9%)
Norway (N = 45)	29 (64.4%)	16 (35.6%)
Poland (N = 49)	35 (71.4%)	14 (28.6%)
Portugal (N = 102)	64 (62.7%)	38 (37.3%)
Spain (N = 248)	152 (61.3%)	96 (38.7%)
Switzerland (N = 501)	330 (65.9%)	171 (34.1%)
United Kingdom (N = 92)	63 (68.5%)	29 (31.5%)
Total (N = 2,055)	**1,294 (63%)**	**761 (37%)**

In what follows, we concentrate exclusively on legislators' speaking *on behalf of women*. Table 4.2 displays the percentage of actors by country. Actors are those legislators who speak at least once every three months on behalf of women or more often in the parliamentary party group. It is obvious that there are some clear country differences. The number of actors is rather low in France, Hungary, Poland, and the Netherlands, whereas a particularly large group of legislators claims to represent women in Austria, Ireland, Israel, and Italy. This lends some preliminary support to our expectations that institutions could play a role in explaining when women's substantive representation occurs.

It should, however, be acknowledged that some of these findings may seem rather surprising at first sight. The relatively low number of respondents in some parliaments should first of all be taken into consideration. Because we have relatively small samples, the likelihood of producing skewed data is high. This means that the increase of just a couple of respondents claiming to speak for women could result in a disproportionately high increase in percentage points.

Secondly, we also have to bear in mind that our findings are based on the self-reported behaviour of representatives. Representatives might be tempted to overstate their accomplishments. Even though we have tried to limit socially desirable answers, we acknowledge the possibility that these attempts have proven insufficient in some of the countries. Nevertheless, even with the possibility of social desirability, only 18.9 to 53.1 per cent of all the respondents report to speak on a regular basis for women (i.e. at least once every three months). If we take into account that 92 per cent of the legislators generally speak at least once every three months during PPG meetings (see Table 4.1) than it is safe to say that we have captured the important category of legislators who are central in the promotion of women's interests in the PPG.

4.4.2 Explaining Legislators' Acting on Behalf of Women in the PPG

Now that we have identified differences across countries and, hence, institutional settings, we go into detail on which institutional variables explain legislators acting on behalf of women. Since our dependent variable is a dummy variable, we ran a binomial logistic regression explaining whether or not legislators speak on behalf of women in the PPG. In order to correct for the differences in response patterns, we use weights in the explanatory parts of the analysis, correcting for differences in answer patterns between parliamentary party groups, differences in answer patterns between regions in the multilevel countries, and for the overrepresentation of Swiss cantonal parliaments. The results of our analyses are reported in Tables 4.3 to 4.5.

TABLE 4.3 *Binomial logistic regression explaining legislators' acting on behalf of women in the PPG (non-actors are the reference category)*

	Model 1: Critical mass Exp.β	Model 2: Institutions Exp.β	Model 3: Control Exp.β
Sex Male (Ref.) Female	3.144***	3.122***	3.147***
Proportion of women	n.s.	0.984**	n.s.
Electoral formula No PR (Ref.) PR		1.617**	1.484+
Devolution National/federal (Ref.) Regional		1.551***	1.369*
Gender committee No committee (Ref.) Committee		n.s.	n.s.
Nagelkerke R^2	8.5%	10.9%	19.4%
N	1,851	1,851	1,851

Note: *** $p < 0.001$; ** $p < 0.01$; * $p < 0.05$; + $p < 0.10$. Control variables in model 3 are age (in years), seniority (log), left–right self-placement, and country dummies (United Kingdom is the reference category).

TABLE 4.4 *Binomial logistic regression explaining the impact of list type on legislators' acting on behalf of women in the PPG (non-actors are the reference category)*

	Model 4: List type Exp.β	Model 5: Interaction Exp.β
Sex	3.071***	2.690***
Male (Ref.)		
Female		
Proportion of women	n.s.	n.s.
PR list type	n.s.	n.s.
Closed list (Ref.)		
Open list		
Devolution	1.342+	1.351+
National/federal (Ref.)		
Regional		
Gender committee	n.s.	n.s.
No committee (Ref.)		
Committee		
PR list type * Sex		2.361*
Open list * Female		
Nagelkerke R²	18%	20.4%
N	1,537	1,537

Note: *** $p < 0.001$; ** $p < 0.01$; * $p < 0.05$; + $p < 0.10$. In models 4 and 5, we only include legislators in PR-list systems. Control variables are age (in years), seniority (log), left–right self-placement, and country dummies (United Kingdom is the reference category).

TABLE 4.5 *Association between membership of gender-related (sub)committees and legislators' acting on behalf of women in the PPG, in row percentages*

	Non actors	Actors	Total
No committee, no member	448 (61.1%)	285 (38.9%)	733 (100%)
Committee, no member	529 (65.7%)	276 (34.3%)	805 (100%)
Committee, member	42 (50.6%)	41 (49 4%)	83 (100%)
Total	1,019	602	1,621

Note: Cramer's V = 0.075, $p < 0.05$.

Table 4.3 distinguishes between three models, each of which adds some control variables to the former. Model 1 operates as a model of reference. As we stated in the introduction, scholars have hitherto primarily looked at sex and the number of women in explaining the substantive representation of women. This is why we first run an analysis with the legislators' sex and the proportion of women in parliament.[6] This base model is already relatively strong: the two independent variables explain 8.5 per cent of the variation in acting for women in the PPG, and sex clearly has the strongest effect. Differences between legislators in terms of their sex can thus be considered important predictors of legislators' acting on behalf of women. Female legislators are after all more than three times more likely as their male colleagues to act on behalf of women.

Interestingly, however, the number of women in parliament has a much more limited effect on the behaviour of both male and female legislators. An increase in the number of women does not affect whether male and female legislators discuss women's issues. This means that a critical mass will offer no incentives for legislators to engage in the substantive representation of women.

Building on the initial analysis, we add three institutional variables in model 2: the electoral formula (PR versus majority), devolution (regional parliaments versus national/federal parliaments), and the presence of a gender-related committee. The impact of the fourth institutional variable, namely list type, is only relevant for PR-list systems and is therefore analysed in separate models (Table 4.4).

A first obvious result in Table 4.3, model 2 is that the explanatory power of the model changes compared to model 1: adding institutions leads to an increased R^2. Institutions thus do offer some additional explanatory power to the critical mass model. However, this increase should not be overstated: the R^2 is less than 3 per cent higher, indicating that the overall contribution of institutions to our understanding of acting on behalf of women is very limited. The second finding is that adding institutions does very little to the effect of sex. The strength and direction of sex as an independent variable does not change by adding institutions. Institutions do change the effect of the proportion of women, so much that this proportion now has a significant effect. However, this effect is very weak and it loses its significance in the third model when we add the control variables. The effect is thus not robust.

What interests us most, however, is the strength and direction of the institutional variables. Generally speaking, we can say that some institutions do provide incentives for actors to act on behalf of women. This effect is most outspoken for the distinction between regional and federal/national parliaments. The likelihood that legislators act on behalf of women increases when we shift our attention from the national/federal parliaments to the regional parliaments. For every 100 legislators in national/federal parliaments who promote women's interests in the PPG, there are 155 regional legislators who do so. The fact that regional legislators are more likely than national/federal legislators to speak on behalf of women in the PPG is in line with our expectations.

Besides the distinction between regional and federal/national parliaments, the electoral formula also has a significant impact on the participation of legislators in women's substantive representation. We find that for every 100 legislators who act on behalf of women in majority systems, there are 160 who do so in PR systems. This means that members in majority or plurality systems are significantly less likely to promote women's interests than members of PR systems, and this is in line with our hypothesis.

Finally, according to our results in model 2, the presence of a gender-related committee in parliament does not have a significant impact upon legislators' acting on behalf of women. Legislators who are members of a parliament with a relevant (sub)committee are not more likely than legislators who are members of a parliament without such relevant (sub)committees to represent women's issues.

In model 3, we add a number of control variables to determine the overall robustness of the three institutions. We include legislators' age (in years), legislators' seniority (in years, log transformed), and the left–right self-placement of the legislators (on a ten-point scale with a low score indicating a left-wing position and high score indicating a right-wing position). In addition we also include fourteen country dummy variables in order to control for country effects and to identify some higher-level clustering.[7] The control variables have only a limited impact upon the institutional variables, indicating that the effects we found are fairly robust. Two points are nevertheless important to make. First, we see that the significant effect of the variable measuring the proportion of women in parliament disappears. The effect of the proportion of women was arguably attributable to more general differences in gender regimes between the countries. Second, we also find that the significant difference between PR electoral systems and majority/plurality electoral systems narrows (although it does not disappear). In order to understand this, we need to dig deeper and look for differences that exist between various types of PR systems. Table 4.4 therefore focuses on comparing two different list systems: closed-list systems and open-list systems.

In general, we find no significant difference between PR open-list systems and PR closed-list systems in model 4. However, we do see that the list type variable interacts with legislators' sex in model 5. What we find is that list type does not affect the behaviour of male legislators, but that it does influence the behaviour of female legislators. Female legislators are significantly more likely to promote women's interests under open-list systems than under closed-list systems. This might indicate that women receive more incentives under open-list systems to cultivate a personal vote, which encourages them to solicit the support of female voters by acting on their behalf.

Legislators' membership of regional parliaments, the electoral formula, and the list type are significant predictors for legislators' participation in women's substantive representation. Oddly, the presence of a gender committee appears to have no effect whatsoever on legislators' actions on behalf of women. One explanation for this finding is that we assume that the mere presence of a gender-related (sub)committee will provide incentives for all legislators to speak on behalf of women. However, moving down from the macro to the micro level, it could be that only legislators who actually have a seat on such a committee accumulate gender-related knowledge, and serve as information specializers (Krehbiel 1991; Gilligan and Krehbiel 1990). In order to test this assumption, we looked at the association between legislators' *individual membership* of gender-related (sub)committees and legislators' acting on behalf of women. Table 4.5 confirms that legislators who actually serve on gender-related (sub)committees are more likely than other legislators to promote women's interests. Almost half of the group of legislators (49.4 per cent) who are a member of a gender-related (sub)committee act on behalf of women in the PPG, compared to only 38.9 per cent of the legislators in parliaments without such a (sub)committee, and compared to 34.3 per cent of the legislators in parliaments with a gender-related (sub)committee but who are themselves not a member of this (sub)committee. The association between membership of a gender-related (sub)committee and legislators' acting on behalf of women remains however overall rather weak (Cramer's V = 0.075), and we need to conclude that the presence of a gender-related committee in parliament does not bring any guarantees with regard to legislators' acting on behalf of women.

4.5 DISCUSSION AND CONCLUSION

Our central aim in this contribution was to study whether institutions have a *direct* impact on legislators' acting on behalf of women in the parliamentary party group and whether this impact exists *independently* of the impact of a critical mass of women. There is, after all, a lot of previous scholarship on how institutions mediate the impact of critical mass, but very little research has been done on the direct effects of institutions. We studied the impact of three variables: legislators' membership of regional parliaments, the electoral system (electoral formula and list type), and the presence of a gender-related committee in parliament. Our choice of institutions was limited through pragmatic reasons, but there are certainly other institutions worth exploring, such as institutional sexism (Kanter 1977; Kathlene 1995), the access of the women's movement (Weldon 2002; Beckwith and Cowell-Meyers 2007), and gender quotas (Franceschet and Piscopo 2008; Zetterberg 2008).

In general, we find that some institutions do have a direct and independent impact upon legislators' acting on behalf of women in the PPG, but also that their effect is variable. With regard to the impact of membership of regional parliaments, we find that members of regional parliaments are more likely to speak on behalf of women than members of national/federal parliaments. Regional parliaments are important venues for women's substantive representation.

The results for the electoral system are also clear. On the one hand, there is a significant difference between legislators under proportional systems and legislators under majority or plurality systems with regard to acting on behalf of women, confirming our hypothesis that members under proportional systems are more likely to act on behalf of women. On the other hand, we find that female representatives under open-list systems are more likely to promote women's interests than their female colleagues under closed-list systems. It is clear that the link between descriptive and substantive representation of women is more likely to develop in open-list systems where women are encouraged to solicit the support of female voters.

Finally, the mere presence of a gender-related committee in parliament does not encourage legislators to act on behalf of women; it only incites the members of such committees to do so. Non-committee members are actually less likely than legislators in parliaments without a gender-related committee to promote women's interests.

The results point out that institutions matter but at the same time we should not overstate the impact of institutions. Institutions are certainly not all that matters. Our results reveal that legislators' sex remains the most important explanatory variable in the different models. Notwithstanding that critical mass insufficiently explains the occurrence of women's substantive representation in parliament (see also Childs and Krook 2009), this finding indicates that it matters who the representatives are. Especially in informal settings and during early stages of the decision-making process, agency proves to be a much more important determinant than institutions for understanding the occurrence of women's substantive representation (Phillips 1995; Mansbridge 1999). Hence, reforms aiming at increasing the inclusiveness of the representative systems, and more specifically aiming at the substantive representation of social groups that are at risk of being underrepresented, benefit from a focus on agency and institutions.

Our results point at some interesting questions for future research. Even though we found that institutional variations are significantly linked to legislators' acting on behalf of women, we are intrigued with *how* institutions affect legislators' acting and how institutions affect female legislators 'as women'. In this contribution, we demonstrate that institutions sometimes influence the behaviour of women and men differently. Open-list systems, for instance, give incentives to female legislators to promote women's issues but not to their male colleagues. Understanding the gendered effects of institutions would further allow us to understand how institutional processes either include or exclude women as agents for policy change (Hawkesworth 2003). This would also permit us to consider how institutions privilege the expression of certain interests—the interests of the dominant group—over others.

NOTES

1. The exact question in the PARTIREP survey was: 'How often, would you say, you yourself speak during meetings with your parliamentary party group to signal a situation in society that you consider disadvantageous for women?'
2. In addition to this survey question, we also asked legislators a second question: 'And how often would you say you yourself bring a proposal to your parliamentary party to resolve such a situation in society that you consider disadvantageous for women?' ('(almost) at every meeting', 'at least once a month', 'at least every three months', 'at least once a year', '(almost) never'). Our analyses based on this question provided less stable results, and we therefore chose to work only with the first question.
3. Because women's issues are possibly part of the 'soft' policy competences that are more easily transmitted to the regional level, we have controlled for the possibility that regional parliaments are more likely to have a gender-related (sub)committee. We find that this is however not the case: regional parliaments are as likely as national/regional parliaments to have a gender-related committee.
4. In mixed-member systems, i.e. systems combining proportional and district elements, the coding reflects the level on which the legislator was elected.
5. Note that we exclude PR systems without lists such as PR-STV in this variable.
6. We measure the proportion of women on a metric scale and not as categorical variables because cut-off points are often difficult to determine (Dahlerup 1988; Studlar and McAllister 2002). We do not include the proportion of women in the PPG because this variable correlates strongly with the proportion of women in parliament (see Erzeel forthcoming).
7. Overall, however, we should be aware that the results of our single-level analyses might overestimate the effects of the institutional variables.

REFERENCES

André, A., S. Depauw, and K. Deschouwer (2011), 'Institutional Constraints and Conceptions of Political Representation', paper presented at the annual meeting of the American Political Science Association, Seattle.

Beckwith, K. and K. Cowell-Meyers (2007), 'Sheer Numbers: Critical Representation Thresholds and Women's Political Representation', *Perspectives on Politics*, 53 (3): 553–65.

Carey, J. and M. S. Shugart (1995), 'Incentives to Cultivate a Personal Vote: A Rank Ordering of Electoral Formulas', *Electoral Studies* 14 (4): 417–39.

Celis, K. (2009), 'Substantive Representation of Women (and Improving It): What It Is and Should Be About', *Comparative European Politics*, 7 (1): 95–113.

—— and B. Wauters (2010), 'Pinning the Butterfly: Women, Blue-Collar, and Ethnic Minority MPs vis-à-vis Parliamentary Norms and the Parliamentary Role of the Group Representative', *Journal of Legislative Studies*, 16 (3): 380–93.

—— and A. Woodward (2003), 'Flanders: Do It Yourself and Do It Better? Regional Parliaments as Sites for Democratic Renewal and Gendered Representation', in J. Magone (ed.), *Regional Institutions and Governance in the European Union: Subnational Actors in the New Millenium*. Westport: Praeger, 173–91.

—— et al. (2008), 'Rethinking Women's Substantive Representation', *Representation*, 44 (2): 113–24.

Chaney, P. (2006), 'Critical Mass, Deliberation and the Substantive Representation of Women: Evidence from the UK's Devolution Programme', *Political Studies*, 54 (4): 691–714.

Chappell, L. (2006), 'Comparing Political Institutions: Revealing the Gendered "Logic of Appropriateness"', *Politics & Gender*, 2 (2): 223–35.

Childs, S. and M. L. Krook (2009), 'Analysing Women's Substantive Representation: From Critical Mass to Critical Actors', *Government and Opposition*, 44 (2): 125–45.

Dahlerup, D. (1988), 'From a Small to a Large Minority: Women in Scandinavian Politics', *Scandinavian Political Studies*, 11 (4): 275–98.

Diamond, I. and N. Hartsock (1981), 'Beyond Interests in Politics: A Comment on Virginia Sapiro's "When Are Interests Interesting?"', *American Political Science Review*, 75 (3): 717–21.

Diermeier, D. and R. B. Myerson (1999), 'Bicameralism and Its Consequences for the Internal Organization of Legislatures', *American Economic Review*, 89 (5): 1182–96.

Erzeel, S. (forthcoming), 'Explaining Legislators' Acting on Behalf of Women in the Parliamentary Party Group: The Role of Attitudes, Resources, and Opportunities', *Journal of Women, Politics and Policy*.

Esaiasson, P. (2000), 'How Members of Parliament Define their Task', in P. Esaiasson, and K. Heidar (eds.), *Beyond Westminster and Congress: The Nordic Experience*. Columbus: Ohio State University Press, 51–82.

Franceschet, S. and J. Piscopo (2008), 'Gender Quotas and Women's Substantive Representation: Lessons from Argentina', *Politics & Gender*, 4 (3): 393–425.

Gilligan, T. W. and K. Krehbiel (1990), 'Organization of Informative Committees by a Rational Legislature', *American Journal of Political Science*, 34 (2): 531–64.

Hall, P. A. and R. C. Taylor (1996), 'Political Science and the Three New Institutionalisms', *Political Studies*, 44: 936–57.

Hawkesworth, M. (2003), 'Congressional Enactments of Race-gender: Toward a Theory of Raced-gendered Institutions', *American Political Science Review*, 97 (4): 529–50.

Heath, R. M., L. A. Schwindt-Bayer, and M. M. Taylor-Robinson (2005), 'Women on the Sidelines: Women's Representation on Committees in Latin American Legislatures', *American Journal of Political Science*, 49 (2): 420–36.

Heidar, K. and R. Koole (eds.) (2000), *Parliamentary Party Groups in European Democracies: Political Parties behind Closed Doors*. London: Routledge.

Jónasdóttir, A. G. (1988), 'On the Concept of Interest, Women's Interests, and the Limitations of Interest Theory', in K. B. Jones and A. G. Jónasdóttir (eds.), *The*

Political Interests of Gender: Developing Theory and Research with a Feminist Face. London: Sage, 33–65.

Kanter, R. M. (1977), 'Some Effects of Proportions on Group Life: Skewed Sex Ratios and Responses to Token Women', *American Journal of Sociology*, 82 (5): 965–90.

Kanthak, K. and G. A. Krause (2010), 'Can Women's Caucus Solve Coordination Problems among Women Legislators? Logic, Lessons, and Evidence from American State Legislatures', paper presented at the annual meeting of the APSA, Washington.

Kathlene, L. (1995), 'Position Power versus Gender Power: Who Holds the Floor?' in G. Duerst-Lahti and R. M. Kelly (eds.), *Gender Power, Leadership and Governance*. Minnesota: University of Minnesota Press, 176–94.

Krehbiel, K. (1991), *Information and Legislative Organization*. Ann Arbor: University of Michigan Press.

Leyenaar, M. (2004), 'Vrouwvriendelijk Europees Kiessysteem', in P. Meier and K. Celis (eds.), *Vrouwen vertegenwoordigd, Wetstraat gekraakt? Representativiteit feministisch bekeken. Tweespraak Vrouwenstudies*. Brussels: VUBPress, 49–80.

Lijphart, A. (1999), *Patterns of Democracy: Government Forms and Performance in Thirty-Six Countries*. New Haven: Yale University Press.

Long, J. S. (1997), *Regression Models for Categorical and Limited Dependent Variables*. Thousand Oaks, CA: Sage.

Lowndes, V. and S. Leach (2004), 'Understanding Local Political Leadership: Constitutions, Contexts and Capabilities', *Local Government Studies*, 30 (4): 557–75.

McBride, D. E. and A. G. Mazur (2010), *The Politics of State Feminism: Innovation in Comparative Research*. Philadelphia: Temple University Press.

Mackay, F. (2006), 'Descriptive and Substantive Representation in New Parliamentary Spaces: The Case of Scotland', in M. Sawer, M. Tremblay, and L. Trimble (eds.), *Representing Women in Parliaments: A Comparative Study*. London: Routledge, 171–87.

—— (2008), 'Thick Conceptions of Substantive Representation: Women, Gender and Political Institutions', *Representation*, 44 (2): 125–39.

—— et al. (2002), 'Women and Constitutional Change in Scotland, Wales and Northern Ireland', *Australasian Parliamentary Review*, 17 (2): 35–54.

Mansbridge, J. (1999), 'Should Blacks Represent Blacks and Women Represent Women? A Contingent "Yes"', *Journal of Politics*, 6 (3): 628–57.

March, J. G. and J. P. Olsen (1989), *Rediscovering Institutions: The Organizational Basis of Politics*. New York: Free Press.

Mateo Diaz, M. (2005), *Representing Women? Female Legislators in West European Parliaments*. Essex: ECPR Press.

Matland, R. E. (1998), 'Women's Representation in National Legislatures: Developed and Developing Countries', *Legislative Studies Quarterly*, 23 (1): 109–25.

Mezey, M. L. (2008), *Representative Democracy: Legislators and Their Constituents*. Lanham: Rowman and Littlefield.

Müller, W. C. (2000), 'Political Parties in Parliamentary Democracies: Making Delegation and Accountability Work', *European Journal of Political Research*, 37 (3): 309–33.

Norris, P. (2004), *Electoral Engineering*. Cambridge: Cambridge University Press.

Ortbals, C. D. (2008), 'Subnational Politics in Spain: New Avenues for Feminist Policymaking and Activism', *Politics & Gender*, 4: 93–119.

Peters, G. B. (1999), *Institutional Theory in Political Science: The 'New Institutionalism'*. Continuum: London.

Phillips, A. (1995), *The Politics of Presence*. Oxford: Clarendon Press.

Pitkin, H. F. (1972), *The Concept of Representation*. Berkeley: University of California Press.

Rebouché, R. and K. Fearon (2005), 'Overlapping Identities: Power Sharing and Women's Rights', in I. O'Flynn and D. Russell (eds.), *Power Sharing: New Challenges for Divided Societies*. London: Pluto Press, 155–71.

Rehfeld, A. (2005), *The Concept of Constituency: Political Representation, Democratic Legitimacy, and Institutional Design*. Cambridge: Cambridge University Press.

Reingold, B. (2000), *Representing Women: Sex, Gender and Legislative Behavior in Arizona and California*. Chapel Hill: University of North Carolina Press.

Rosenthal, C. S. (1998), *When Women Lead: Integrative Leadership in State Legislatures*. Oxford: Oxford University Press.

Rule, W. (1987), 'Electoral Systems, Contextual Factors and Women's Opportunity for Election to Parliament in Twenty-three Democracies', *Western Political Quarterly*, 40 (3): 477–98.

Sapiro, V. (1981), 'Research Frontier Essay: When Are Interests Interesting? The Problem of Political Representation of Women', *American Political Science Review*, 75 (3): 701–16.

Sawer, M. (1998), 'Loading the Dice: The Impact of Electoral Systems on Women', in Women Into Politics (ed.), *Here We Come, Ready or Not!* North Sydney: Women Into Politics, 46–53.

Schwindt-Bayer, L. A. and M. M. Taylor-Robinson (2011), 'Introduction'. *Politics & Gender*. 7 (3): 417–18.

Steele, J. F. (2002), 'The Liberal Women's Caucus', *Canadian Parliamentary Review*, 25 (2): 13–19.

Studlar, D. T. and I. McAllister (2002), 'Does a Critical Mass Exist? A Comparative Analysis of Women's Legislative Representation since 1950', *European Journal of Political Research*, 41 (2): 233–53.

Swers, M. L. (2002), *The Difference Women Make: The Policy Impact of Women in Congress*. Chicago: University of Chicago Press.

—— (2005), 'Connecting Descriptive and Substantive Representation: An Analysis of Sex Differences in Cosponsorship Activity', *Legislative Studies Quarterly*, 30 (3): 407–33.

Thomas, S. (1991), 'The Impact of Women on State Legislative Policies', *Journal of Politics*, 53 (4): 958–76.

—— (1994), *How Women Legislate*. Oxford: Oxford University Press.

Thomassen, J. and R. Andeweg (2004), 'Beyond Collective Representation: Individual Members of Parliament and Interest Representation in the Netherlands', *Journal of Legislative Studies*, 10 (4): 1–23.

Tremblay, M. (2003), 'Women's Representational Role in Australia and Canada: The Impact of Political Context', *Australian Journal of Political Science*, 38 (2): 215–38.

—— (2006), 'The Substantive Representation of Women and PR: Some Reflections on the Role of Surrogate Representation and Critical Mass', *Politics & Gender*, 2 (4): 502–11.

Urbinati, N. and M. E. Warren (2008), 'The Concept of Representation in Contemporary Democratic Theory', *Annual Review of Political Science*, 11: 387–412.

Waylen, G. (2008), 'Enhancing the Substantive Representation of Women: Lessons from Transitions to Democracy', *Parliamentary Affairs*, 61 (3): 518–34.

—— (2010), 'Researching Ritual and the Symbolic in Parliaments: An Institutionalist Perspective', *Journal of Legislative Studies*, 16 (3): 352–65.

Weldon, S. L. (2002), 'Beyond Bodies: Institutional Sources of Representation for Women in Democratic Policymaking', *Journal of Politics*, 64 (4): 1153–74.

Williams, M. (1998), *Voice, Trust, and Memory: Marginalized Groups and the Failings of Liberal Representation*. Princeton: Princeton University Press.

Young, I. M. (2002), *Inclusion and Democracy*. Oxford: Oxford University Press.

Zetterberg, P. (2008), 'Do Gender Quotas Foster Women's Political Engagement? Lessons from Latin America', *Political Research Quarterly*, 62 (4): 715–30.

5

Electoral Rules and Legislators' Personal Vote-seeking

Audrey André, André Freire, and Zsófia Papp*

5.1 INTRODUCTION

Electoral institutions, it has commonly been argued, shape the behaviour, attitudes, and orientations of members of parliament. Legislators, Mayhew (1974) famously observed, are foremost driven by the desire to retain their seat in parliament—a necessary condition for achieving other, more intrinsically valuable goals (see also Fenno 1978). The focus of legislators' 'permanent campaign' (Blumenthal 1980; Butler and Collins 2001) is, however, affected by the electoral institutions they compete under for re-election. Mayhew's (1974) Congressional study on the 'electoral connection' has inspired a vast body of literature exploring the manner in which electoral institutions affect what legislators do in parliament and beyond. Electoral institutions, Carey and Shugart (1995) specified, determine the relative value of personal and party reputations to legislators in securing re-election and thereby restrict the range of vote-seeking strategies they can successfully pursue. Individualized campaign strategies may translate into (at least) two personal vote-seeking actions: constituency service and dissent from the party line. On the one hand, legislators can develop a reputation for being good constituency members by helping individual constituents with their demands for casework and by advocating the constituency's collective economic and social needs (e.g. Searing 1994). On the other hand, legislators may feel the need to differentiate themselves from their parliamentary party by taking positions countering party stands or even

* As national director of the national branch of the PARTIREP project in Portugal, André Freire gratefully acknowledges the support of all the sponsors of the project 'Portuguese MPs in Comparative Perspective: Elections, Leadership and Political Representation', 2007–10 (Portuguese Foundation for Science and Technology—FCT, Portuguese Parliament, Ministry of Internal Affairs—Department for Electoral Administration, Gulbenkian Foundation, National Electoral Commission), for their logistic and financial support, and the Portuguese MPs that participated in the web survey, for their cooperation. A new Portuguese research project on political representation is still going on, 2012–15: 'Elections, Leadership, and Accountability: Political Representation in Portugal in a Longitudinal and Comparative Perspective' (FCT project reference: PTDC/CPJ-CPO/119307/2010).

by voting against their party on issues that are salient to constituents (especially when government survival is not at stake) (e.g. Carey 2007).

Besides suffering from an Anglo-American bias, most existing studies dealing with the connection between electoral rules, member attitudes, and behaviour are either theoretical (e.g. Carey and Shugart 1995) or are case studies in which electoral rules are a constant rather than a variable (e.g. Fenno 1978; Cain, Ferejohn, and Fiorina 1987). Comparative studies are scarce and often include a very limited number of cases with only slightly diverse electoral systems (e.g. Heitshusen, Young, and Wood 2005; Pilet, Freire, and Costa 2012). In addition, the current literature linking electoral systems, personal vote-seeking incentives, and legislative behaviour has been hindered by the lack of 'direct evidence of a personal vote' (Shugart 2008: 46). Empirical studies typically go directly from the electoral rules to various—often aggregate-level—proxies. The effect electoral rules have on any single indicator tends to be obfuscated by the simple fact that legislators trade off various activities contributing to a personal vote (André and Depauw 2013).

Aiming to address these shortcomings in the current literature, this chapter performs a systematic two-step analysis of how electoral systems affect legislators' attitudes on an unprecedented scale using data from the PARTIREP comparative legislators' survey. In the first step, we test the impact of different electoral system features on the incentives to cultivate a personal vote *as legislators perceive them*. In line with Zittel and Gschwend's (2008) notion of 'campaign norms', legislators were asked to assess the relative utility of personal compared to party campaigns in attaining re-election. In the second step, the chapter uses this arguably more direct measurement of personal vote-seeking incentives as a mediator variable to explain the impact formal electoral rules have on two oft-cited indicators of personal and partisan vote-seeking: legislators' commitment to constituency representation and to upholding party discipline. The findings clearly establish that the type of electoral system has a significant impact on the person or party-centred character of the vote-seeking strategies legislators pursue: personal vote-seeking is strongest in strong preferential systems and/or systems with small districts (in at least one tier), whereas it is weakest in closed-list systems and/or systems with large districts. Constituency service and dissent in parliament, the analysis demonstrates, are two common ways to cultivate a personal reputation among constituents. Now, before turning to the two-step analysis in sections 5.4 and 5.5, the theoretical foundations are discussed, more precise hypotheses are formulated and the data are presented.

5.2 THEORETICAL FRAMEWORK AND EXPECTATIONS

Most existing typologies classify electoral rules based on the electoral formulae, distinguishing between majoritarian and proportional representation (PR) systems (e.g. Farrell 2001). That is, previous research has focused by and large on the binary distinction between single-seat and multi-seat districts (e.g. Heitshusen, Young, and Wood 2005). It has been the dominant assumption that the personal vote incentives facing legislators in multi-seat districts are weaker than those facing legislators in single-seat districts. Where each legislator represents a distinct geographical area, the accountability linkage is strongest (Lancaster 1986; Scholl 1986; Pilet, Freire, and Costa 2012). On the one hand, elected representatives can directly be rewarded for promoting constituents' interests. Blame, on the other hand, is equally indivisible: constituents can easily sanction their representative for shirking their demands (Buck and Cain 1990; Bowler and Farrell 1993). In the context of dyadic representation (Thomassen and Andeweg 2004), as a result developing a favourable personal reputation among constituents is key to a legislator's electoral success. In multi-seat districts, by contrast, representation has a more collective, partisan dimension. Legislators have the opportunity to either free ride on the achievements of other representatives or pass them the buck. They, thereby, obfuscate the ability of rationally ignorant voters to monitor their actions and assign them credit and blame. Competition for votes, as a consequence, will quickly become less personalized as districts grow in magnitude (Weßels 1999; Pilet, Freire, and Costa 2012), in turn decreasing the electoral utility of constituency service and voting dissent in parliament.

> Hypothesis 1: Personal vote-seeking grows weaker as district magnitude increases.

Carey and Shugart (1995) argued, however, that the relative value of personal compared to party reputations in securing re-election depends critically on the openness of the electoral system, which is strongly connected with the way voters' options are structured by the ballot. *Ceteris paribus*, legislators' personal vote-seeking incentives will be stronger in systems that allow voters to express a preference for individual candidates than in systems that only allow them to endorse the party list as a whole (Bowler and Farrell 1993; Carey and Shugart 1995). Few studies have attempted to take into account the rich variety in electoral institutions represented by Carey and Shugart's (1995) seminal argument. Previous studies have either focused on the dichotomy between majoritarian and PR systems, or they have concentrated on the effect of district magnitude collapsing a wide variety of electoral formulae into 'open-list' or 'closed-list' systems.

Based on the choices voters face in the voting booth, we distinguish four types of electoral systems: non-preferential systems, mixed-member systems, weak preferential systems, and strong preferential systems. Non-preferential systems and strong preferential systems represent the opposite ends of the continuum. The distinction between them is starkest: in the former systems voters cannot disturb the party-preferred order in which seats are allocated among co-partisan candidates and personal vote-seeking on their part is therefore weakest. In the latter systems the order in which seats are allocated is determined only by their ability to attract preference votes. Whereas mixed-member systems have been studied extensively in recent years, we know little in particular about weak preferential systems, except that they fall somewhere between the two opposites. In contrast with previous studies (see for example Shugart 2008; Carey and Shugart 1995) we do not sidestep the thorny issue, but instead intend to meet it head on. We discuss the four types of electoral systems in turn.

Legislators' incentives to nurture a personal reputation among constituents are weakest in *non-preferential systems*. Voters can only endorse the party ticket and are not offered the opportunity to express a preference for one or more co-partisan candidates. Under these circumstances, the (re-)election prospects of candidates are inextricably tied to their party's electoral performance. Both in terms of their selection and election, representatives have but one principal: the party (Carey 2007). As a result elected representatives will concentrate on strengthening the party's collective reputation (Bowler and Farrell 1993; Carey and Shugart 1995). There is one caveat, however: in addition to closed-list PR systems the category of non-preferential systems comprises also single-member plurality or majority systems (Carey and Shugart 1995). In neither system can a vote for a candidate be separated from a vote for the party (Karvonen 2004). Voters can only sanction individual legislators at the high cost of changing party affiliation (Mitchell 2000). But in such low-magnitude districts constituents likely constitute competing principals and legislators may still have an incentive to pursue individualized campaigns (Carey 2007). Or alternatively, by putting a face to the party, a legislator may draw additional votes to the party and in turn increase his own probability of maintaining a seat in parliament (Shugart 2008).

'Pure' or *'strong' preferential systems* constitute the opposite end of the continuum. Legislators' incentives to pursue an individualized campaign are expected to be strongest when voters may cast one or more preference votes and nominal votes alone determine the order in which seats are allocated to candidates (Karvonen 2004; Shugart 2008). Intra-party preference voting, by definition, rules out voters' ability to rely solely on the shared party label as a readily available voting cue and requires legislators to set themselves apart from co-partisan competitors in constituents' minds (Shugart, Valdini, and Suominen 2005). Both single-transferable vote and open-list PR systems fall within the category of strong preferential systems. In PR-STV, all candidates appear on the ballot in alphabetical order, discouraging voters to organize their ordinal preferences along party lines. In this highly competitive electoral environment, co-partisans compete with each other for the first preferences of loyal party voters and undecided voters, and for the lower preferences of voters committed to other parties (Gallagher 2008). In open-list PR systems, on the other hand, candidates are grouped on ordered or (partly) alphabetical party lists. As the party-preferred ranking of candidates is merely an advice voters may choose to disregard, a high list position does not translate into a formal electoral advantage (Katz and Bardi 1980).

Hypothesis 2: Personal vote-seeking is strongest in strong preferential systems and weakest in non-preferential systems.

But what about the systems in between? In *'weak' preferential systems* or flexible-list PR elected representatives should be more inclined to cultivate a personal reputation than legislators in non-preferential systems, but less so than legislators in strong preferential systems. The allocation of seats to candidates is based on the number of preference votes they gathered as well as on their position on the party list (Marsh 1985; Karvonen 2004). Therefore, the electoral utility of running an individualized campaign depends to a large extent on the number of preference votes required to 'leapfrog' past higher ranked candidates and voters' propensity to utilize their possibility to express one or more candidate preferences (Marsh 1985; Katz 1986; Norris 2006). A good personal score in any case increases a legislator's probability of being assigned to a legislative, executive, or party post with high visibility and raises his chances of obtaining a more secure position near the top of the list at the next election.

Hypothesis 3: Personal vote-seeking in weak preferential systems is weaker than in strong preferential systems, but stronger than in non-preferential systems.

Mixed-member systems, in conclusion, are frequently classified as a distinctive type of non-preferential system. Although mixed systems encompass quite some institutional variation,[1] they have (at least) two separate overlapping tiers in common: one tier entails allocation of seats *nominally* whereas seats in the other tiers are allocated by proportional representation from *party lists* (Shugart and Wattenberg 2001: 10). On the one hand, these systems are often characterized as the 'best of both worlds'. That is, the incentive structure facing legislators elected in the PR and in the nominal tiers are assumed not to differ from those in pure closed-list and single-member plurality/majority systems (e.g. Lancaster 1986). On the other hand, scholars increasingly point at spillover or contamination effects as a result of combining several tiers. It is the assumption that the position of mixed-member systems on the continuum differs at the individual level, as political actors respond strategically to the unique competing incentives generated by the majoritarian and proportional components (Herron and Nishikawa 2001; Cox and Schoppa 2002).

In particular, the relative value of personal and party reputations in these systems depends on the mode of candidacy—that is, whether legislators simultaneously stand for election in both tiers or whether they only pursue one type of mandate (Bawn and Thies 2003; Zittel 2012). Dual-listed candidates can be expected to respond to the incentives generated by the majoritarian tier, even if they wind up being elected off the party list (Pekkanen, Byblade, and Krauss 2006). Running an individualized constituency campaign not only increases a candidate's chances of winning the more prestigious district seat, it also increases the likelihood of obtaining a more secure list position in future elections (Patzelt 2007; Zittel and Gschwend 2008). In addition, the campaign strategies of district representatives in mixed systems may well be even more personalized than those of legislators in pure single-member district (SMD) systems. In the latter system, legislators are the sole incumbents running in their district and face less resourceful challengers. In mixed systems, on the other hand, the incumbency effect is less strong: members elected in the second tier often end up 'shadowing' the district member who defeated them by organizing and soliciting casework (Lundberg 2007; Carman and Shephard 2007). Heightened competition will make these district members invest even more resources in order to bolster up their personal reputation.

> Hypothesis 4: Personal vote-seeking in mixed-member systems depends on the mode of candidacy. Personal vote-seeking among list candidates is as weak as in closed-list systems, but personal vote-seeking among district (and dual-listed) candidates is at least as strong as in single-member plurality.

To their categorization of ballot structures, Carey and Shugart (1995), moreover, added that district magnitudes' effect is contingent upon the ballot structure. That is, the balance legislators strike between candidate-centred and party-centred vote-seeking strategies depends on the interaction between district magnitude and ballot structure. Personal vote incentives are expected to decrease with magnitude in closed-list systems, but increase with magnitude in systems with intra-party candidate choice. As the number of candidates running in a district increases in systems with fixed party lists, on the one hand, voters will increasingly rely on parties' labels to reach an 'informed' decision. Strengthening the party's collective reputation gains relevance under these circumstances. Legislators in non-preferential and mixed-member systems, as a result, will step up their efforts promoting the party's achievements and policy pledges as lists grow longer. In systems where preference votes are effective in determining the order of intra-party seat allocation, on the other hand, voters increasingly turn to candidate-specific information in the voting booth. The more co-partisan candidates a legislator competes against, the harder it is to distinguish himself from the throng, and the more effort he will have to put into developing a personal reputation. Whether the same positive effect of district magnitude is to be found in weak preferential systems remains an open question.

> Hypothesis 5: Personal vote-seeking grows weaker in non-preferential systems as district magnitude increases, but grows stronger in strong (and weak) preferential systems.

5.3 DATA

The study of how electoral rules shape legislators' incentives to cultivate a personal or party reputation among constituents has largely been hindered by the unavailability of appropriate data (Shugart 2008). Comparative research is scarce and empirical studies typically resort to various—often aggregate-level—proxies. To explore how electoral rules shape legislators' personal-vote incentives and how these incentives translate into legislative behaviour, we rely on the extensive data collection efforts of the PARTIREP project. The cross-national legislator survey covers fifteen national and fifty-eight regional parliaments in a range of European democracies. The selected parliaments, Table 5.1 indicates, map onto different electoral system contexts in terms of electoral formula and ballot structure. District magnitude also varies widely across and generally even within cases—ranging from single-member districts to at-large region or nationwide districts. In some countries, different systems are combined to elect the legislators of a single parliament. In others, a different set of rules applies across levels of government and/or across regions. Variation in the response rate across cases, moreover, is not systematically related to the type of electoral system in use.

Members of the UK House of Commons and the French National Assembly are elected in single-seat districts respectively using a 'first-past-the-post' system and two-round majority system, respectively. Multi-seat districts with closed party lists are employed in Austria (for the upper tiers), France (for the regional assemblies), Italy (for the *Camera dei Deputati* and the Tuscan regional council), Israel, Norway,[2] Portugal, and Spain. The mixed electoral systems used in Germany, Hungary, Scotland, and Wales combine single-member districts and closed party lists. Strong preferential systems are found in Ireland (PR-STV), Italy (some regional councils), Poland, and Switzerland (open-list PR). But, there is substantial variation in the way voters can express a preference for individual candidates. In Poland, voters have to cast a single preference vote. Voters' choice of candidates is similarly constrained to one in Calabria, Lazio, and Lombardy.[3] Two candidates can be selected in Campania and three in Valle d'Aosta. In Switzerland, by contrast,

TABLE 5.1 *Electoral rules in fifteen European democracies*

		Ballot structure				District magnitude		
		closed	mixed	flexible	open	min.	max.	mean
Austria	nat.	X		X		1	36	7.5
	reg. (9)	X		X		1	26	6.6
Belgium	nat.			X		4	24	13.6
	reg. (4)			X		2	72	35.1
France	nat.	X				1	1	1
	reg. (2)	X				8	25	15.6
Germany	nat.		X			1	65	2
	reg. (4)		X			1	65	1.9
Hungary			X			1	64	1.9
Ireland					X	3	5	3.9
Israel		X				120	120	120
Italy	nat.	X				1	44	24.2
	reg. (6)	X			X	1	42	8.9
Netherlands				X		150	150	150
Norway		X				4	17	8.9
Poland					X	7	19	11.2
Portugal	nat.	X				2	47	10.5
	reg. (2)	X				2	47	26.4
Spain	nat.	X				1	35	6.7
	reg. (4)	X				11	85	23.2
Switzerland	nat.				X	1	34	7.7
	reg. (25)				X	1	100	19.6
United Kingdom	nat.	X				1	1	1
	reg. (2)		X			1	7	1.5

Note: The table summarizes the electoral rules used by country and level of government. The number of regional parliaments is indicated between brackets. 'Closed' denotes the non-preferential systems; 'mixed' the mixed-members systems; 'flexible' the weak preferential systems; and 'open' the strong preferential systems.

voters have two options: they may support a party list without indicating a candidate preference or they may cast as many preference votes as there are seats to be filled in the district. They can, moreover, vote for candidates of different parties (i.e. panachage) and/or vote for the same candidate twice (i.e. cumulative voting). Flexible-list systems, finally, are used in Austria, Belgium, and the Netherlands, but here too there are important differences in the method by which preference votes may alter the party's predetermined list ranking. In Austria[4] and the Netherlands,[5] candidates reaching a particular quota of preference votes are elected regardless of their list position—provided of course their party has won sufficient seats. The remaining seats are allocated in the order candidates appear on the list (Andeweg 2008; Müller 2008). In Belgium, on the other hand, half of the votes cast for the party list (i.e. ballots without a candidate preference) are transferred to the highest ranked candidates until they clear the electoral quota. When the supply of list votes in exhausted, the process of intra-party seat allocation proceeds in the order of preference votes (De Winter 2008).[6]

5.4 ELECTORAL RULES AND CAMPAIGN STRATEGIES

To capture legislators' incentives to cultivate a personal or party reputation, we build on Zittel and Gschwend's (2008: 988) notion of campaign norms. The question in the PARTIREP survey assessing whether legislators 'subjectively seek personal votes' was worded as follows:

> To retain their seat in the Parliament, Members of Parliament often face hard choices. How would you choose to allocate your limited resources? Would you choose to spend more effort and money on achieving the goal on the left-hand side, would you choose to spend more effort and money on the goal on the right-hand side, or would the allocation of resources to both goals be about equal?

A scale was offered ranging from 1 [a personal campaign] to 5 [a party campaign].

To ease interpretation of the results, the dependent variable was trichotomized and reversed: a value of '1' indicates a party-centred campaign, '3' indicates an individualized campaign strategy, and '2' reflects a combination of both campaign styles.[7] Table 5.2 presents the proportion of legislators in each of the three categories and shows the distribution of legislators' preferred campaign strategy by country and by ballot type. Even though there exists substantial variation in legislators' campaign norms, the figures underline a strong partisan component in the process of representation in Europe: 41 per cent of all legislators place themselves at the party-centred end of the continuum and 26 per cent gravitate towards the centre of the scale.[8] But, electoral rules seem to matter in shaping a legislator's perceived utility of personal and party reputations in securing re-election. Elected representatives in countries with non- or weak preferential systems clearly prefer party-centred campaigns (e.g. Austria, Israel, the Netherlands, Norway, Portugal, Spain), whereas in countries with strong-preferential electoral rules (e.g. Ireland, Poland), the importance of personal campaigning is emphasized. In Germany and Hungary legislators, it seems, try to keep a balance between person and party in response to mixed electoral incentives. In case distinct rules are applied at different levels of government, however, percentages aggregated at the country level might obscure within-country variation. The same picture crystallizes when the data are sorted by ballot type. More

TABLE 5.2 *Campaign strategies in fifteen European countries*

	Party versus personal campaigns		
	1	2	3
Country			
Austria	50.08	32.32	17.61
Belgium	29.52	37.74	32.74
France	19.22	26.44	54.34
Germany	19.07	45.21	35.73
Hungary	22.24	49.62	28.14
Ireland	16.19	32.40	51.42
Israel	41.59	29.76	28.65
Italy	45.62	21.96	32.42
Netherlands	73.93	9.84	16.23
Norway	77.95	18.94	3.11
Poland	8.37	39.22	52.41
Portugal	53.95	37.55	8.49
Spain	72.21	21.40	6.39
Switzerland	38.41	30.66	30.93
United Kingdom	22.29	42.07	35.64
Ballot structure			
Closed	54.98	26.08	18.94
Mixed	20.16	46.69	33.15
Flexible	46.01	30.47	23.52
Open	30.03	32.16	37.81
Overall average	40.81	32.84	26.35

Note: Entries are the frequencies in each category (percentages).

than one in two legislators elected in closed-list systems favour cultivating the party's collective reputation, whereas approximately two in five legislators elected in strong preferential systems actively seek personal votes. As expected, the two 'hybrid' systems fall somewhere in between 'pure' open and closed systems. Elected representatives in mixed-member systems tend to gravitate towards the middle and candidate-centred end of the scale, while those in flexible-list systems run more party-intensive campaigns.

To isolate the effect of electoral rules, we estimate partial proportional odds models (Williams 2006), which is the most parsimonious estimation technique to analyse a three-category ordinal dependent variable.[9] This type of model relaxes the parallel lines assumption only for those independent variables violating the assumption, uncovering their differential effect across categories of the dependent variable. Constrained variables, that meet the assumption, have one line of estimates in Table 5.3 and their interpretation does not differ from interpreting ordered logit coefficients. Unconstrained variables, that do not, on the other hand, have two lines of estimates: the

TABLE 5.3 *Electoral rules and campaign strategies*

	Model 1		Model 2		Model 3	
	b.	s.e.	b.	s.e.	b.	s.e.
Open-list	0.899	(0.349)***	1.441	(0.538)***	1.059	(0.362)***
			1.368	(0.533)***		
Flexible-list	0.468	(0.431)	0.625	(0.666)	0.542	(0.409)
			0.205	(0.706)		
Mixed-member	1.546	(0.352)***	1.744	(0.417)***	1.397	(0.279)***
	0.687	(0.431)	0.577	(0.533)	0.453	(0.360)
Open-list*DM			−0.449	(0.268)*		
			−0.519	(0.337)		
Flexible-list*DM			−0.122	(0.531)		
			0.195	(0.383)		
Mixed-member*DM			−0.165	(0.263)		
			0.124	(0.388)		
District Magnitude (log)	−0.588	(0.172)***	−0.486	(0.275)*	−0.151	(0.224)
			−0.627	(0.361)*		
Single-member district					1.094	(0.360)***
Ideological proximity	0.141	(0.061)**	0.138	(0.060)**	0.135	(0.062)**
	0.254	(0.069)***	0.249	(0.070)***	0.250	(0.071)***
Party's left–right position	0.143	(0.039)***	0.146	(0.039)***	0.135	(0.036)***
Governing party	0.208	(0.091)**	0.217	(0.085)**	0.234	(0.079)***
Mainstream party	0.370	(0.261)	0.372	(0.259)	0.355	(0.253)
Seniority (in years)	0.012	(0.008)	0.012	(0.008)	0.009	(0.008)
Regional parliament	−0.070	(0.118)	−0.057	(0.132)	−0.025	(0.137)
Constant (1)	−0.827	(0.515)	−0.973	(0.548)*	−1.420	(0.471)***
Constant (2)	−2.323	(0.570)***	−2.274	(0.676)***	−2.927	(.524)***
N	1,996		1,996		1,996	
Log pseudo-likelihood	−1,971.94		−1,968.98		−1,956.81	
LR(df)	372.13	(12)***	378.04	(12)***	402.40	(12)***
Nagelkerke r^2	0.192		0.195		0.206	

Note: The table displays the parameter estimates and robust standard errors (in parentheses) of a partial proportional odds model. * p ≤ 0.10; ** p ≤ 0.05; *** p ≤ 0.01, using two-tailed t-values.

first line represents the coefficient for campaigns with at least some personal component (2 and 3) in contrast with party-focused campaigns (1); the second line displays the coefficient for a predominantly individualized campaign strategy (3) in contrast with categories 1 and 2. As it is not inconceivable that there are country differences in campaign styles, standard errors are clustered at the country level.[10]

In testing the effect electoral rules have on the balance legislators strike between cultivating personal and party reputations, it is important to acknowledge that a number of other factors will shape the focus of their campaign strategy that need to be controlled for in the analysis. First, a legislator's *perceived ideological distance* from his or her party should increase the attractiveness of developing a distinct personal profile (Zittel and Gschwend 2008). About 43 per cent of the legislators in the sample fully share their party's ideological values and platform. Their self-placement on an eleven-point left–right scale does not deviate from the score they assigned their party. Another 37 and 14 per cent perceive a distance of respectively one and two scale points. Second, the campaign focus of legislators affiliated to right-wing political parties might be more personal in nature than that of left-wing party representatives. *Party ideologies* on the right of the political spectrum are often characterized as individualistic, whereas leftist ideologies tend to promote collectivism (Özbudun 1970).

Third, members of *governing parties* can be expected to pursue more individualized campaigns than those in opposition parties. The discrepancy between campaign promises and unredeemed expectations typically results in vote loss for governing parties—mid-term being the nadir of popularity (e.g. Van Der Eijk 1987). In this uncongenial re-election context, legislators may try to protect themselves from broader partisan swings by putting more emphasis on one's personal characteristics and achievements as compared to the party's collective record (Cain, Ferejohn, and Fiorina 1987; Kam 2009). Fourth, elected representatives of large *mainstream parties* will likely favour more candidate-centred campaigns. While small and niche parties lack local embedment, mainstream parties have a well-developed organization at the grassroots. These local structures and networks facilitate legislators' efforts in developing and maintaining high visibility and name recognition among constituents (Zittel and Gschwend 2008). In line with Ezrow's (Ezrow 2010: 12) definition, political parties belonging to the social democratic, liberal, Christian democratic, and conservative party families are coded as mainstream.[11]

The analysis further controls for a legislator's *seniority*. Veteran legislators have entered the protectionist stage of their career and try to consolidate the measure of trust and political support they have established among constituents over the years (Fenno 1978; Norton and Wood 1993). In addition, seniority and apprenticeship go hand in hand: senior parliamentarians are more likely to be assigned posts in parliament, in the committees, in the party, and possibly in the executive (Johannes 1980; Heitshusen, Young, and Wood 2005). The number of years a legislator has served in parliament should therefore be negatively related to his propensity to pursue an individualized campaign. A final control we add to the model is a dichotomous variable indicating *regional parliaments*. Members of regional assemblies are generally elected in districts with smaller constituent-to-representative ratios which should result in more direct contact (Patzelt 2007; Curtice and Shively 2009). Candidate-centred campaign strategies can there.ore be expected to be more common at the lower levels of government. We now turn to the results of the multivariate analysis.

The results presented in Table 5.3 provide strong support for the second hypothesis: personal vote-seeking through individualized campaign strategies is markedly more valuable to legislators in strong preferential systems as compared to those elected on fixed party lists. Legislators' predicted probability of cultivating a personal reputation among constituents increases by 17 per cent when preference votes are the sole criterion for allocating seats to candidates.[12] The probability of running a party-centred campaign, on the other hand, decreases from 54 per cent in non-preferential systems to 33 per cent in strong preferential systems, a change significant at the 0.05 level. But no support is found for Carey and Shugart's (1995) oft-cited hypothesis that the effect of district magnitude is contingent upon the ballot structure. Legislators' incentives to pursue a person-intensive campaign in open-list systems do not increase with the scope of intra-party competition. District magnitude, on the contrary, has an invariably negative effect in all list types, corroborating hypothesis 1 rather than hypothesis 5 as demonstrated by the multiplicative interaction terms included in model 2.

This effect is, however, largely driven by districts with a magnitude of one (in a similar vein, see Pilet, Freire, and Costa 2012). A legislator's predicted probability of seeking out personal votes decreases by 19 per cent when multiple seats are allocated in the district. When isolating single-member districts in the analysis, moreover, we can no longer be sure at any level of statistical significance that legislators' campaign norms become increasingly party-centred as magnitude grows (model 3). That is, an increase in district magnitude from one to two seats is more consequential for legislators' behaviour than an increase from twenty-one to twenty-two for instance. As the number of (co-partisan) competitors grows, voters become increasingly unable and unwilling to learn about the characteristics, stands, and records of individual candidates. Even in open-list systems, legislators' personal-vote incentives may therefore quickly be outweighed by the increasing efforts and resources needed to communicate a personal reputation to voters.

The campaign focus of legislators in weak preferential systems seems to be somewhat more candidate-centred than in non-preferential systems (8 per cent) but less so than in open-list systems (9 per cent), in line with hypothesis 3. These changes in predicted probabilities cannot be distinguished from zero at conventional levels of statistical significance, however. This group of systems seems to be too heterogeneous a category to generate a univocal effect. Not only do these systems vary from each other based on the details of the electoral rules (e.g. quota or transfer system), but the same set of formal rules

TABLE 5.4 *The mode of candidacy and campaign strategies in mixed-member systems*

	All parties		Mainstream parties	
	b.	s.e.	b.	s.e.
Mode of candidacy (ref. list-only candidate)				
Successful district candidate	1.590	(0.385)***	2.179	(0.490)***
Defeated district candidate	0.545	(0.385)	1.408	(0.501)***
Constant (1)	−0.414	(0.594)	0.134	(0.860)
Constant (2)	−2.676	(0.614)***	−2.807	(0.871)***
N	357		245	
Log pseudo-likelihood	−348.06		−226.68	
LR(df)	56.28	(8) ***	37.60	(9) ***
Nagelkerke r²	0.166		0.164	

Note: The table displays the parameter estimates and robust standard errors (in parentheses) of a partial proportional odds model. Controls for ideological distance, governing party, year of first entry, regional parliament, and the ratio between district and list seats are not displayed. * $p \le 0.10$; ** $p \le 0.05$; *** $p \le 0.01$, using two-tailed t-values.

may present legislators with different incentives and constraints depending on their position on the party list and the actual number of preference votes required to alter their rank. To scale these weak preferential systems on the continuum between non-preferential and strong preferential systems requires a case-by-case judgment accounting for possible intra-system variation (Shugart, Valdini, and Suominen 2005; Shugart 2008) that is beyond the scope of this chapter.

Table 5.3 further reveals that, in contrast with non-preferential systems, legislators' campaign strategies in mixed-member systems are considerably more candidate-intensive. The predicted probability of running a highly individualized campaign is approximately 12 per cent higher in mixed systems—an increase significant only at a more lenient level of 0.10. But, legislators primarily end up in the middle category responding to the competing incentives generated by the different tiers. They have more than a 50 per cent chance of combining both campaign styles, a probability which is 22 per cent higher than in closed-list systems. Mixed systems appear to be more than a mere sum of their parts—in line with hypothesis 4. The mode of candidacy seems to be an important cause of spillover effects, explaining why legislators in mixed systems more frequently opt to bolster their personal reputation.

When restricting the analysis to mixed-member systems in Table 5.4, we find further evidence in support of hypothesis 4, comparing differences in the campaign focus of successful district candidates, defeated district candidates elected on the party list, and 'list-only' candidates. For district members, the personal-vote incentives generated by the SMD tier always override the incentives emanating from the PR component—even if they are granted a secure position on the party list. They are 41 per cent more likely to run a predominantly candidate-centred campaign than list-only members and 20 per cent more likely to do so than list members simultaneously pursuing a district mandate. On the other hand, the electoral utility of an individualized campaign to dual-listed candidates that were rejected by the district in which they stood for election depends on their party affiliation. Only candidates from the large mainstream parties that have a reasonable chance of winning district seats and have well-developed local branches are more inclined to favour personal over party reputations. Small and niche parties, by contrast, field candidates in the SMD races merely to increase the party's vote share in the PR tier (Cox and Schoppa 2002; Ferrara and Herron 2005). The widespread use of split-ticket voting turns their district candidates into 'hopeless' contestants (Patzelt 2007). But in return, these candidates are rewarded with a higher position on the party list. As a result, the incentives facing small party candidates standing simultaneously in both tiers strongly resemble those facing list specialists: cultivating the party's collective reputation is much more important for securing re-election than seeking out personal votes.

Over and above the effect of electoral rules, party-related factors have an impact on the candidate or party-centred nature of a legislator's campaign. Personal vote-seeking strategies are more appealing to legislators identifying more loosely with their party. Legislators feeling more distant from their party in ideological terms are significantly more likely to favour personal over party reputations. But the effect is rather small substantively: the predicted probability of running a predominantly individualized campaign is only 3 per cent lower for the strongest identifiers than for legislators perceiving a one-point deviance between their own and their party's position on the left–right scale and 12 per cent lower for those perceiving a three-point deviance. In addition, representatives from left-wing parties are considerably more party-centred in their campaign focus than those from right-wing parties. Changing a party's position on the left–right scale from 3 to 7—that is the mean minus and plus one standard deviation—decreases a legislator's likelihood of prioritizing a more collective party campaign by 13 per cent. Elected representatives from governing parties, moreover, have a slightly higher likelihood of pursuing a candidate-intensive campaign. A favourable personal reputation might help individual legislators to compensate for the generally lower levels of party popularity at the end of the term either by winning personal votes or by giving the party a human face in the district. Personal campaigning, finally, is also more common among legislators affiliated to the large mainstream parties with established local structures and vital grassroots but the effect does not reach conventional levels of statistical significance. Seniority and the level of government hardly affect a legislator's campaign choices.

5.5 CAMPAIGN STRATEGIES, CONSTITUENCY SERVICE, AND PARTY DISCIPLINE

In the previous section we linked electoral rules to legislators' campaign norms as they perceive them—arguably a more direct measure of personal vote incentives. In the second step of the analysis, we assess whether and to what extent differences in the candidate- or party-centred nature of campaign strategies translate into attitudinal and behavioural differences in the way legislators perceive their representative tasks. We will focus on two oft-cited indicators of personal and partisan vote-seeking: legislators' commitment to constituency service on the one hand, and to upholding party discipline on the other. Based on the extensive literature reviewed in the first sections of our chapter, we hypothesize that legislators who prioritize cultivating their personal reputation in their campaigns will be more eager to show constituents that they care about their needs. As a result, personal vote-seekers are expected to focus on their constituencies to a greater extent than those pursuing predominantly party-centred campaigns. Additionally, we expect them to be more relaxed in their attitudes towards party discipline as well: they should be more willing to desert the party opinion when it conflicts with the interest of their districts.

The relation of personal vote-seeking to constituency service is two-fold: on the one hand, it relates to the strength of a legislator's constituency orientation and it shows in the activities carried out in district, on the other hand. First, we find a significant relationship between the campaign strategies legislators pursue and the focus of representation they choose. The PARTIREP survey asked legislators to indicate on a seven-point scale how important they consider it to promote the views and interests of all the people who voted for their party and of the people in their constituency.[13] Table 5.5 shows the importance the average legislator in the sample attaches to promoting the interests of the two different groups of people. In addition, party promoters put greater emphasis on representing the party voters, whereas legislators pursuing a more individualized campaign favour looking after the people in their districts. Overall averages (5.77 and 5.7 points) indicate that respondents rated both categories generously: both the party electorate and the constituents seem exceptionally important to represent. For this reason, the relative importance of party and constituency representation was calculated by a simple division of ratings to show whether individual campaigners are indeed more inclined to focus on their constituencies. The results support the initial hypothesis: personal vote-seekers actually consider the promotion of constituency interests more important than both party campaigners and those who try to balance between the two strategies.

Second, legislators' decision as to whether or not to engage in certain constituency-oriented activities that bolster up their reputation and visibility

TABLE 5.5 *The average importance of promoting the interests of different groups of people*

	Importance of promoting the interests of ...		
	all the people who voted for his/her party	all the people in his/her constituency	relative importance (constituency/party)
Campaign strategy			
Party	5.96 (1.171)	5.56 (1.420)	0.986 (0.506)
Both	5.77 (1.201)	5.79 (1.257)	1.054 (0.477)
Personal	5.47 (1.342)	5.79 (1.476)	1.147 (0.681)
Overall average	5.77 *(1.243)*	5.70 *(1.387)*	1.051 *(0.552)*
Significance	$p < 0.01$	$p < 0.01$	$p < 0.01$
Eta	0.157	0.081	0.117

Note: Entries are mean values, standard deviations in parentheses.

among constituents also varies under different campaign strategies. Personal vote-seekers are significantly ($p < 0.05$) more likely to '*attend (or send out letters on the occasion of) weddings, wedding anniversaries, and funerals*', '*send out personal newsletters*', and '*meet with local businesses and action groups*' and they do so more frequently than members prioritizing a more party-intensive campaign. Additionally, representatives favouring personal over party reputation appear to be more likely to '*meet with (small parties of) constituents in their private home to talk about their wants and needs*', '*hold surgeries*', '*advertise...) constituency work services*' and '*publicize... successes in attracting business and obtaining government grants for the local area*' as well. But the frequency for these activities is the same under the different campaign strategies.

Personal vote-seeking is not only connected to legislators' behaviour in the district, but it has implications for party discipline in parliament as well. We measure dissent on the attitudinal level using the concept of the style of representation, capturing a legislator's willingness to desert the party line. Representatives were asked, in case of conflict, to trade off their party's opinion with their personal judgment on the one hand and their voters' opinion on the other. Table 5.6 shows the distribution of answers over the different campaign strategies. Figures indicate that the average legislator would choose to vote in line with the party's opinion in case of conflict with either his/her own opinion or with that of the voters: 60.4 per cent of all representatives report that they would follow the party, even if this implies setting aside their personal judgment. The partisan preference is even stronger when it comes to choosing between the voter and the party: 64.7 per cent think that they should vote with the PPG. The results demonstrate the same pattern when we examine the distribution of answers over the different campaign strategies. In every category, the party's opinion prevails. There are, however, significant differences in the dominance of the party-centred answers. Fifty

TABLE 5.6 *Dissent in parliament under different campaign strategies*

	If his/her opinion does not correspond with the opinion of the party, the MP should vote according to the opinion of the…		If his/her opinion does not correspond with the opinion of the voters, the MP should vote according to the opinion of the…	
	MP	party	voters	party
Campaign strategy				
Party	31.3	68.7	31.1	68.9
Both	41.4	58.6	34.9	65.1
Personal	50.0	50.0	42.5	57.5
Overall	39.6	60.4	35.3	64.7
Significance	$p < 0.01$		$p < 0.01$	
Kendall's tau-c	−0.164		−0.095	

Note: Entries are the frequencies in each category of campaign strategies (percentages).

per cent of the personal vote-seekers think that they should take their own opinion as a guideline, and 42.5 per cent would stick with the voters' will in case of conflict. Both percentages exceed the proportion of those who would vote against the party in the other two groups. This indicates that personal vote-seekers are more willing to desert the party line than members pursuing party-centred campaigns.

5.6 CONCLUSION

In the recent wave of reform debates, it has often been argued that the quality of political representation depends not only on the ideological congruence between the represented and those acting on their behalf, but also on the strength of the representative relationship (e.g. Norris 2006; Shugart 2008; Freire and Meirinho 2012). This chapter has sought to contribute to this topical discussion by studying, on an unprecedented scale, how electoral systems affect the legislators' vote-seeking strategies and behavioural patterns. Electoral institutions, it was demonstrated, affect legislators' campaign strategies. Legislators elected on the basis of their preference votes alone are considerably more likely to pursue an individualized campaign that distinguishes themselves from co-partisan competitors than those elected in closed-list systems. Hybrid systems, on the other hand, fall somewhere in-between open- and closed-list systems: legislators elected in flexible-list systems and mixed-member systems tend to combine both campaign strategies. As districts increase in magnitude, however, legislators' predicted probability of running a candidate-centred campaign decreases. More than being a difference of degree, the effect of district magnitude is a difference of kind: legislators' campaign strategies in multi-seat districts are more party-focused than in single-seat districts.

Legislators' decision as to the type of campaign to pursue, moreover, has important consequences for what they do in and outside parliament in-between election campaigns. Electoral rules that incentivize legislators to run a personalized campaign not only increase the amount and quality of services offered to constituents, but also enhance members' potential to desert the party line. Personal vote-seeking was found to increase the value of being congruent with constituents' preferences in terms of voting behaviour in parliament, whenever there is a conflict between voters' and party's preferences. In sum, the recent trend towards systems that allow for effective intra-party choice might strengthen the constituent–representative relationship, but might also increase the potential dissolution of party unity and thereby challenge the responsible party model, the dominant theory explaining representation and governance in contemporary Europe. Perhaps the problem here is one of balance and admitting that the 'best of both worlds' might not be entirely possible.

NOTES

1. The German, Scottish, and Welsh parliaments use a two-tiered system with single-member plurality at the lowest level, whereas at the time the data were collected, the Hungarian mixed system complemented a two-round majority system with two PR tiers. In all parliaments (including the Hungarian one), voters cast two ballots: one for a candidate in the first tier and one for a party list in the second tier. The ratio of district to list seats varies across parliaments however: the German Bundestag, Brandenburg, Rhineland-Palatinate, and Thuringia have a 50:50 ratio, Lower Saxony a 65:35 ratio, Wales a 67:33 ratio, Scotland a 57:43 ratio, and Hungary a 46:54 ratio. Only in Wales dual candidacies are not allowed. There are further differences in the linkage mechanism between tiers, and the district magnitude, legal threshold, and electoral formula in the PR tier (Shugart and Wattenberg 2001).
2. The Norwegian electoral law allows voters to alter the list order of candidates or strike out names. For these changes to take effect, more than half of the party electorate should indicate a preference for the same candidate. This has never occurred so far.
3. Members of these regional councils use open-list PR, but a majority bonus is allocated to the coalition or party list elected for presidency.

4. For the Austrian Nationalrat, candidates running in the lowest tier need at least as many preference votes as half of the Land-level Hare quota or one sixth of the party vote in the district to be elected in defiance of the list order. In the second tier, candidates need to reach the full Hare quota. At the regional level, all parliaments use a flexible-list system in the lowest tier. Burgenland, Lower Austria, and Vienna use that system in the second tier as well. The quotas specified vary widely.

5. In the Netherlands, candidates move to the top of the list when their preference votes reach 25 per cent of the Hare quota.

6. In Belgium, the 'eligibility threshold' equals the party's total district vote divided by the number of seats won plus one.

7. The scores of '4' and '5' on the original scale are recoded as '1', whereas the scores of '1' and '2' are collapsed in '3'.

8. To correct the bias resulting from the inclusion of all Swiss cantonal parliaments, that high number of responses is down-weighted to a level comparable with the responses in the other countries. We further correct for the over and underrepresentation of particular political parties by weighing the responses by the size of the parliamentary party in each parliament.

9. We use Williams' (2006) software package 'gologit2' in Stata.

10. The data have a multilevel structure with individual MPs nested in countries. Using clustered standard errors is a good way to correct for the non-independence of observations at the country level. Clustering avoids inflated standard errors and decreases the likelihood of committing Type I errors (Steenbergen and Jones 2002).

11. In addition, a handful of parties that would be coded as mainstream, based on party family, but that systematically receive a small share of the votes are added to the reference category (e.g. the FDP in Germany).

12. To compute predicted probabilities as well as the 95 per cent confidence intervals for discrete changes, continuous variables were fixed at their mean values (log of district magnitude = 1.03; ideological distance = 0.87; party's left–right position = 4.97; number of years served in parliament = 5.27). All dichotomous variables were set to zero, save for mainstream party.

13. For the sake of presentational purposes, equal distance between scale values is assumed.

REFERENCES

Andeweg, R. B. (2008), 'The Netherlands: The Sanctity of Proportionality', in M. Gallagher and P. Mitchell (eds.), *The Politics of Electoral Systems*. Oxford: Oxford University Press, 491–510.

André, A. and S. Depauw (2013), 'District Magnitude and Home Styles of Representation in European Democracies', *West European Politics*, 36 (5): 986–1006.

Bawn, K. and M. F. Thies (2003), 'A Comparative Theory of Electoral Incentives Representing the Unorganized under PR, Plurality and Mixed-member Electoral Systems', *Journal of Theoretical Politics*, 15 (1): 5–32.

Blumenthal, S. (1980), *The Permanent Campaign: Inside the World of Elite Political Operatives*. Boston: Beacon Press.

Bowler, S. and D. Farrell (1993), 'Legislator Shirking and Voter Monitoring: Impacts of European Parliament Electoral Systems upon Legislator-Voter Relationships', *Journal of Common Market Studies*, 31 (1): 45–70.

Buck, J. V. and B. E. Cain (1990), 'British MPs in their Constituencies', *Legislative Studies Quarterly*, 15 (1): 127–43.

Butler, P. and N. Collins (2001), 'Payment on Delivery—Recognising Constituency Service as Political Marketing', *European Journal of Marketing*, 35 (9/10): 1026–37.

Cain, B., J. Ferejohn, and M. Fiorina (1987), *The Personal Vote: Constituency Service and Electoral Independence*. Cambridge, MA: Harvard University Press.

Carey, J. M. (2007), 'Competing Principals, Political Institutions, and Party Unity in Legislative Voting', *American Journal of Political Science*, 51 (1): 92–107.

—— and M. S. Shugart (1995), 'Incentives to Cultivate a Personal Vote: A Rank Ordering of Electoral Formulas', *Electoral Studies*, 14 (4): 417–39.

Carman, C. and M. Shephard (2007), 'Electoral Poachers? An Assessment of Shadowing Behaviour in the Scottish Parliament', *Journal of Legislative Studies*, 13 (4): 483–96.

Cox, K. and L. J. Schoppa (2002), 'Interaction Effects in Mixed-Member Electoral Systems Theory and Evidence From Germany, Japan, and Italy', *Comparative Political Studies*, 35 (9): 1027–53.

Curtice, J. and W. P. Shively (2009), 'Who Represents Us Best? One Member or Many?' in H.-D. Klingemann (ed.), *The Comparative Study of Electoral Systems*. Oxford: Oxford University Press, 171–92.

De Winter, L. (2008), 'Belgium: Empowering Voters or Party Elites?' in M. Gallagher and P. Mitchell (eds.), *The Politics of Electoral*. Oxford: Oxford University Press, 417–32.

Ezrow, L. (2010), *Linking Citizens and Parties: How Electoral Systems Matter for Political Representation*. New York, NY: Oxford University Press.

Farrell, D. M. (2001), *Electoral Systems: A Comparative Introduction*. New York: St Martin's Press.

Fenno, R. F. (1978), *Home Style: House Members in Their Districts*. Boston: Little, Brown.

Ferrara, F. and E. S. Herron (2005), 'Going It Alone? Strategic Entry under Mixed Electoral Rules', *American Journal of Political Science*, 49 (1): 16–31.

Freire, A. and M. Meirinho (2012), 'Institutional Reform in Portugal: From the Perspective of Deputies and Voters Perspectives', *Pôle Sud—Revue de Science Politique*, 36 (1): 107–25.

Gallagher, M. (2008), 'Ireland: The Discreet Charm of PR-STV', in M. Gallagher and P. Mitchell (eds.), *The Politics of Electoral Systems*. Oxford: Oxford University Press, 511–32.

Heitshusen, V., G. Young, and D. M. Wood (2005), 'Electoral Context and MP Constituency Focus in Australia, Canada, Ireland, New Zealand, and the United Kingdom', *American Journal of Political Science*, 49 (1): 32–45.

Herron, E. S. and M. Nishikawa (2001), 'Contamination Effects and the Number of Parties in Mixed-superposition Electoral Systems', *Electoral Studies*, 20 (1): 63–86.

Johannes, J. R. (1980), 'The Distribution of Casework in the US Congress: An Uneven Burden', *Legislative Studies Quarterly*, 5 (4): 517–44.

Kam, C. J. (2009), *Party Discipline and Parliamentary Politics*. Cambridge: Cambridge University Press.

Karvonen, L. (2004), 'Preferential Voting: Incidence and Effects', *International Political Science Review*, 25 (2): 203–26.

Katz, R. S. (1986), 'Intraparty Preference Voting', in B. Grofman and A. Lijphart (eds.) *Electoral Laws and Their Political Consequences*. New York, NY: Agathon Press, 85–103.

—— and L. Bardi (1980), 'Preference Voting and Turnover in Italian Parliamentary Elections', *American Journal of Political Science*, 24 (1): 97–114.

Lancaster, T. D. (1986), 'Electoral Structures and Pork Barrel Politics', *International Political Science Review*, 7 (1): 67–81.

Lundberg, T. C. (2007), *Proportional Representation and the Constituency Role in Britain*. Basingstoke: Palgrave Macmillan.

Marsh, M. (1985), 'The Voters Decide? Preferential Voting in European List Systems', *European Journal of Political Research*, 13 (4): 365–78.

Mayhew, D. R. (1974), *Congress: The Electoral Connection*. New Haven, CT: Yale University Press.

Mitchell, P. (2000), 'Voters and Their Representatives: Electoral Institutions and Delegation in Parliamentary Democracies', *European Journal of Political Research*, 37 (3): 335–51.

Müller, W. C. (2008), 'Austria: A Complex Electoral System with Subtle Effects', in M. Gallagher and P. Mitchell (eds.) *The Politics of Electoral Systems*. Oxford: Oxford University Press, 397–416.

Norris, P. (2006), 'Ballot Structures and Legislative Behavior: Changing Role Orientations via Electoral Reform', in T. J. Power and N. C. Rae (eds.), *Exporting Congress? The Influence of the US Congress on World Legislatures*. Pittsburgh, PA: University of Pittsburgh Press, 157–84.

Norton, P. and D. M. Wood (1993), *Back from Westminster: British Members of Parliament and Their Constituents*. Lexington, MA: University Press of Kentucky.

Özbudun, E. (1970), *Party Cohesion in Western Democracies: A Causal Analysis*. Beverly Hills, CA: Sage Publications.

Patzelt, W. J. (2007), 'The Constituency Roles of MPs at the Federal and Länder Levels in Germany', *Regional & Federal Studies*, 17 (1): 47–70.

Pekkanen, R., B. Byblade, and E. S. Krauss (2006), 'Electoral Incentives in Mixed-Member Systems: Party, Posts, and Zombie Politicians in Japan', *American Political Science Review*, 100 (2): 183–93.

Pilet, J.-B., A. Freire, and O. Costa (2012), 'Ballot Structure, District Magnitude and Constituency-Orientation of MPs in Proportional Representation and Majority Electoral Systems', *Representation*, 48 (4): 359–72.

Scholl, E. L. (1986) 'The Electoral System and Constituency-Oriented Activity in the European Parliament', *International Studies Quarterly*, 30 (3): 315–32.

Searing, D. (1994), *Westminster's World: Understanding Political Roles*. Cambridge, MA: Harvard University Press.

Shugart, M. S. (2008), 'Comparative Electoral Systems Research: The Maturation of a Field and the New Challenges Ahead', in M. Gallagher and P. Mitchell *The Politics of Electoral Systems*. Oxford: Oxford University Press, 25–55.

—— M. E. Valdini, and K. Suominen (2005), 'Looking for Locals: Voter Information Demands and Personal Vote-earning Attributes of Legislators under Proportional Representation', *American Journal of Political Science*, 49 (2): 437–49.

—— and M. P. Wattenberg (ed.) (2001), *Mixed-member Electoral Systems: The Best of Both Worlds?* Oxford: Oxford University Press.

Steenbergen, M. R. and B. S. Jones (2002), 'Modelling Multilevel Data Structures', *American Journal of Political Science*, 46 (1): 218–37.

Thomassen, J. and R. B. Andeweg (2004), 'Beyond Collective Representation: Individual Members of Parliament and Interest Representation in the Netherlands', *Journal of Legislative Studies*, 10 (4): 47–69.

Van Der Eijk, C. (1987), 'Testing Theories of Electoral Cycles', *European Journal of Political Research*, 15 (2): 253–70.

Weßels, B. (1999), 'Whom to Represent? Role Orientations of Legislators in Europe', in H. Schmitt and J. J. A. Thomassen (eds.), *Political Representation and Legitimacy in the European Union*. Oxford: Oxford University Press, 209–34.

Williams, R. (2006), 'Generalized Ordered Logit/Partial Proportional Odds Models for Ordinal Dependent Variables', *STATA Journal*, 6 (1): 58–82.

Zittel, T. (2012), 'Legislators and Their Representational Roles: Strategic Choices or Habits of the Heart?' in M. Blomgren and O. Rozenberg (eds.), *Parliamentary Roles in Modern Legislatures*. Oxford: Routledge, 101–20.

—— and T. Gschwend (2008), 'Individualised Constituency Campaigns in Mixed-Member Electoral Systems: Candidates in the 2005 German Elections', *West European Politics*, 31 (5): 978–1003.

Agreement, Loyalty, and Discipline: A Sequential Approach to Party Unity

Cynthia M. C. van Vonno, Reut Itzkovitch Malka, Sam Depauw,
Reuven Y. Hazan, and Rudy B. Andeweg

6.1 PARTY AND PERSONAL REPRESENTATION

In 2006, a Citizens' Assembly set up by the Dutch government to evaluate the electoral system proposed to give more weight to preference votes for individual candidates, and at the same time to oblige legislators who split from their party to give up their seat in parliament. The first proposal would have strengthened individual legislators vis-à-vis their party while the second proposal would have had the opposite effect. The example illustrates the tension between party representation and personal representation that is inherent in representative democracy. The balance between parties and individual legislators varies across time and across countries. In many countries the emphasis shifted from individual legislators to political parties with the introduction of universal suffrage, but even before that time like-minded legislators formed loosely structured parliamentary groups to coordinate their activities and increase their chances of legislative success. And even after the arrival of well-organized mass parties, individual legislators are more than just 'lobby fodder' and continue to provide an elite-mass linkage, albeit less visibly (Thomassen and Andeweg 2004). The relative weakening of political parties in society in recent decades has led to speculation about a concomitant shift back towards more personal representation as witnessed by increasing preference voting (Karvonen 2009: 41–63) and by electoral reforms favouring personal representation (Carey 2009: 23–42).

Political parties are meant to solve collective action problems in both the electoral and the legislative arena (Bowler 2000; Bowler, Farrell, and Katz 1999), and thus shifts in the balance between individual legislators and their parties have important consequences. In the electoral arena, it is likely that an emphasis on personal representation will attract candidates with different qualities than a system dominated by parties, and that political competition will focus more on valence issues and legislators' past performance than on position issues and party programmes (Colomer 2011). In the legislative arena, an emphasis on personal representation will weaken party unity and make the outcome of legislative decision-making less predictable. In parliamentary systems of government, dissent among the governing parties will not only jeopardize the government's policy agenda, but the survival of the government itself (Strøm 2000).

Currently, parties vote in near perfect unity in recorded parliamentary votes, with measures frequently surpassing 99 per cent (e.g. Carey 2009; Depauw and Martin 2009; Heidar 2006; Sieberer 2006), but this very absence of variance has hampered the study of the relationship between personal and party representation. Cross-national analysis is further hindered by selection bias and measurement error related to the diverse rules governing recorded (roll-call) votes in parliament (Hug 2010; Carrubba et al. 2006; Saalfeld 1995a). Finally, the study is complicated by conceptual confusion, in particular between the concepts 'party discipline' and 'party cohesion' (Hazan 2003). As a consequence, as Skjæveland (2001) noted, comparative research has not comprehensively studied micro-level explanations of party unity, let alone tied them to institutions. This study uses interviews with legislators in several countries, where relevant in both national and regional parliaments, to provide a better understanding of an individual legislator's *sequential decision-making process* in determining whether or not to toe the party line—relating each stage of the decision-making process to government and electoral institutions in particular. The inclusion of sub-national legislators also remedies the fact that previous research has largely ignored the puzzle of party unity at the regional level (but see Könen 2009; Davidson-Schmich 2003).

6.2 CONCEPTS AND SEQUENCE

The theoretical literature on party unity suffers from severe conceptual confusion, as there is no widely accepted terminology among scholars. Terms such as party unity, party cohesion, party discipline, party agreement, party loyalty, party socialization, and party homogeneity are ill defined and used by different scholars in different ways (Andeweg and Thomassen 2011). However, it appears that we can point to some common ground between scholars in their understanding of the core concepts. First, most scholars view party unity as an outcome, not a process; hence they try to explain party unity using other factors which may influence it. Party unity is thus defined in this chapter as the 'observable degree to which members of a group act in unison' (Sieberer 2006: 151).

Second, most scholars acknowledge that party unity can be achieved in (at least) two different ways—by legislators adhering to the party line voluntarily, or alternatively involuntarily by the threat or the actual use of positive and negative sanctions by the party leadership. The voluntary pathway to party unity is often referred to by scholars as *party cohesion*, while the involuntary determinant is typically referred to as *party discipline* (Andeweg and Thomassen 2011; Hazan 2003; Krehbiel 1993; Norpoth 1976; Özbudun 1970).

Even if one is able to distinguish cohesion from discipline, the conceptual confusion does not end there but goes further into the meaning of the term cohesion itself. While some scholars conceptualize cohesion as stemming from homogeneous policy preferences among legislators of the same party—hence the extent to which co-partisans agree with one another when voting on legislation—others use it also to describe legislators' subscription to the norm of party unity in the absence of shared policy preferences. The former situation—that of shared preferences—is referred to as *party agreement*, while the latter situation—that of legislators' adherence to the norm of party unity—is referred to as *party loyalty*. Party agreement and party loyalty thus comprise the two main facets of party cohesion. Note that both parts of party cohesion—party agreement and party loyalty—are voluntary behavioural strategies, which matches the general understanding of party cohesion in the literature.

This sets party cohesion apart from party discipline which is defined as the use of sanctions—more precisely the threat of negative sanctions or the promise of positive incentives, in order to oblige legislators to toe the party line. It is easy to confuse party loyalty with party discipline—a fact which also contributes to the conceptual confusion—as many scholars attribute any instance in which legislators toe the party line, in the absence of shared preferences, to the anticipation of sanctions and ignore the possibility that it is the role perceptions internalized by the legislators that cause them to stay loyal to the party. However, while party loyalty entails that legislators' behaviour is led by a 'logic of appropriateness', party discipline entails that such behaviour is led by a 'logic of consequentiality' resulting from the anticipation of sanctions (Andeweg and Thomassen 2011; Kam 2009; Jensen 2000; Crowe 1983).

Party cohesion (both agreement and loyalty) and party discipline are usually conceived as characteristics of the parliamentary party group, but we explore these variables at the individual level looking at how individual legislators contribute to party unity by agreeing with the party position, by remaining loyal to the party in case of disagreement, or by being subjected to party discipline. In this chapter we argue that these pathways to party unity are not so much alternative strategies, but constitute a process of sequential reasoning whenever a legislator faces a decision about policy (Figure 6.1). Deciding how to vote in parliament, a legislator first determines whether his or her personal policy preferences are in line with those of the party.[1] In case

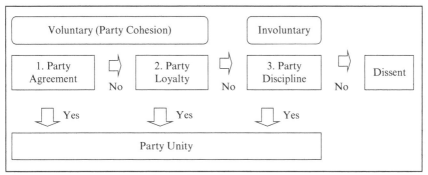

F IGURE 6.1 Legislator's sequential decision-making model

there is no conflict the legislator acts in concert with the party as a result of party agreement. If, however, the legislator's policy preferences differ from those of the party, party agreement is no longer relevant and legislators must decide whether to vote with the party out of loyalty. In other words, her internalized role conceptions and norms may bring her to vote with her party, even when she does not agree with its position. She appreciates the value of party unity and is willing to exchange her individual policy preferences for the greater good of the party she has long identified with (Crowe 1986). In such cases it is party loyalty which generates party cohesion. Party discipline comes in at the third and final stage of a legislator's decision-making process regarding a vote in parliament. Party discipline becomes relevant only when a legislator does not share the same policy preferences as the party and either the salience of the issue up for vote or the distance between personal and party position is so great that it makes the legislator's own policy preferences trump party loyalty.

6.3 THE SEQUENTIAL MODEL

We now move to a discussion of each of the three steps of a legislator's sequential decision-making model, and the distribution of legislators in each step among the fifteen national parliaments and nine sets of regional legislatures.

6.3.1 Step 1: Party Agreement

The most basic source of legislators' toeing the party line on their own accord is their simple agreement with their party's policy position. Party positions are to a large extent specified in the party programme or electoral manifesto and, if the party participates in government, in the government (coalition) agreement. Parties select candidates whose preferences are most in line with that of the party, and candidates self-select into parties (Hazan and Rahat 2010), adopting the party label that most closely suits their own policy preferences (Bowler, Farrell, and Katz 1999). Furthermore, the party's position on a specific topic is often developed during the parliamentary term by the parliamentary party group leader(s), the parliamentary party group as a whole, the party as a whole, or the parliamentary party specialist. If a legislator feels strongly about an issue, he or she may have had an opportunity to contribute to the internal decision-making process. If a legislator lacks a strong opinion on an issue, he or she may simply follow the cues provided by the party specialist in that area (Andeweg and Thomassen 2011; Skjæveland 2001). In our survey, 64 per cent of legislators indicated that the MP acting as the parliamentary party spokesperson for a policy domain determines the position of the party on topics within that domain (62 per cent of national legislators and 65 per cent of regional legislators). In all instances of a priori agreement, involvement in the formulation of the party's position, or indifference, legislators are unlikely to feel at odds with their party's position.

Policy preferences, however, have proven difficult to measure. One measure that is often used is votes in the legislature, but using roll-call votes to explain voting behaviour is tautological (Jackson and Kingdon 1992) and in addition one cannot distinguish between the relative effects of preferences versus other determinants that may contribute to legislators' voting behaviour (Krehbiel 1993). Another potential way to gauge policy preferences is through the use of legislators' self-placements on left–right or other policy scales found in elite surveys to determine the policy distance of legislators from their party's position (Kam 2001), or to calculate party agreement coefficients through which the policy homogeneity of a party can be ascertained (Andeweg and Thomassen 2011; Kam 2009). In this chapter we use a different measure for party agreement. We asked legislators 'How often, in the last year, would you say you have found yourself in the position that your party had one opinion on a vote in Parliament, and you personally had a different opinion?' We combined the response categories of 'about once a month' and 'about every three months' into 'frequently disagree', and those of 'about once a year' and '(almost) never' into 'infrequently disagree'.

In order to validate our measure of party agreement, we compared the legislators' frequency of disagreement with the absolute distance they perceived between themselves and their party on the ideological left–right scale,[2] which has been used in previous studies as a measure of party homogeneity (Kam 2009). Our expectation was that the larger the absolute distance legislators perceived between their own position and that of their party, the more frequently they will disagree with their party. Indeed, there is a negative linear relationship between the two. Among those national-level legislators who placed themselves at the same position as their party on the left–right scale, 72 per cent frequently agreed with their party on votes in parliament and 28 per cent frequently disagreed. Of legislators who experience a one-point difference, 58 per cent usually agree and 42 per cent frequently disagree. And, among those who perceived a two-point difference or more, 47 per cent frequently agreed and 53 per cent frequently disagreed. At the regional level the relationship between party agreement and perceived ideological distance is weaker, but also present. Among legislators who placed themselves either at the same position as their party or perceived a one-point difference the distributions are identical: 76 per cent frequently agreed with their party and 24 per cent frequently disagreed. However, among those legislators who experienced a two-point difference or more, 63 per cent frequently agreed and 37 per cent frequently disagreed, showing the same negative linear pattern found at the national level.

In our study, 66 per cent of legislators indicated that they usually agreed with their party, and 34 per cent frequently disagreed with their party's positions, but this figure hides considerable variation across parliaments (Figure 6.2). Party agreement was highest among national legislators from Ireland (81 per cent), Spain (79 per cent), Austria (78 per cent) and the Netherlands (72 per cent), and only in Italy, Israel, and Portugal did a (small) majority of legislators indicate that they experienced frequent disagreement with their party on a vote in parliament. With the exception of Belgium and Switzerland, party agreement was higher in the regional parliaments than in the national parliaments, with substantial differences in France, Portugal, and the United Kingdom.

Our first impression is that political parties in these parliamentary democracies can, to a large extent, rely on their representatives' agreement with the party line for the unity of their party in parliament. Nonetheless, political parties are commonly broad churches capable of widespread disagreement over policy goals, or over the means and the timing to achieve them. Around one-third of legislators frequently disagreed with their party line which, given the high levels of voting unity found in previous studies, is more than one would expect if party agreement was the sole determinant of legislators' voting behaviour. Parties, it seems, must also rely on other mechanisms to achieve party unity in Parliament.

6.3.2 Step 2: Party Loyalty

Even when legislators disagreed, they frequently toed the party line—but not because they were persuaded (through positive incentives) or coerced (through negative sanctions) to do so involuntarily. They did so voluntarily

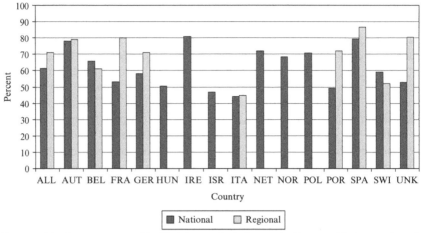

F igure 6.2 Party agreement (% of legislators who infrequently disagree with the party's position)

because they acknowledged the importance of party unity for parliamentary government. They accepted party unity as part of their role conception as elected representatives. Previously we identified party loyalty as the second stage of a legislator's sequential decision-making process. Among those who usually agreed with their party line, party loyalty was rarely relevant. However, among those who frequently disagreed with the party line, the norm of party loyalty was likely to be an important, regularly occurring determinant of their voting behaviour.

Again, the influence of party loyalty on legislators' voting behaviour is difficult to measure. Party loyalty is theorized to be the result of processes of socialization and internalization. As a result, legislators identify with their party: they *should not* 'rock the boat' and harm their party. Legislators *should* vote with their party. Failure to live up to this norm is not caused by their ignorance of what is expected of them. Party unity norms are learned, not in the first years of apprenticeship in the legislature, but long before that (Asher 1973; Crowe 1983). As such seniority in the legislature is a common, but not very valid proxy to tap into differences in party loyalty among legislators. When legislators fail to live up to the norm, it is because they feel that this time an exception is warranted. There are, however, important differences among legislators as to what warrants such an exception: some feel that under most circumstances a legislator *should* vote the party line, while others feel entitled to vote according to their own conscience or opinion (Andeweg and Thomassen 2011; Converse and Pierce 1979; Wahlke et al. 1962): because of the ethical nature of the issue, for instance, or because of strong public opinion in their district. In our survey, we asked legislators whether in the case of a disagreement an MP *should* vote according to his own opinion or that of his party.

In order to validate our measure of party loyalty we compared the answers to this voting dilemma with the importance legislators attached to promoting the views and interests of the party. Our expectation was that the more importance legislators attached to promoting the views and interests of their party, the stronger their subscription to party loyalty. Not surprisingly, a majority of all legislators considered this important, with 82 per cent scoring this at least a five on the seven-point scale, seven representing the greatest importance. But there is a linear relationship between how legislators answered the two questions—the more importance they ascribed to promoting the views and interests of their party, the more they indicated that an MP ought to vote according to the party's opinion in the case of a disagreement.[3] Of those national legislators who situated themselves at the extreme end of the scale in assigning greater importance to representing the party (thus scoring a seven on the scale), 75 per cent answered that an MP should vote according to the party's opinion and 25 per cent felt that an MP should follow his own opinion. The pattern is identical among regional legislators: among those who thought it is of great importance to represent the interests of the party, three-quarters felt that an MP should follow the party line when there is a disagreement.

In our sequential model, party loyalty is only of relevance in the absence of party agreement. Consequently, we confined our analysis of party loyalty to those MPs who indicated that they frequently disagreed with their party (Figure 6.3a). Strictly speaking, however, even MPs who reported infrequent disagreement are likely to experience some disagreements during their career, at which point the question of party loyalty arises for them too. For that reason we also report the distribution of party loyalty for all MPs (Figure 6.3b).

In our study, 51 per cent of legislators who frequently disagreed responded that a MP should vote according to the party's opinion when it conflicts with his own opinion, but here too we find considerable variation across countries and between national and regional parliaments. Party loyalty among national legislators who frequently disagreed is highest in the Netherlands (93 per cent), Norway (88 per cent), Spain (86 per cent), Belgium (85 per cent), and Ireland (81 per cent). In Switzerland, however, only 9 per cent of national legislators who frequently disagreed with their party felt that one should toe the party line in such cases. Similarly, in France, Italy, Israel, the United Kingdom, Germany, and Austria, only a minority of frequently disagreeing legislators indicated that an MP ought to vote according to the party position in the case of a disagreement with the party.

In general, party loyalty seems to be more widespread in regional parliaments, in particular among legislators who frequently disagree with their party. The pattern for all legislators is quite similar to that for MPs who frequently find themselves at odds with their party. Interestingly, disagreement does not appear to have an impact on loyalty: in many countries the percentage of MPs subscribing to party loyalty is even higher among those experiencing frequent disagreement with their party. In summation, it appears that even when parliamentary party groups are not homogeneous in terms of legislators' political preferences, they can count on the loyalty of most MPs who differ with their party. If we combine national and regional legislators, the two components of party cohesion account for 81 per cent of party unity. Nevertheless, this still leaves almost one in five legislators who are unlikely to toe the party line voluntarily.

6.3.3 Step 3: Party Discipline

When legislators do not agree with the party position and will not vote with the party out of loyalty, party leaders may resort to disciplinary measures. The observation and measurement of the use of positive incentives and negative sanctions is, however, problematic. First, their threat or promise alone may be enough to elicit submission to the party line. Second, when discipline is applied, this is usually done behind the closed doors of the parliamentary party group, as public disciplining can usually produce media attention which is assumed to have negative effects on the electoral prospects of the party as a whole. Finally, it is difficult to distinguish between behaviour resulting from the use of sanctions or other determinants (e.g. not being placed on the candidate list for the upcoming elections may be a negative sanction, but may also result from other relatively innocent factors, such as retirement).

We asked legislators to evaluate party discipline in their parliamentary party group in terms of strictness: Should party discipline be stricter, remain as it is, or should it be less strict? It is surprising, from the perspective of the literature that emphasizes discipline as the main pathway to party unity, that around 70 per cent of legislators were satisfied with their parliamentary party's level of discipline, indicating that it should remain as it is (Table 6.1). Even more unexpected, from the perspective that associates party discipline with coercion, is that out of those who were not satisfied two-thirds answered that party discipline should be more strict. Legislators' responses to the questions pertaining to specific aspects of party discipline may provide us with some additional insight into the circumstances under which party discipline is more or less likely to be applied, accepted, or even desired. Table 6.1 shows that when it comes to sticking to the party line when voting in parliament— the question that is most in line with our two facets of party cohesion (both refer specifically to voting in parliament)—79 per cent of national legislators and 84 per cent of regional legislators were satisfied with party discipline as it is, and the remaining legislators were distributed almost equally between those who thought that party discipline ought to be either stricter or less

a) Legislators who frequently disagree

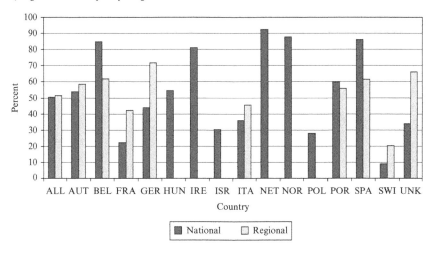

b) All legislators

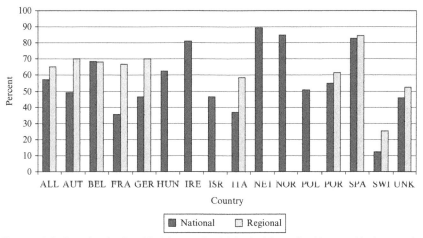

FIGURE 6.3 Party loyalty (% of legislators who think a legislator should vote with the party in case of a disagreement)

strict. One could infer from this that when it comes to voting behaviour, the requirement of party unity is both largely undisputed and understood by a vast majority of legislators. Almost the same distribution holds for another aspect of party discipline, when we asked legislators about taking political initiatives only with the parliamentary party's authorization.

TABLE 6.1 *Party discipline (% total)*

		More strict	As it is	Less strict
General party discipline	national	21	69	10
	regional	22	70	8
Taking parliamentary initiatives	national	12	76	13
	regional	10	78	12
Internal party discussions	national	54	45	2
	regional	50	49	1
Voting in parliament	national	10	79	11
	regional	8	84	8

The one exception to this pattern is legislators' evaluation of party discipline when it comes to keeping internal party discussions confidential: only 45 per cent of national legislators and 49 per cent of regional legislators were satisfied with this aspect of party discipline, and among those who were dissatisfied almost all wanted it to be stricter. This high level of dissatisfaction, in the direction of wanting stricter party discipline, highlights that party unity is more than merely the end vote in parliament but a much broader requirement that includes the entire policymaking process: the party must be united (or at least appear to be). Whereas the requirement of party unity in the final vote in parliament is fairly undisputed, it seems that party unity in the process of forming the party position is disregarded, or at least considered less salient, by some legislators. Apparently, there are legislators who do breach confidential intra-party discussions, which leads to the relatively low satisfaction with party discipline and a desire by half or more for stricter party discipline.

These assessments of the current situation with regard to party discipline are clearly of a different nature than our data on party agreement and party loyalty. Nevertheless, we can distil an indicator of the occurrence of party discipline from these evaluations. For that purpose, we suggest that legislators who feel that their behaviour is indeed limited by the parliamentary party group will most likely hold the opinion that party discipline should be less strict (because they presumably have had sanctions used against them or operate under the threat of sanctions); whereas legislators who feel that they personally, or the parliamentary party group as a whole, suffer from the behaviour of fellow group members will likely hold the opinion that party discipline ought to be more strict.[4]

Since we are most interested in legislators who thought party discipline ought to be less strict (because we believe that these are the ones who are regularly disciplined), we combined those who indicated that party discipline ought to be more strict with those who wished it to remain as is into one category. When it comes to general party discipline, we expected that legislators who regularly disagreed with their party and who did not subscribe to the norm of party loyalty would prefer party discipline to be less strict than their colleagues who voluntarily voted with their party. Indeed, only 79 per cent of legislators who did not contribute to party cohesion believed party discipline should be stricter or remain as is, while 21 per cent thought it ought to be less strict. Of legislators who frequently disagreed but who were loyal to their party, 91 per cent felt that party discipline should be more strict or stay the same, while only 9 per cent thought it should be less strict. From this we can deduce that our interpretation of the question has some validity, legislators who do not voluntarily toe the party line are more likely to be disciplined and thus more likely to indicate that party discipline should be less strict, whereas legislators who toe the party line voluntarily value the collective benefits of the party being unified and would like to see them remain as is or even be increased.

As with party loyalty, we present the data both for those legislators for whom discipline is relevant (i.e. the MPs who disagreed with their party frequently, and who did not subscribe to the norm of party loyalty), and for all legislators (Figures 6.4a and 6.4b). There is an added reason for also presenting the data on all legislators: at the third stage of the sequential model the number of legislators left is rather small, especially at the country and national versus regional level (the 100 per cent preferring party discipline to be less strict in the Netherlands in Figure 6.4a, for example, represents a single respondent). Combining the two figures, it would seem that party discipline plays a relatively big role in the UK, Spain, Portugal, and Poland, but is a relatively marginal phenomenon in Austria, Germany, Norway, and Switzerland. In the UK and Italy in particular, party discipline seems to be more prevalent at the regional level than at the national level, whereas the opposite seems to hold true in Portugal.

6.4 THE THREE STEPS TO PARTY UNITY

We can now combine the results of the three steps in the sequential model and assess their relative contribution to party unity (Table 6.2).

Two thirds of the legislators in our survey usually agreed with their party. Nearly one in five disagreed frequently, but felt that they nevertheless ought to vote the party line. Nearly one in twenty frequently disagreed with the party and did not internalize the norm of party loyalty, but was subjected to party discipline. This leaves us with 13 per cent of all legislators who disagreed frequently, and who were neither loyal nor disciplined. These are the legislators whom we predicted will dissent frequently. For some parliaments, for example Switzerland, our findings are in line with earlier studies which

a) Legislators who frequently disagree and who are not loyal

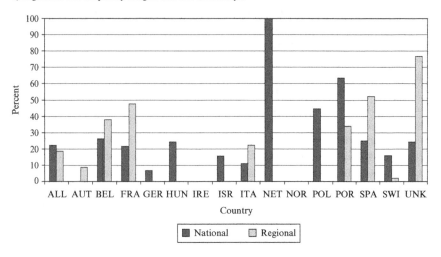

b) All legislators

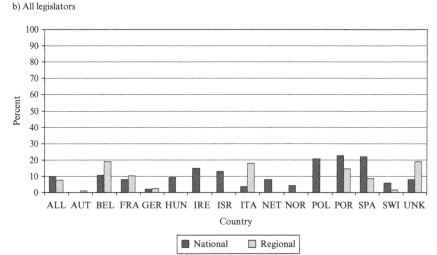

FIGURE 6.4 General party discipline (% of legislators who prefer less strict party discipline)

reveal lower average levels of party voting unity (Lanfranchi and Lüthi 1999). However, if our prediction is correct, studies of roll-call votes in most other countries should have found much higher levels of party dissension, which is not the case (see Andeweg and Thomassen 2011 for the Netherlands; and Depauw and Martin 2009 for Austria, Belgium, France, Germany, Ireland, Israel, Italy, Norway, and the United Kingdom). It seems likely that we underestimated the contribution to party unity of at least one of the three components. Given the different nature of the data on party discipline, and the assumptions we had to make in order to use our data as an indicator of being disciplined, it seems most likely that we underestimate party discipline. However, even if party discipline could completely fill the gap in assessing party unity, it would still make only a relatively modest contribution to party unity, almost of the same magnitude as party loyalty and far below the impact of party agreement. Moreover, although we find considerable variation across countries and across levels within countries here too, the conclusion of a limited effect by party discipline is robust.

Party agreement is the most important pathway to party unity in all parliaments, party loyalty usually comes second and party discipline last. Only in the Swiss *Nationalrat* is party discipline of more importance than party loyalty, and even then it only accounts for 7 per cent (and in Poland the two are equally important). Of course, this is partly the result of our sequential model, in which we entered party agreement first and party discipline last, but not entirely: if we had turned the model around and had started with discipline, this would still not have made party discipline the biggest contributor to party unity.

6.5 THE EFFECTS OF INSTITUTIONS

So far we have argued that party unity is brought about through party agreement, party loyalty, and party discipline. Some legislators toe the party line because they invariably agree with the party line; others decide not to rock the boat out of loyalty to the party even when they disagree; and still others return to the flock out of fear of being disciplined. In this section we move further down the causal chain to find out to what extent the institutional context explains agreement, loyalty, and discipline. Our argument is that institutions affect party unity because they shape legislators' sequential reasoning. We will focus on the two institutions most often mentioned in the study of party unity, namely, electoral systems and participation in government. In addition, we consider how regionalized institutions affect these pathways.

First, electoral systems shape the conditions that legislators compete under for re-election. In this respect they are expected to affect party agreement, party loyalty, and party discipline—albeit for different reasons. Electoral systems affect party agreement; party control of the order in which candidates running under the party label are elected allows the leadership to select candidates who are in agreement with the party line. In electoral systems in which voters have the option to indicate a preference among co-partisans and

TABLE 6.2 *The relative contribution of party agreement, party loyalty, and party discipline to party unity (%)*

Country	Level	Agreement	Loyalty	Discipline	Unaccounted
All	national	62	19	5	15
	regional	71	15	3	11
Austria	national	80	11	0	9
	regional	79	13	1	8
Belgium	national	64	29	2	5
	regional	64	21	6	9
France	national	54	8	8	29
	regional	82	4	7	7
Germany	national	57	18	2	23
	regional	70	21	0	9
Hungary	national	51	28	5	16
Ireland	national	82	14	0	4
Israel	national	47	17	7	30
Italy	national	42	22	5	32
	regional	45	25	6	24
The Netherlands	national	76	22	2	0
Norway	national	70	26	0	5
Poland	national	71	9	9	11
Portugal	national	49	28	14	9
	regional	70	18	3	9
Spain	national	78	19	1	2
	regional	87	8	3	3
Switzerland	national	59	2	7	32
	regional	51	10	1	38
United Kingdom	national	59	11	7	24
	regional	71	15	3	11

Note: The percentages may deviate from earlier tables and figures because these include only legislators who answered all three questions. Unfortunately, the party discipline question was near the end of the survey.

can effectively alter the order in which legislators are elected, the co-partisan competitors may face 'competing principals' demanding different policies from them (Carey 2009). In so far as the constituencies that legislators represent differ from the national party electorate in their social and economic make-up, party agreement is likely to suffer (Kam 2009). For the latter reason electoral systems also affect party loyalty. Legislators who face a 'product differentiation' problem (Cox and Thies 1998), having persuaded voters to support them and not some co-partisan, are likely to feel that this warrants some leeway on the part of the leadership for them to vote with their personal constituency when at odds with the party line. Legislators who were (re)elected on the coat-tails of the party, on the other hand, benefit more from the collective benefits of a unified party reputation and are therefore more likely to toe the party line out of loyalty, and if not, out of fear of being disciplined. Party control of the ballot is used as a—oftentimes silent, some-times noisy—disciplinary tool to prevent rebels being returned to parliament (Laver 1999; Saalfeld 1995b).

Hypothesis 1.1: Legislators are more likely to frequently agree with the party in party-centred electoral systems than in candidate-centred elec-toral systems;

Hypothesis 1.2: Of the legislators who frequently disagree with the party, those in party-centred electoral systems are more likely to subscribe to the norm of party loyalty, than those in candidate-centred electoral systems;

Hypothesis 1.3: Of the legislators who frequently disagree with the party and do not subscribe to the norm of party loyalty, those in party-centred electoral systems are more likely to anticipate discipline (and hence feel that party discipline should be less strict), than those in candidate-centred electoral systems.

The conditions that legislators compete under for re-election affect legislators' incentives to nurture a personal constituency in two manners. On the one hand, the formal properties of electoral systems favour, or do not favour, personal vote-seeking on the part of legislators. These properties can be tapped into by the differential effect of district magnitude (Carey and Shugart 1995). When voters can alter the order in which candidates running under the same party label are elected, the 'product differentiation' problem that legislators face increases with the number of competitors running under the same party label; that is, with district magnitude. When voters cannot, alternatively, the incen-tive to nurture a personal constituency grows weaker as district magnitude increases. On the other hand, it is arguably legislators' perceptions of the value of a personal vote, rather than the value itself, that shapes their behaviour. Even in similar circumstances legislators' perceptions are likely to be different, tak-ing into account their standing in the party and prior career trajectories. Per-ceptions can be tapped into more directly by looking at the kind of campaign legislators would like to run, whether they would run a personal campaign or a party campaign. Taking a position against the party line may yield legislators name recognition and support in constituencies unfavourable to the party line (Kam 2009). Where such support can make the difference between (re)election and defeat, legislators are less likely to agree with the party, less likely to feel that they should toe the party line regardless, and more likely to anticipate discipline (and hence to feel that party discipline should be less strict).

Hypothesis 2.1: Legislators who do not engage in personal vote-seeking are more likely to frequently agree with the party than legislators who do engage in personal vote-seeking;

Hypothesis 2.2: Of the legislators who frequently disagree with the party, those who do not engage in personal vote-seeking are more likely to subscribe to the norm of party loyalty, than those who do engage in personal vote-seeking;

Hypothesis 2.3: Of the legislators who frequently disagree with the party and do not subscribe to the norm of party loyalty, those who engage in personal vote-seeking are more likely to anticipate discipline (and hence feel that discipline should be less strict), than those who do engage in personal vote-seeking.

Second, parliamentary government is defined by the fact that the cabinet can be voted out of office by a plurality in the legislature by means of an ordinary or constructive vote of no confidence (Strøm 2000: 265). Cabinet stability thus directly depends on the cabinet's ability to maintain party unity in its supporting parties. The evidence in this respect is contradictory, however. On the one hand, party unity is thought to be stronger in governing parties (e.g. Saalfeld 1995b). Disunity in the opposition undercuts its public record as a viable alternative, but dissent in the ruling parties may bring down the government and result in early elections. On the other hand, whereas opposition legislators find it easier to duck votes on which there is disagreement; ruling parties cannot outrun their responsibility in a similar manner (Jackson 1968). The 'sequential reasoning' approach proposed here can disentangle both: government legislators can be expected to disagree more often with the party line than opposition legislators (Rahat 2007); after all, circumstances may oblige governing parties to take unpopular measures, and in case of coalition government, governing parties have to defend compromises rather than their own ideology. However, the threat of bringing down the government and the ensuing early elections will most likely elicit government legislators to support their party on these votes voluntarily out of loyalty, and government party leaders will more readily apply disciplinary mechanisms to get their legislators to toe the party line involuntarily if needed. In fact, we expect both party loyalty and party discipline to grow stronger the smaller the margin the cabinet has in the legislature over the opposition. When the margin is large, a few lone government dissenters cannot jeopardize the outcome of the division. When the margin is small, dissent may be voiced but government legislators will not stray in their vote from the party line (Crowe 1980).

Hypothesis 3.1: Legislators in governing parties are less likely to frequently agree with their party than legislators in opposition parties;

Hypothesis 3.2a: Of the legislators who frequently disagree with the party, those whose party is in government are more likely to subscribe to the norm of party loyalty, than those whose party is in opposition;

Hypothesis 3.2b: Of the legislators who frequently disagree with the party and do not subscribe to the norm of party loyalty, those whose party is in government are more likely to anticipate discipline (and hence feel that discipline should be less strict), than those whose party is in opposition;

Hypothesis 3.3a: The smaller the margin of seats of the government over the opposition, the more likely it is that legislators in governing parties who frequently disagree with the party, subscribe to the norm of party loyalty;

Hypothesis 3.3b: The smaller the margin of seats of the government over the opposition, the more likely it is that legislators in governing parties who frequently disagree with the party and do not subscribe to the norm of party, anticipate discipline (and hence feel that discipline should be less strict).

Finally, it seems likely that we should find differences between national and regional legislatures. First, disagreement over public policy tends to increase with population size (Weßels 1999). In this respect, regions tend to be more homogeneous than countries and disagreement between regional legislators may erupt less often as a result. In a similar vein, disagreement may be reduced among national legislators in multilevel democracies when particularly divisive issues have been devolved to the regions. Second, party loyalty and party discipline may be expected to prevail more often when more is at stake. That is, because there is more at stake at the national level in unitary states, we expect legislators there to subscribe more to the norm of party loyalty and to be less likely to feel party discipline should be less strict than national and regional legislators in multilevel democracies. Furthermore, in unitary systems the strongest level of party organization is generally the national level (Carey 2007). This means that the national party organization commonly controls candidate selection, which can serve as a source of loyalty, and can also be used as a disciplinary mechanism. In multilevel systems the national party organization usually has less control, and the loyalty of legislators may be diffused by loyalty to the party organization at lower levels of government.

Hypothesis 4.1: National legislators in unitary states are less likely to frequently agree with their party than national and regional legislators in multilevel settings;

Hypothesis 4.2: Of those legislators who frequently disagree with their party, national legislators in unitary states are more likely to subscribe to the norm of party loyalty, than national and regional legislators in multilevel settings;

Hypothesis 4.3 Of those legislators who frequently disagree and do not subscribe to the norm of party loyalty, national legislators in unitary states are more likely to anticipate discipline (and hence feel that discipline should be less strict), than national and regional legislators in multilevel settings.

Institutions constrain legislators' behaviour, but institutions do not determine party unity. Institutions are but the rules of the game and do not prescribe legislators' strategies and stratagems. In order to demonstrate this point, we present legislators' sequential reasoning by means of three logistic regression models, focusing on party agreement, party loyalty, and party discipline in turn. In line with the sequential model the analyses disregard at each stage those who observe party unity for reasons of party agreement or party loyalty. That is, the party loyalty model excludes those who do not frequently disagree with the party position and will vote with the party as a result. The party discipline model further excludes those who feel loyalty demands that they vote with the party, even when in disagreement. However, for the same reasons outlined in our presentation of the sequential model, we compare these findings to the estimations on the basis of all respondents. Given the dichotomous nature of the dependent variables, logistic regression is the proper estimation method. To take into account the hierarchical nature of the data three-level random intercept models are used or we risk underestimating standard errors (Steenbergen and Jones 2002).[5] Individual legislators are part of parliamentary party groups in the fifteen different countries and at least some of the variance in their responses can be explained by factors at the level of the party group or at the country level. That variance, the intra-class correlations demonstrate, is modest, though significant.

The estimated regression coefficients and robust standard errors are presented in Table 6.3.[6] First, the incentives to nurture a personal constituency are captured in two ways. On the one hand, the formal properties of electoral institutions are measured by the decimal logarithm of district magnitude and a dichotomous indicator coded '1' for effective preferential systems and '0' for closed-list systems. On the other hand, individual perceptions of the value of personalized electoral support are measured by a five-point scale, '1' being the intention to spend scarce time and resources running a party campaign and '5' being the intention to run a personal campaign. With regard to the effect of being in government or in opposition, a dichotomous indicator is used, while the government's command of a majority in the legislature is captured by the number of seats its supporting parties hold above the 50 per cent +1 seat threshold. We also use two dichotomous variables to distinguish between three groups: national legislators in unitary states, national legislators in multilevel democracies, and regional legislators by definition in multilevel democracies. In addition, the size of the parliamentary party is controlled for.

First, we find that electoral systems, and in particular the incentives for personal vote-seeking they generate, shape legislators' frequency of agreement with the party line and their attitude vis-à-vis party discipline. But contrary to our expectations legislators do not toe the party line less often out of loyalty when they face competing principals. Moreover, individual perceptions better capture legislators' incentives than the formal properties of electoral systems do. District magnitude does not have the predicted differential effect on party agreement or party loyalty. But legislators who do not agree with the party line and do not subscribe to the norm of party loyalty are more likely to think that party discipline should be less strict as district magnitude increases in systems where voters have the option to alter the order in which candidates running under the same party label are elected; legislators are less likely to think that when voters do have that option. Individual perceptions, on the other hand, affect both party agreement and party discipline. Legislators who run a personal campaign are more often in disagreement with the party line. While they may not feel they should not vote against the party when they disagree, they do feel party discipline should be less strict in the circumstances. That is, the incentive to nurture a personal constituency as perceived by legislators affects their sequential reasoning. The incentive as captured by the formal properties of electoral systems on the other hand affects only the final stage of the process: how legislators feel about the use of disciplinary measures to secure party unity in the face of dissent.

Second, the institutions of parliamentary government shape party agreement, party loyalty, and party discipline—but not always as we put forward. Legislators in government parties are less likely to agree with the party line than legislators in opposition parties. They are also more likely to toe the party line out of loyalty. The effects are weak, however, and do not reach conventional levels of statistical significance. We further hypothesized that the impact of participation in government might be dependent on the size of the majority it commands in the legislative arena. That is what we find: the more seats the government parties command in the legislature, the less likely legislators in the governing parties are to agree with the party line and to toe the party line out of loyalty when they do. Remarkably, legislators in the opposition parties are similarly affected: with the margin by which governing parties rule the legislature razor thin, opposition parties close ranks in order to topple the government and force early elections. In the circumstances, when the margin is thin, legislators from both governing and opposition parties do not feel that party discipline should be less strict; they accept that, when the stakes are high, the leadership ultimately will preserve party unity even if that party unity is involuntary.

Third, there are important differences between national and regional legislators with regard to party agreement. In multilevel democracies, either

TABLE 6.3 *Institutional explanations of party agreement, party loyalty, and party discipline (multilevel logistic regression)*

	Party agreement	Party loyalty		Party discipline	
	Model 1	Model 2a	Model 2b	Model 3a	Model 3b
	(all legislators)	(only legislators who frequently disagree with their party)	(all legislators)	(only legislators who frequently disagree with their party and who do not subscribe to the norm of party loyalty)	(all legislators)
Electoral system					
Preferential voting (preferential voting = 1)	0.236 (0.371)	1.336 (0.635)**	0.786 (0.636)	−1.530 (0.968)	−0.908 (0.676)
District magnitude (logged)	−0.167 (0.087)*	0.024 (0.172)	0.017 (0.162)	−0.506 (0.251)**	−0.215 (0.303)
Preferential voting * district magnitude	−0.021 (0.268)	−0.605 (0.405)	−0.393 (0.374)	1.808 (0.744)**	0.948 (0.520)*
Campaign strategy					
Party (1) versus personal campaign (5)	−0.258 (0.050)***	−0.187 (0.177)	−0.260 (0.075)***	0.453 (0.225)**	0.437 (0.107)***
Government					
Government participation (gov = 1)	−0.296 (0.132)**	0.287 (0.504)	0.574 (0.265)**	0.545 (0.667)	−0.005 (0.381)
Size of government majority (decimal logarithm)	−0.511 (0.147)***	−1.681 (0.349)***	−0.532 (0.255)**	−1.411 (0.420)***	−0.626 (0.203)***
Government participation * size of government majority	0.328 (0.135)**	0.346 (0.510)	−0.021 (0.315)	−0.346 (0.656)	−0.049 (0.355)
System level					
Level of government (reg = 1)	0.620 (0.221)***	−0.323 (0.372)	0.017 (0.239)	−0.531 (0.636)	−0.268 (0.434)
National legislators (multilevel = 1)	0.463 (0.182)**	0.327 (0.482)	−0.758 (0.229)***	0.647 (0.500)	0.166 (0.459)
Party					
Size of PPG (logged)	−0.016 (0.190)	−0.342 (0.462)	0.431 (0.305)	−0.643 (0.451)	−0.230 (0.436)
Constant	1.504 (0.388)***	2.007 (1.142)*	0.667 (0.702)	−0.389 (0.851)	−2.981 (1.116)***
N (countries)	15	15	15	15	15
N (PPGs)	303	242	303	181	303
N (legislators)	1,860	685	1860	386	1860
−2log	2,896.620	998.718	2,601.010	196.864	−667.168

TABLE 6.4 *Institutional explanations of party agreement, party loyalty, and party discipline: summary of the findings*

| | | Personal vote | | | | Government | | | | | System level | | | |
| | | Electoral system | | Campaign | | Govt. participation | | Govt. party only | | Level of govt. | | National only | | |
		Candidate-centred	Party-centred	Personal	Party	Governing party	Opposition party	Safe margin	Narrow margin	National	Regional	Unitary	Multilevel	
Step 1: all legislators	Party agreement			-	+					-	+	-	+	
Step 2: legislators who frequently disagree with their party	Party loyalty							-	+			+	-	
Step 3: legislators who frequently disagree with their party and are not loyal to the party	Party discipline	-	+	-	+			-	+					

through federal design or as a result of institutional reform, some policy areas are dealt with by the national legislature and others by the regions. Regional and national legislators are both more likely to agree with the party line in the circumstances as a result than legislators in unitary states. In the unitary states there is also more at stake in the national legislature. But there are few differences between national and regional legislators with regard to party loyalty or party discipline. Table 6.4 summarizes our findings, indicating that we find support for most, but not all of our hypotheses. Moreover, the importance of taking into account the sequential reasoning of legislators is emphasized by comparing these findings with the models including all legislators.

6.6 CONCLUSION

Day after day parliamentary parties vote in near perfect unity. It is the assumption that institutions shape the tension that frequently arises between what is in the interest of the party and what is in the interest of the individual elected representatives. But the research has not been very successful in identifying the institutions' impact on legislators' behaviour. One reason is that party unity on roll-call votes, more often than not, is so close to 100 per cent and thus 'there was no longer any point in measuring it' (Beer 1969: 350). More importantly, however, party unity results from different processes. Institutions, in particular electoral institutions and government participation, affect these processes differently. That is, a legislator's vote is but the end product of their *sequential reasoning* when making up their mind. In large part legislators share the policy preferences set out by the party, for example, in its election manifesto or in the government agreement. And thus in large part they toe the party line *because* they agree with it. Only when they disagree, legislators may decide to toe the party line voluntarily, out of loyalty, anyway. They may decide that they *should not*, in this case, harm the party. Finally, legislators may toe the party line despite their disagreement out of anticipation of positive or negative sanctions on the part of the leadership. Voluntary cohesion may then give way to involuntary discipline.

Institutions, we demonstrated, impact these processes differently. Electoral institutions shape the constituencies that legislators seek to represent and thereby affect their propensity to share their party's policy preferences. When they cultivate a personal vote, legislators are more prone to find themselves in conflict with their party and are more likely to feel that party discipline should be less strict. Government legislators, in addition, cannot duck their responsibility for public policy as the opposition can. They are more prone to conflict with their party, but are more swayed by party loyalty to toe the party line. The loyalty of legislators, both in government and in opposition, is dependent on the possibility of government alternation and therefore on the number of votes the government commands in the legislature.

NOTES

1. This is assuming that the only choice legislators have to make is between their own preferences and those of their party. There may, of course, be other preferences as a result of other potential foci of representation, such as the legislator's constituency, the party members, or the entire electorate. For the purposes of this chapter we do not look at these other foci but assume that they are nested in the legislators' personal preferences.
2. We asked legislators to place both themselves and their political party on the left–right ideological scale and this allows us to calculate the absolute ideological distance legislators perceive between their own position and their party's position. For all legislators, the perceived position of their 'closest' political party is used. At the national level in unitary systems, legislators were only asked to position their 'political party'. In multilevel systems, however, legislators were asked to place both their 'national' and 'regional' political parties. For the national legislators in multilevel systems, we use the distance to the former. The fact that the questions are placed consecutively in the survey allows us to interpret the distance that respondents perceive as meaningful.
3. A one step increase on the seven-point scale towards ascribing more importance to promoting the views and interests of the party increased the odds of a legislator agreeing with the statement that in the case of disagreement an MP ought to vote with the party's opinion as opposed to her own by a factor of 1.341 (sig. = 0.000) at the national level and 1.830 (sig. = 0.000) at the regional level.
4. This reading is related to the distinction between individual damages and collective benefits based on Andeweg and Thomassen's (2011) analysis of party discipline in the 1990 Dutch Parliamentary Study. In that study, legislators were asked an open question about the pros and cons of party discipline. Positive aspects of party discipline generally referred to the collective benefits of presenting a unified front to the outside world and making clear where the political party stands, whereas negative aspects were placed primarily at the individual level (such as curtailing individual legislators' freedom and obstructing creativity). Andeweg and Thomassen (2011: 661) deduce that '"party discipline" is considered rational from a collective point of view, not from an individual point of view'. Therefore, it may be that those legislators who prefer that party discipline be stricter value these collective benefits and would like to see them increased, whereas those who would prefer that party discipline be less strict focus on how it limits the individual legislators' freedom. Those who think party discipline should remain as it is are

probably those who perceive a good balance between the two, or they may value one above the other but are content with how they are maintained in the parliamentary party group.

5. To improve the parameter estimates penalized quasi-likelihood (PQL) iterative estimation with a second-order linearization is used.

6. In the multilevel model we use the same weight as used in the univariate and bivariate analyses, which corrects for the differences in answer patterns between party groups, regions in multilevel countries, and the overrepresentation of Swiss cantonal parliaments. In addition to the independents and (junior) ministers who were excluded from the univariate and bivariate analyses, legislators who constitute the only response for their parliamentary party are also excluded in the multilevel model.

REFERENCES

Andeweg, R. B. and J. A. Thomassen (2011), 'Pathways to Party Unity: Sanctions, Loyalty, Homogeneity, and Division of Labour in the Dutch Parliament', *Party Politics*, 17 (5): 655–72.

André, A., S. Depauw, and K. Deschouwer (2013), 'Legislators' Local Roots: Disentangling the Effect of District Magnitude', *Party Politics*. DOI 10.1177/1354068812458617.

Asher, H. B. (1973), 'The Learning of Legislative Norms', *American Political Science Review*, 67 (2): 488–503.

Beer, S. H. (1969), *British Politics*. London: Faber.

Bowler, S. (2000), 'Parties in Legislatures: Two Competing Explanations', in R. J. Dalton and M. P. Wattenberg (eds.), *Parties Without Partisan: Political Change in Advanced Industrial Democracies*. Oxford: Oxford University Press, 157–79.

—— D. Farrell, and R. S. Katz (1999), *Party Discipline and Parliamentary Government*. Columbus: Ohio State University Press.

Carey, J. M. (2007), 'Competing Principals, Political Institutions, and Party Unity in Legislative Voting', *American Journal of Political Science*, 51 (1): 92–107.

—— (2009), *Legislative Voting and Accountability*. New York: Cambridge University Press.

—— and M. S. Shugart (1995), 'Incentives to Cultivate a Personal Vote: A Rank Ordering of Electoral Formulas', *Electoral Studies*, 14 (4): 417–39.

Carrubba, C. J., M. Gabel, L. Murrah et al. (2006), 'Off the Record: Unrecorded Legislative Votes, Selection Bias and Roll-Call Vote Analysis', *British Journal of Political Science*, 36 (4): 691–704.

Colomer, J. M. (2011), 'Introduction: Personal and Party Representation', in J. M. Colomer (ed.), *Personal Representation: The Neglected Dimension of Electoral Systems*. Colchester: ECPR Press, 1–19.

Converse, P. E. and R. Pierce (1979), 'Representational Roles and Legislative Behavior in France', *Legislative Studies Quarterly*, 4 (4): 525–62.

Cox, G. W. and M. F. Thies (1998), 'The Cost of Intraparty Competition: The Single, Nontransferable Vote and Money Politics in Japan', *Comparative Political Studies*, 31 (3): 267–91.

Crowe, E. W. (1980), 'Cross-voting in the British House of Commons: 1945–1974', *Journal of Politics*, 42 (2): 487–510.

—— (1983), 'Consensus and Structure in Legislative Norms: Party Discipline in the House of Commons', *Journal of Politics*, 45 (4): 907–31.

—— (1986), 'The Web of Authority: Party Loyalty and Social Control in the British House of Commons', *Journal of Legislative Studies*, 9 (4): 161–85.

Davidson-Schmich, L. K. (2003), 'The Development of Party Discipline in New Parliaments: Eastern German State Legislatures 1990–2000', *Journal of Legislative Studies*, 9 (4): 88–101.

Depauw, S. and S. Martin (2009), 'Legislative Party Discipline and Cohesion in Comparative Perspective', in D. Giannetti and K. Benoit (eds.), *Intra-Party Politics and Coalition Governments*. New York: Routledge, 103–20.

Hazan, R. Y. (2003), 'Does Cohesion Equal Discipline? Towards a Conceptual Delineation', *Journal of Legislative Studies*, 9 (4): 1–11.

—— and G. Rahat (2010), *Democracy within Parties: Candidate Selection Methods and their Political Consequences*. Oxford: Oxford University Press.

Heidar, K. M. (2006), 'Parliamentary Party Group Unity: Does the Electoral System Matter?' *Acta Politica*, 41 (3): 249–66.

Hug, S. (2010), 'Selection Effects in Roll Call Votes', *British Journal of Political Science*, 40 (1): 225–35.

Jackson, J. E. and J. W. Kingdon (1992), 'Ideology, Interest Group Scores, and Legislative Votes', *American Journal of Political Science*, 36 (3): 805–23.

Jackson, R. (1968), *Rebels and Whips: An Analysis of Dissension, Discipline and Cohesion in British Political Parties*. London: Macmillan.

Jensen, T. (2000), 'Party Cohesion', in P. Esaiasson and K. Heidar (eds.), *Beyond Westminster and Congress: The Nordic Experience*. Columbus: Ohio State University Press, 210–36.

Kam, C. J. (2001), 'Do Ideological Preferences Explain Parliamentary Behaviour? Evidence from Great Britain and Canada', *Journal of Legislative Studies*, 7 (4): 89–126.

—— (2009), *Party Discipline and Parliamentary Politics*. New York: Cambridge University Press.

Karvonen, L. (2009), *The Personalisation of Politics: A Study of Parliamentary Democracies*. Colchester: ECPR Press.

Krehbiel, K. (1993), 'Where's the Party?' *British Journal of Political Science*, 23 (2): 235–66.

Könen, S. (2009), *Wo Sind Die Rebellen Hin? Dissentierendes Abstimmungsverhalten in Ost- und Westdeutschen Landtagen*. Heidelberg: Springer.

Lanfranchi, P. and R. Lüthi (1999), 'Cohesion of Party Groups and Interparty Conflict in the Swiss Parliament: Roll Call Voting in the National Council', in S. Bowler, D. M. Farrell, and R. S. Katz (eds.), *Party Discipline and Parliamentary Government*. Columbus: Ohio State University Press.

Laver, M. (1999), 'Divided Parties, Divided Government', *Legislative Studies Quarterly*, 24 (1): 5–29.

Norpoth, H. (1976), 'Explaining Party Cohesion in Congress: The Case of Shared Policy Attitudes', *American Political Science Review*, 70 (4): 1156–71.

Özbudun, E. (1970), *Party Cohesion in Western Democracies: A Causal Analysis*. Beverly Hills: Sage Publications.

Rahat, G. (2007), 'Determinants of Party Cohesion: Evidence from the Case of the Israeli Parliament', *Parliamentary Affairs*, 60 (2): 279–96.

Saalfeld, T. (1995a), 'On Dogs and Whips: Recorded Votes', in H. Döring (ed.), *Parliaments and Majority Rule in Western Europe*. New York: St Martin's Press, 528–65.

—— (1995b), *Parteisoldaten Und Rebellen. Fraktionen Im Deutschen Bundestag* 1949–1990. Opladen: Leske and Budrich.

Sieberer, U. C. (2006), 'Party Unity in Parliamentary Democracies: A Comparative Analysis', *Journal of Legislative Studies*, 12 (2): 150–78.

Skjæveland, A. (2001), 'Party Cohesion in the Danish Parliament', *Journal of Legislative Studies*, 7 (2): 35–56.

Steenbergen, M. R. and B. S. Jones (2002), 'Modeling Multilevel Data Structures', *American Journal of Political Science*, 46 (1): 218–37.

Strøm, K. (2000), 'Delegation and Accountability in Parliamentary Democracies', *European Journal of Political Research*, 37 (3): 261–89.

Thomassen, J. and R. B. Andeweg (2004), 'Beyond Collective Representation: Individual Members of Parliament and Interest Representation in the Netherlands', *Journal of Legislative Studies*, 10 (4): 47–69.

Wahlke, J. C., H. Eulau, W. Buchanan et al. (1962), *The Legislative System: Explorations in Legislative Behavior*. New York: Wiley.

Weßels, B. (1999), 'Whom to Represent? Role Orientations of Legislators in Europe', in H. Schmitt and J. Thomassen (eds.) *Political Representation and Legitimacy in the European Union*. Oxford: Oxford University Press, 209–34.

MPs' Inter-party Contacts and the Operation of Party Democracy

*Marcelo Jenny, Wolfgang C. Müller, Jonathan Bradbury,
Nikolaus Eder, and Gabriella Ilonszki*

7.1 INTRODUCTION[1]

European democracies have been organized as party democracies for about a century and despite much gloomy talk about the decline or crisis of political parties no real alternative has yet emerged of how democracy could be practised in the modern state. In such systems representation is collective, building on political parties, their programmes and candidates selected within the parties. Likewise, within political institutions political parties are the main units of action, with party representatives mostly showing unity in taking positions and making decisions. Party systems then are commonly understood as systems of inter-party relations (Sartori 1976)—a perspective that assumes a holistic view of party. There are many good practical reasons to work with political parties as the units of analysis (Laver and Schofield 1990).

The dominant holistic view of political parties in inter-party politics, useful as it is for capturing most observable party behaviour, leaves us in the dark about much of the actual *how* of inter-party relations. For instance, how do parties get to cooperate on political projects such as enacting specific legislation, electing candidates to parliamentary or other offices (such as speaker, committee chair, or ombudsman), or forming government coalitions? The constitution and other rules provide a framework for many of these processes that would allow players to conclude them with a minimum of interaction. This is reflected in game-theoretic modelling where one party makes a proposal and the other parties accept or reject it. However, while game theory is a powerful analytical tool for analysing complex processes, real actors face great information problems ahead of making decisions. For instance, actors do not know what content will get their proposal accepted (or rejected, as both can be useful outcomes) and do not know the best time to make their proposal. In writing successful game plans political actors greatly depend on information on the other players, their preferences and constraints. Formal modelling often assumes fully informed actors, satisfying itself with a fiction. Equally, more conventional analyses of party interaction typically do not fill this gap and often remain silent about the information problems of actors. Of course, party actors can infer some information from the objective interests of other parties (such as the composition of their electorate), formal rules (such as the party statute), behavioural records (i.e. from what the party in question did in similar situations in the past), and from what is in the public domain (e.g. newspaper reports). But how do party actors make sense of this information? In this chapter we take the first systematic look at a key source of mutual information: inter-party contacts (or ties) at the level of individual MPs. Although this source is likely to produce soft information, we argue that it is crucially important for making sense of the harder information mentioned above. In assessing inter-party contacts we address a key missing dimension in our understanding of party democracies as a whole.

Currently, the research literature reveals very little on the quantity and quality of inter-party contacts of MPs in European parliaments. Consequently, a pioneering role of the chapter is to provide an estimate of these characteristics. In so doing, we are mindful that working together in one institution clearly exposes each MP to a myriad of interactions with MPs from other parties. We are not interested in superficial or fully role-determined interactions but rather 'good contacts', which typically require frequency, duration, and a level of mutual trust derived from experiences in previous interactions. Ultimately, having such contacts is very much a matter of individual choice and the 'chemistry' between MPs. It is therefore difficult to predict for social scientists with the help of their conventional arsenal of methods. Although we cannot unravel personalities we can nevertheless expect that the frequency and precise nature of good contacts between MPs from different parties will be influenced by the context in which they interact. For example, given the importance of the government–opposition divide in parliamentary systems, we would expect better contacts on the government side of this divide rather than across it.

The chapter proceeds as follows. In the next section we discuss current explanations of inter-party contacts among MPs. We then describe our data and our methods of analysis. Next we use the data to present a descriptive analysis of cross-party contacts of national and regional MPs in fifteen European countries. In the penultimate section we then attempt to explain variations in inter-party contacts between MPs and subject our data to regression analysis. In the conclusion we summarize the main results and discuss possible implications for the operation of party democracies at the system level as a basis for future research on this much under-studied issue.

7.2 THEORY: WHAT MAKES MPS BUILD BRIDGES WITH MPS FROM OTHER PARTIES?

What are the conditions that provide individual MPs with the opportunity and incentive to build up and maintain good contacts with MPs from other parties? While the literature on inter-party contacts on the whole is scarce and offers little guidance, as so often US research offers some ways forward. In particular, research going back to the 1960s has revealed that as a result of them lacking strong pre-structuring of parliamentary business by disciplined parliamentary parties, state legislatures rely on cross-party ties for their functional operation.

> Because legislative institutions must process a multitude of complex and controversial issues in an orderly and civil fashion, their effective performance rests upon strong networks of friends. Interpersonal ties among members define the legislature, laying the basis for the dynamics of legislative leadership, supplying the texture for partisan and other aggregations of members, establishing channels of communication, and providing the connections through which bargaining, exchanges of cues, and decision making transpire. (Caldeira and Patterson 1987: 954)

This strand of research has focused on finding and explaining friendship and instrumental relations between legislators, documenting who seeks advice and cooperation with whom in parliamentary work (e.g. Routt 1938; Patterson 1959; Wahlke, Eulau et al. 1962; Kingdon 1973; Baker 1980; Caldeira and Patterson 1987, 1988; Caldeira, Clark, and Patterson 1993; Arnold, Deen, and Patterson 2000; Cho and Fowler 2010). Factors identified behind purposefully forged ties were the similarity of political views, respect for the expertise of colleagues or a rational acknowledgement of their power in the legislature (Caldeira and Patterson 1987, 1988; Caldeira, Clark, and Patterson 1993). 'Certain attributes of legislators—such as partisan identification, location in the hierarchy of leadership, or position among active members—make a member more attractive to colleagues' (Caldeira and Patterson 1987: 954). Apolitical factors like sitting next to each other in the legislature or joint travel from the same district to parliamentary sessions helped in explaining friendships between legislators, though they easily blended with instrumental motivations (Patterson 1959, 1972; Baker 1980). We would expect such factors to cause similar effects in European parliaments.

In the European context inter-party relations are explicitly addressed in Anthony King's (1976) well-known work on executive–legislative relations. King's important contribution was to systematically introduce 'party' to the study of executive–legislative relations, further differentiating the relations between the government and parliament (Andeweg 1992; Müller 1993). Building on King's work Andeweg and Nijzink (1995) arrive at a broader classification of actor–actor relations unfolding in parliaments. These comprise the *inter-party mode* (sub-dividing into the *intra-coalition* and *opposition modes*), the *cross-party mode*, and the *non-party mode*. Each mode identifies one politically relevant type of actor–actor relations and a different line of division running either between the institutions (government vs. parliament), between parties, or between MPs acting as representatives of sectoral interests. What is important in our context is that the different modes identify conflict situations in parliaments where MPs of different parties find themselves on the same side. We need to explore how such experiences are likely to foster 'good relations' between MPs from different parties. At the same time the existence of such relations may make actual instances of particular types of conflict more likely.

In the *non-party mode* the focus is on the boundaries of institutions. The main line of conflict runs between the cabinet/ministers and parliament/MPs. This is a residual of classic parliamentarism 'before the arrival of disciplined mass parties' (Andeweg 1997: 117). It finds its expression in MPs displaying 'a certain *institutional* pride' (Esaiasson and Holmberg 1996: 315) and devoted to defending the prerogatives of parliament vis-à-vis the executive regardless of their party affiliation—Searing's (1994) 'Parliament Men'. Such attitudes and behaviour may indeed foster cross-party respect and good relations between MPs who find themselves united in a common cause. Yet, as a result of the arrival of disciplined mass parties MPs have to assume that respect from their peers for defending parliamentary rights may be less important for their future career than the goodwill of party leaders. This mode therefore may contribute to good inter-party contacts between MPs but in all likelihood it is of marginal importance.

We now turn to the two versions of the inter-party mode. The permanent confrontation of government and opposition parties (opposition mode) may lead to mutual respect among MPs for debating skills but is unlikely to create good contacts between them. In contrast, being teamed-up in a government coalition (the intra-coalition mode) may force MPs to fight parliamentary battles shoulder-to-shoulder and to coordinate before committee and plenary meetings to foster their common goals. This may be particularly so if the government parties are close to each other ideologically. Yet coalition politics also knows mutual mistrust, scrutiny, and confrontation; indeed many coalitions end in conflict and are remembered as unhappy episodes by their protagonists (Strøm et al. 2008). Thus the long-term effects on interpersonal relations among MPs in a coalition are not all that easy to predict.

In the *cross-party mode* sectoral interests cut across party and government–opposition lines. MPs who share a concern for a common cause of a functional or regional nature join forces to achieve desired goals such as passing a clause in a piece of legislation or making public investment in a region. It is easy to understand that such cooperation, in particular if it is successful, will result in durable high-quality contacts between the MPs involved.

The most relevant empirical study of inter-party contacts among MPs in the European context of multi-party systems and high levels of party unity is a comparative study of the Nordic parliaments (Jensen 2000). The author describes cross-party cooperation as 'a rather common phenomenon' (Jensen 2000: 228). However, the breadth of cross-party contacts varied considerably in the five countries across six different issue areas and between countries. Finland took the lead in cooperation across party lines, followed by Norway, Denmark, and Iceland. This left Swedish MPs as the ones least willing to build bridges across parties with at best a third of them reporting recent cross-party cooperation. Cooperation in all countries was most common on local and regional issues and least common on religious or ethical issues. 'More than half of the Danish and Icelandic MPs, more than two thirds of Norwegian MPs, and more than four-fifths of Finish MPs have actively cooperated across party lines during the last year on localization and other local and regional issues' (Jensen 2000: 230). Jensen stresses that 'the existence of high party cohesion does not forbid or prevent contacts and cooperation across party lines'. Indeed, he finds extensive cooperation and coalition-building among MPs from different parties within various policy areas. In Jensen's analysis 'the norms of party unity regulate these interactions—they do not stop them—and they might even facilitate cooperation, in that they provide norms for how far individual MPs may go when exchanging information and taking political initiatives'. In this author's conclusion 'the Nordic parliaments are working parliaments in which the *interparty mode* exists side by side with the *cross-party mode*' (Jensen 2000: 234–5).

We can see that existing research suggests that the extent of contacts between MPs across parties is an important issue for more systematic comparative research. We now consider how conditions fostering inter-party contacts of MPs can be located at the system level (and hence affect all MPs), at the party level (and hence affect only MPs who belong to the respective party or parties), and at the individual level (and hence affect only those MPs who share the relevant characteristics).

7.2.1 System-level Factors

Number of parliamentary parties. The number of parties represented in parliament should have a straightforward effect on most measures of MPs' inter-party contacts. More parties mean that the total number of technically possible party contacts is higher and that individually the MPs can have contacts with a greater number of parties. More parties also creates the functional need for each party to interact with a greater number of other parties. More parties may also mean more choice in terms of a greater spectrum of preferences and groups being represented within different parties who can then become the focus for cross-party contacts. For instance, each party may want to have a medical doctor, a professor, a farmer, etc. who, in turn, might find it easy to communicate with representatives of these professions in other parties. Consequently, a straightforward hypothesis is that the more parliamentary parties there are the more individual inter-party contacts there will be.

Electoral systems. Electoral systems may pit candidates of different parties against each other in a 'winner-takes-all' manner. Once they are elected though, MPs do not serve with direct electoral competitors in parliament, which should have a positive effect on their relations. In principle this should be helpful for inter-party cooperation on regional issues (i.e. issues relevant to more than one constituency). However, majority systems conventionally provide for a one-party government which may address such concerns, which in turn may reduce the value of inter-party cooperation among MPs anyway. In contrast, list systems with large constituencies should encourage inter-party cooperation between MPs for a number of reasons. List systems are likely to reduce tensions between MPs from different parties as the gains and losses of parties affect only those MPs at the bottom of the lists and those of marginal parties. List systems also bring to parliament MPs from different parties who share regional and group interests; and parliaments elected from such lists normally create coalition governments that make inter-party cooperation between MPs more attractive. Mixed member systems add additional complexity by creating contamination effects (i.e. when prospective MPs cannot neatly be divided into those running in single member districts and those running on party lists). In such situations their attitude towards other parties' MPs might be influenced by their more confrontational experience of single member district competition.

Parliamentary committees. Cross-party contacts are also likely if MPs are members of the same policy network and jointly develop, scrutinize, and amend legislation in their area of expertise (Andeweg and Nijzeng 1995; Thomassen and Andeweg 2004). Parliamentary committees constitute institutionalized arenas in which policy specialists from different parties meet on a regular basis. The argument that strong committees strengthen cross-party ties has been repeatedly made (e.g. Shaw 1979). Some empirical evidence supports this view although the number of committees, their functions and legal powers and their political importance vary greatly across countries (Mattson and Strøm 1995; Martin and Depauw 2011). The reputation of the German Bundestag as a 'working parliament' stems from the amount of legislative work done and the time spent in committee sessions (e.g. Shaw 1998: 236). Studies of Norwegian minority governments emphasize the significance of committee work in parliament (Strøm 1990: 209–11). As Matthews and Valen stress, the standing committees in the Storting are 'unusually strong for a parliamentary system' with most members' time and energy being devoted to committee work. 'The parties stress their differences in the ceaseless competition for votes. But the Storting requires cooperation across party lines if the country is to be governed' (1999: 59, 178). 'Committee work not only enhances specialization and provides a setting for compromise on concrete issues, it also serves to integrate the opposition into the power structures of the state (Heidar 1997: 96).

Old or new democracies. We must take some account of the comparative historical context and specifically we consider the significance of whether states are new or old democracies. Here a key factor to take into consideration is the stability of the party system. A wealth of research shows that on the whole new democracies show greater electoral volatility, higher MP turnover and more party splits (Bielasiak 1997; Tóka 1998; Kitschelt et al. 1999; Kostadinova 2003; Sikk 2005; Tavits 2005; Enyedi et al. 2011). Given the fluidity of the party system and its units, we might expect to see more inter-party contacts in new as opposed to old democracies. However, we remain aware that because new parties in new democracies have to clearly differentiate themselves to make distinct offers to voters another assumption might be that they neglect contacts or even overplay confrontation.

Non-political opportunities. While almost all European parliaments seat their members according to party affiliation (Andeweg and Nijzink 1995) the Norwegian parliament is distinctive in seating the MPs by region. According to Rommetvedt (1992: 89), 'it is quite possible that the seating arrangement in the Norwegian *Storting* has contributed to the widespread consensus which has characterized Norwegian politics in much of the post-war period. When political opponents share a two-seated chair during debates they have considerable time for informal communication, reducing the political tension between them. This communication may reduce the conflicts between the parties and strengthen the cooperation between county representatives across party cleavages'. Of course, other factors such as no recourse to early elections, frequent rule by minority government, the importance of local and regional issues, and joint travel to the capital may also be influential. Our cross-national research design now allows us to test the non-political opportunities hypothesis comparatively, though given its geographical extension and limited opportunities to travel we still would expect these factors to be particularly important in Norway.

Parliamentary culture. Parliaments are also distinguished from each other by the culture that each has evolved. Yet culture is a slippery concept, difficult to define and even more difficult to measure. To get a handle on it we turn to the claim in feminist studies of representation that women do politics differently from men (Wängnerud 2009). In this perspective, female legislators are similar to each other in their political views, preferences and parliamentary behaviour, but differ systematically from their male colleagues. If so, female MPs from different parties might have a stronger incentive than men to cooperate across party lines. This is particularly the case as women MPs are minorities in most parliaments and parliamentary parties, though this varies quite widely from only a few token female MPs to a figure above the theorized 'critical mass' threshold (Dahlerup 1988; Studlar and MacAllister 2002; Bratton 2005). It is often assumed that the presence of women has a 'civilizing' effect on parliamentary culture. First, their presence is theorized to 'elicit at least a veneer of civility' atypical for the dynamics of an all-male group. Second, women themselves are theorized to 'bring a less confrontational approach as a consequence of their gender socialization and family roles' (Sawer, Tremblay, and Trimble 2006: 16–17; also Dahlerup 1988: 290). This suggests that in a less confrontational culture contacts bridging party boundaries should be easier to sustain. We will use sex as an individual variable and the share of female MPs as a proxy variable for parliamentary culture in our multivariate models.

National versus regional assemblies. As our empirical study covers both types of assemblies, are there factors distinguishing the two that can be expected to be potentially relevant for our research question? Given the primacy of national politics, we take it that the most controversial issues are dealt with at the national level. Keeping such issues off the agenda should work to the benefit of inter-party relations on both institutional and personal levels in regional chambers. Similarly, we expect regional assemblies to be less diverse than national ones in terms of both the socio-cultural and economic backgrounds of MPs. Following the assumptions of other chapters in this book we note the claims that regional parliaments are closer to publics, and often geared by a politics of regional mobilization to show that regional parliaments can work more closely together than national parliaments. All this should make good cross-party contacts between MPs more likely.

7.2.2 Party Factors

Majority versus minority government. Minority governments need to reach out to the opposition to survive and pass legislation. At the same time minority government provides incentives for the opposition parties to reach out to other parties to make policy gains, to get included in the cabinet or to unseat the government. While such issues are normally considered to be 'high politics' and decided between party leaders (King 1976), mutual sounding out and work to prepare the ground for top-level decisions may well fall on ordinary MPs who are less likely to compromise their party if the attempt fails or gets unwanted publicity. In such conditions, therefore, we would expect more contacts between MPs from different parties over legislation or even over government composition. Equally, we might expect good contacts to be higher in systems with frequent minority government.

Single-party versus coalition government. Systems with frequent coalition government alert parties and MPs to the fact that good inter-party relations may have an instrumental value when the main prize of parliamentary systems—government office—is at stake. As coalition governments often witness changes in composition both government and opposition parties have incentives not to abandon contacts that have built up between them. At the same time, coalition government forces government parties to coordinate their activities and present a joint front in parliament. All of these factors encourage contacts and civilized inter-party relations, and thus provide a suitable background for building up good personal contacts. In contrast, systems with frequent single-party government encourage inter-party confrontation and only change through wholesale replacement (Mair 1997: ch. 9). Building bridges between the parties may simply be considered unnecessary or even dangerous (as they allow for infiltration). Thus we would expect MPs from systems with frequent government coalitions, in particular in pivotal party systems, to have better contacts with colleagues from other parties than MPs from systems that cultivate single-party government.

Government or opposition. Parliamentary systems of government are characterized by a more or less clear-cut divide between the government and the parliamentary opposition. In the case of majority governments, government parties do not have much reason to seek contacts with the opposition, but parties within coalition governments have a myriad of reasons to coordinate between themselves. At the same time, opposition parties may find coordination with other opposition parties important on some issues that relate to the rights of the parliamentary minority or executive–legislative relations. Even so, in most instances achieving something would require the cooperation of the government or convincing MPs of the government party or parties to join forces with the opposition. While this may occasionally happen, as suggested by the non-party mode, we might expect the camaraderie of power to forge stronger ties among MPs from government parties than the camaraderie of being powerless among the MPs of non-government parties, with limited opportunities to achieve their own goals.

Ideology. MPs from parties with more extreme ideologies have more incentives to seek contact with MPs from other parties than those from more centrist ones. However, they face more severe constraints. Assuming that ideological closeness provides a good starting point for inter-party cooperation, we should expect that the more extreme parties are the less their MPs should be able to actually build such contacts (although they may try). Extremist parties are not necessarily the smallest parties but these two attributes often overlap, and MPs from smaller parties also might be assumed to have more incentives to establish good contacts with MPs from other parties as a key way to acquire influence and political opportunities. Another take on the ideology of parties is the distinction between mainstream and niche parties (Meguid 2008). Minimally defined, niche parties emphasize policy areas that their competitors do not (Meyer and Miller, forthcoming). Party 'nicheness' might reduce the cross-party contacts of their MPs in two ways: they might have fewer contacts and might be less frequently contacted by other parties.

7.2.3 Individual Characteristics

We have already introduced gender as an individual-level variable above, suggesting that we should expect women MPs to have more good contacts with MPs from other parties than male representatives. In addition, we need to consider two further key individual-level variables. First, we should expect that MPs in parliamentary leaderships will have more cross-party ties than backbenchers. For some leadership roles it is part of the role description to hold contacts with all parties (Searing 1994; Strøm 2012). The Speaker of Parliament in most European systems clearly epitomizes such a role description (Jenny and Müller 1995). In addition, as US studies have demonstrated, MPs in leadership roles are important for other MPs to court. Thus we would expect leaders of parliamentary party groups, and, to a lesser degree, committee chairmen to be approached by MPs from other parties. Although the phrasing of our question was intended to avoid the reporting of mere functional cross-party interactions, this group of respondents may still be inclined to claim their contacts as good ones if these interactions are frequent and not conflictual. Finally, we expect seniority to play a role. Quite simply, more seasoned MPs have had more time to build up contacts and accumulate goodwill from MPs of other parties.

Secondly, data collected in the PARTIREP survey include respondents' answers on role perceptions and background data on institutional variables. We used these to understand the political purposes for which MPs hoped to use good contacts. Of particular interest in discussing the relevance of role perceptions is whether there is an association between the MPs' self-understanding as a 'policy advocate' and their contacts with MPs from other parties. 'Policy advocate' is indeed the most significant of all non-party-based role orientations in our sample of MPs with good contacts. This fact may suggest that the contacts we record reflect more than just frequent encounters in which MPs are merely messengers for their party.

Overall, therefore we consider a series of hypotheses which seek to explain why MPs vary in the amount of good contacts they have with MPs from other parties. But we are suitably sceptical of how strongly based each of these propositions are. The chapter seeks to confirm, revise, or nullify these propositions and to provide further analysis to clarify the relative significance of institutional factors in determining variation in MPs' contacts with MPs from other parties at both national and regional parliament levels.

7.3 DATA

MPs were introduced to the issue of cross-party contacts in the PARTIREP survey in the following way: 'Parliaments are often said to be institutions that allow building bridges to other parties and some MPs do indeed have very good contacts also with MPs from other parties. What is the case with you? Are there other parties which include MPs with whom you have had good contacts?' They were then given the choice of saying whether they did or did not have very good contacts with MPs from other parties. Those who reported good contacts were asked to write in the names of those parties and then to itemize whether the contacts had been helpful politically. In response to the latter question they were given the option of saying 'No, contacts have a purely private nature' or if yes, they were invited to tick up to ten possible ways in which they had been helpful politically. These were (written in the order they appeared in the survey question): to do something for my local area; for understanding internal affairs of another party; for sending informal messages between parties; to ensure fair play between parties; to seed ideas within the other party; to get concessions in inter-party negotiations; to start joint initiatives in parliament; to create coalition government; when in opposition, to get information about government policy; and to promote women's interests.

It is noteworthy how the question used the language of building bridges between parties and asked for information on very good contacts only. Consequently, while the survey could not establish precisely the depth of contacts, it could establish that contacts reported both in terms of the other party and the type of contact were indeed significant ones. The wording of the question did not denote simply coming into contact with MPs from other parties that might follow for example from sitting on the same committee. It is also noteworthy that the contact uses included several which focused on party interest. These included specific and potentially high profile contacts (to create coalition government; to get concessions in inter-party negotiations) as well as more routine ones (for understanding internal affairs of another party; for sending informal messages between parties; to ensure fair play between parties; to seed ideas within the other party; when in opposition to get information about government policy). The list of options also highlighted cross-party contacts related to policy advocacy (to start joint initiatives in parliament; to promote women's interests) and to local representation (to do something for my local area).

MPs were not asked to identify their contact partners, which in some instances would have amounted to a request for highly sensitive information. Thus the survey's product is dyadic data that relate individual MPs at one end to collectives of MPs—parties—at the other end. In this respect the PARTIREP dataset differs from the standard approach in the United States which maps networks between individual legislators. At the planning stage, data collection over the entire cross-party network was considered unobtainable or at least a high-risk question that could lead to a low-response rate in parliaments with many parties. At the time of the survey their numbers varied from five in Germany to twelve in Israel. The PARTIREP group decided to provide respondents uniformly with four write-in slots, assuming that MPs would list the parties with whom they had their most important or most frequent contacts. Given the finite goodwill of survey respondents, party systems with many parties and practical constraints of written questionnaire design, the limit and the write-in format were reasonable choices. However, some MPs were eager to map their complete network of contacts and ingeniously found ways to overcome the imposed restriction by grouping parties and by re-interpreting the question format. We have recoded these instances to obtain a uniform dataset. The existence of party alliances, for instance in Italy, constituted another challenge. As far as possible we have disaggregated the alliances into their component parts. In a small number of cases we have also recoded 'I have no good contacts' and 'contacts were of a purely private nature' answers if an MP indicated some other contact reasons as well. The first two options were intended to be strictly 'either/or' options. However, we take a conservative attitude by including only MPs in our analyses whose data express a discernible attempt to answer the two questions rather than skipping them completely. We do not want to interpret complete item non-response, which may stem from fatigue or an unwillingness to answer the questions, as evidence that the respective MP did not enjoy good contacts with MPs from other parties. Omitting these cases reduces the number of MPs covered by the analyses in this chapter from 983 to 934 national MPs and from 1,343 to 1,235 regional MPs.

7.4 RESULTS

Cross-party contacts between national and regional MPs are shown in Table 7.1. The huge variation in the percentage of national MPs who have

TABLE 7.1 *Cross-party contacts of national and regional MPs*

		Good contacts				Mean of 'good contact' parties	Mean relative coverage (%)	N
	No good contacts (%)	Politically helpful (%)	Of a purely private nature (%)	Not specified (%)	Number of PPGs			
National MPs								
Norway	4	96	0	0	7	2.9	41	45
Switzerland	4	88	3	4	12	3.6	30	47
Portugal	4	87	7	1	6	2.6	44	72
Israel	5	86	9	0	12	3.8	31	34
Netherlands	7	93	0	0	11	2.8	26	65
Germany	9	89	1	1	5	2.6	53	130
Belgium	10	86	0	4	11	2.7	24	66
Austria	15	83	2	0	5[2]	2.2	43	52
Poland	16	75	7	2	8[1]	2.0	25	53
Spain	17	74	2	7	6	2.4	41	94
United Kingdom	18	70	8	4	7[1]	2.3	34	56
Hungary	23	73	1	3	5[1]	1.8	36	99
Ireland	26	72	3	0	7[1]	2.0	29	29
France	41	44	7	7	7	1.1	17	49
Italy	42	51	2	5	6	1.2	20	43
Total	15	79	3	2	7.7	2.4	31	934
Regional MPs								
Switzerland	5	91	2	2	7.0[1]	2.6	37	491
France	7	90	0	4	5.5	2.4	43	31
Italy	8	69	9	14	8.3	2.4	29	82
Spain	10	86	1	4	5.5	2.3	41	165
Belgium	12	82	1	5	7.3[1]	2.5	34	88
Germany	12	81	2	5	4	1.6	41	135
Portugal	14	71	5	19	6.5	2.3	35	36
Austria	15	85	1	0	4.2	2.3	54	163
United Kingdom	19	74	7	0	5.5[1]	2.3	43	44
Total	11	81	3	5	6.7	2.3	35	1,235

Notes: Data are weighted according to party composition of parliaments.

[1] Independents are grouped and counted as one PPG.

[2] A party split-off from the Alliance for the Future of Austria is not counted as a separate PPG.

good cross-party contacts is striking. Regional parliamentarians (drawn from nine of the fifteen countries covered in the PARTIREP survey) vary considerably less. At one extreme more than 90 per cent of the surveyed national MPs in Switzerland, Norway, Portugal, Israel, and the Netherlands reported good contacts with MPs from other parties, whereas in France and Italy a large minority of national MPs had no good cross-party contacts. We have coded MPs reporting at least one instrumental use as having politically helpful contacts. The remaining columns refer to MPs who indicated that contacts with

MPs from another party were of a purely private nature. The highest levels of purely private contacts at the national level are reported from MPs in Israel, the United Kingdom, Portugal, and France, and at the regional level from members of Italian and British regional parliaments. Although the match is not perfect, we see that politically useful contacts are more frequent in pivotal coalition systems than systems with traditions of single-party government or competition between blocs of parties. While we cannot properly test the idea that parliamentary seating arrangements are important, we see that the single parliament in our sample with seating according to region rather than party, Norway, is the one with most MPs having good cross-party contacts all of which are politically useful.

At the national level Swiss and Israeli MPs listed the highest number of parties with whom they had contacts with means of 3.8 and 3.6 respectively. Their parliaments also have the largest number of parliamentary parties with twelve parties each. For the rest of the countries there appears to be no relationship between the number of contact parties and the number of parties in the parliament. For example, the multi-party systems of the Netherlands and Belgium produced mean values of 2.8 and 2.7, slightly below the mean of 2.9 contact parties reported by Norwegian MPs, despite the fact that Norway has a smaller party system. The latter's personal networks consequently cover a larger share of the parliamentary parties. German national MPs exhibit the widest reach, on average covering more than half of the parliamentary parties. We have already noted the high percentages of French and Italian national MPs who have no good cross-party contacts. They also appear to have a very narrow reach, having good contacts with means of 1.1 and 1.2 contact parties respectively.

In six of the nine countries regional MPs claimed to have good cross-party ties about as often as their national colleagues, but the relative reach tends to be larger due to the fact that there are smaller party systems at the regional level. There is a striking contrast between responses from national and regional MPs in France and somewhat less so in Italy. Unlike their isolated national colleagues, Italian and French regional MPs indicate more and broader cross-party contacts. The low mean for German regional MPs seems to be a result of overrepresentation in the data of assemblies from the more polarized Eastern part of the 'split' German party system (Dalton and Jou 2010). Of course, we note that our indicator of relative coverage of the parliamentary parties is sensitive to the rules used in counting them. In addition, there might be a ceiling effect due to the survey-imposed limit of four party slots. However, the ceiling effect cannot be strong given the modest means for most countries.

We now turn to country results on the distinct purposes served by cross-party contacts. Instead of a detailed item-by-item analysis of distinct purposes served by cross-party contacts, in Table 7.2 we present two indices

TABLE 7.2 *Breadth of contact uses at the network level and party status of MPs*

	All MPs	Government party MPs	Opposition party MPs	Difference	N
National MPs	6.9	7.1	6.8	−0.3	60
Netherlands					
Norway	6.2	5.8	6.7	−0.9	43
Switzerland	5.8	5.7	6.7	−1.0	45
Germany	5.6	5.4	5.8	−0.4	116
Belgium	5.3	5.1	5.7	−0.6	59
Hungary	5.0	5.5	4.5	+1.0	77
Austria	4.6	4.3	4.9	−0.6	44
Poland	4.4	5.0	3.6	+1.4	42
Spain	4.4	4.6	4.2	+0.4	83
Ireland	4.3	4.6	4.0	+0.6	21
United Kingdom	4.2	4.0	4.5	−0.5	46
Portugal	3.9	3.6	4.1	−0.5	69
Israel	3.4	3.7	2.6	+1.1	32
Italy	2.9	2.8	3.1	−0.3	25
France	2.8	2.0	3.7	−1.7	29
Total	4.8	4.7	4.9	−0.2	795
Regional MPs					
Switzerland	6.1	6.0	6.6	−0.6	470
Belgium	5.7	6.0	5.0	+1.0	81
Austria	5.5	5.4	5.8	−0.4	141
Germany	5.0	5.2	4.7	+0.5	117
France	4.8	4.3	5.1	−0.8	29
Spain	4.6	4.1	5.0	−0.9	147
United Kingdom	4.5	3.8	5.1	−1.3	37
Portugal	3.7	3.2	4.4	−1.2	29
Italy	3.6	3.6	3.8	−0.2	75
Total	4.9	4.8	5.0	−0.2	1,126

Note: Index of ten distinct 'politically helpful' uses of cross-party contacts acknowledged at least once by
MPs. Theoretical range is from zero to ten. Data are weighted according to party composition of parliaments

to illustrate (a) the breadth of use for MPs' contacts network and (b) the
breadth of use of contacts with specific parties. The first index aggregates
all the cross-party ties an individual MP has, while the second index looks
at the specific party dyads. The network-level index has a theoretical range
of zero to ten points, to cover the ten contact purposes outlined in the survey question. Consequently an MP with a network index value of zero has
described all cross-party contacts as purely private (or provided no additional
information). Thereafter, each acknowledged distinct use raises the network
index by a point, regardless of the number of contact parties to whom it
applies. Table 7.2 provides separate mean index scores for MPs belonging
to government and opposition parties at the time when the PARTIREP survey
was conducted. We expected MPs from opposition parties to show a broader

spectrum of contact uses than MPs from government parties. One of the purposes for contact specifically addresses MPs from opposition parties ('When in opposition, to get information about government policy'). Indeed, in nine countries the contacts of national opposition MPs did indeed serve a broader range of uses. However, in most cases differences between the groups are rather minor.

Tables 7.1 and 7.2 considered together reveal that having ties with many parties tends to correlate with having ties with a wider spectrum of politically helpful uses. The exceptions are national MPs from Israel and Portugal. A significant proportion of them characterized their contacts as purely private, which leads to low mean index values. In most federal or regionalized countries the relationship between the numbers of ties with other parties and number of politically helpful uses, if not the level of mean values for the government–opposition divide, is similar on both levels. However, Belgium and Germany are notable exceptions, where the patterns of breadth of use and party status differ.

Table 7.3 differs from the network-level values shown in the previous table. Here the breadth of the 'use' index is calculated over all individual party dyads reported by MPs. The index score indicates again the multiple ways in which contacts have been politically helpful. By analysing the specific party dyads reported by MPs and their party's status in or out of government we can distinguish four perceived relationships in cross-party contacts: between government parties, between opposition parties, and in contacts that bridge the government–opposition divide, between government party MPs and opposition parties and vice versa. As might be expected countries with single-party government at the time of the survey do not show up in the first column, and one country with a small government coalition party is not represented due to missing data. We should also note that MPs from opposition parties might have been prone to exhibit higher average index scores due to the specific reason of 'When in opposition, to get information about government policy' which has no equivalent for government MPs. (The question did not include a temporal restriction, thus allowing for the reporting of earlier experiences. However, many MPs lack these.) Opposition-party MPs tend to report more contacts with government MPs, supporting our hypothesis that government MPs might be more attractive to have contacts with for obvious political and policy reasons.

An assessment of the results shows that national-level government-party MPs from countries ruled by coalitions described their contacts with colleagues from other government parties on average as more fruitful than their contacts with colleagues from opposition parties. Swiss government MPs constitute an exception. A more diverse pattern emerges for opposition MPs who found contacts with MPs from government parties more

TABLE 7.3 *Breadth of contact uses in party dyads and party status of MPs*

	Government party MPs with MPs from		Opposition party MPs with MPs from	
	Other government parties	Opposition parties	Government parties	Other opposition parties
National MPs	6.4	5.8	5.4	5.0
Netherlands				
Norway	4.8	3.3	5.2	5.9
Switzerland	4.4	5.3	6.2	5.8
Germany	4.8	2.7	3.5	4.4
Belgium	4.5	3.4	3.9	3.2
Poland	4.5	3.7	2.9	2.4
Austria	4.0	2.7	4.9	3.9
United Kingdom	3.3	2.3	2.9	1.5
Israel	2.5	2.7	2.2	1.6
Italy	2.4	2.0	3.8	3.0
Hungary	—	3.9	3.9	3.3
Spain	—	3.8	3.9	3.0
Ireland	—	3.8	2.5	2.9
Portugal	—	2.9	3.4	3.1
France	—	1.6	4.1	2.3
Total	4.1	3.5	3.8	3.6
Regional MPs				
Switzerland	5.0	5.0	5.2	5.1
Germany	4.9	3.2	4.2	3.9
Belgium	4.7	4.9	3.3	2.6
Austria	4.2	4.3	5.2	3.8
Italy	4.2	2.6	2.8	3.0
France	4.1	4.3	4.3	2.3
Spain	3.8	3.8	4.4	3.9
United Kingdom	2.5	2.2	4.0	3.7
Portugal	2.0	—	3.1	2.8
Total	4.5	3.4	4.1	3.4

Note: Index sums over ten distinct uses acknowledged in contact with other party. Data are weighted according to party composition of parliaments.

fruitful in twelve countries and less fruitful in Germany, Ireland, and Norway. The latter three cases were all examples of states where there were two blocs of parties competing and entering government or opposition together. Hungary, which is usually another case of long-lasting bloc politics, did not fall into this group at the time of the survey because the governing party was supported from outside by its former coalition ally, making the government–opposition divide more blurred. The pattern at the regional level is similar to the national level, but looking at specific countries there is almost no difference in contacts within and across the government divide.

7.5 MULTIVARIATE ANALYSES

An analysis of the reasons for variation in inter-party contacts between MPs from seventy-two different parliaments, fifteen countries at the national level and nine countries at the regional level has to take into account huge contextual variation and provides a considerable challenge. To address this we use multilevel regression modelling to take the clustered, multilevel nature of our data into account in testing our expectations of the influence of individual attributes, role perception, party characteristics, and institutional differences between countries (Steenbergen and Jones 2002).

In the models that we present we use covariates that measure attributes of individual MPs, of parties or party dyads and of political systems. A continuous individual attribute is seniority measured in years. Several others are binary variables. Three of them record specific parliamentary leadership roles of (deputy) Speaker of Parliament, parliamentary party leader, or committee chair. Another variable is gender (coded 1 for female MPs). We include MPs' role orientation as a binary variable measuring their role description as 'policy advocate'. It is coded 1 for those MPs who chose 'influencing government policy' as their most important task (with 'providing assistance to individual voters in their dealings with public authorities', 'looking after collective, social, and economic needs of the local area', and 'liaising and managing Parliament's business' as the alternatives).

Three variables measure party attributes: government party status, left–right extremism, and thematic nicheness. The first variable is binary, the other two continuous. The extremeness score comes from a survey question asking MPs to place their party and other parties on an eleven point left–right scale. We calculate a median party position for MPs belonging to a party and then its absolute distance from the midpoint of the scale. A party with a large score is positioned near one of the end points of the left–right dimension. In addition, we use a saliency-based 'nicheness' measure that shows how different a party's thematic profile is compared to all other parties in a party system (Meyer and Miller 2012). Party nicheness scores are based on saliency data from the expert survey of Benoit and Laver (2006). Only a few small or more recently founded parties are missing from the data.

In our final regression model we use inter-party contacts as reported by MPs as the unit of analysis. We include characteristics of the party dyads as covariates. They are based on the parties' status as a government or an opposition party and their respective locations on the left–right dimension. We distinguish contacts between two government parties, contacts from government party to opposition party, and vice versa in the form of dummy variables (see our discussion of the data above). The base category is contact between two opposition parties. For each pair of parties we employ inter-party distance as calculated from the parties' medians.

Our last group of covariates consists of political system attributes. We distinguish between new and established democracies, assuming Spain, Portugal, Hungary, and Poland to be the only states in the former category covered by the survey. We include electoral systems by distinguishing between majoritarian ones (France and the United Kingdom) and the rest. In addition to using gender as an individual characteristic we include the share of female MPs in parliament as a proxy variable for parliamentary culture. Recent patterns of government formation are covered by variables measuring the relative time a country has been ruled by coalition governments and minority governments in the last twenty years. We also include the mean number of parliamentary parties and government parties to define the opportunity structure of parties with which MPs can connect. The last four variables are based on the European Representative Democracy Dataset (Andersson, Bergman, and Errson 2012). We lack these data as well as nicheness scores for regional parliaments and therefore estimate separate models for the two levels. All variables are mean-standardized, and continuous variables are divided by two standard deviations to put them on a similar scale to the binary variables (Gelman 2008).

Our first regression model in Table 7.4 explores whether an MP reports good contact with other parties or not. We employ a two-level model specification with random intercepts at the country level. In a perfect world of balanced data with adequate sample sizes for all parliamentary parties we would report a three-level model specification with individual MPs as the unit of analysis, parties at the second, and parliament at the third level, and covariates at the party-level and political system-level to explain higher-level variation. However, such complex models did not work when applied to our data. Therefore we employ a much simpler random intercept model with covariates at the individual level on all MPs without missing data.

At the national level all Speakers of Parliament reported having good contacts with MPs from other parties. This leads to the statistical problem of perfect separation and produces exorbitantly large coefficients and standard errors (Zorn 2005). To circumvent the problem we simply take note of the strong association between that office and cross-party contacts and estimate a model without Speakers at the national level. In progressing the analysis further we note that the standard deviation of the country random intercepts drops from a reference value of 0.65 estimated for a multilevel null model with random intercepts to a value of 0.25 in the multivariate model. The difference tells us that we have made some steps forward in replacing country labels by substantive variables. Having said that,

TABLE 7.4 *Multilevel logit regression models of 'having good contacts' with other parties*

Covariates	National MPs	Regional MPs
Individual attributes		
Most important task: influence government policy	1.91 (0.46)***	1.14 (0.27)
Speaker	—	3.00 (3.11)
Parliamentary party group leader	0.53 (0.39)	1.92 (1.18)
Committee chair	1.36 (0.59)	1.16 (0.45)
Seniority	1.24 (0.30)	1.86 (0.52)**
Female	0.72 (0.19)	0.78 (0.18)
Party attributes		
Government party	1.50 (0.37)	0.82 (0.20)
Party left–right extremeness	0.55 (0.21)	0.82 (0.24)
Saliency nicheness	1.02 (0.29)	—
Political system attributes		
% female MPs in parliament	2.22 (0.64)***	1.09 (0.33)
% rule by coalition government in last 20 years	2.88 (1.48)**	—
% rule by minority government in last 20 years	0.91 (0.41)	—
Mean number of parliamentary parties in last 20 years	1.03 (0.59)	—
Mean number of government parties in last 20 years	0.47 (0.44)	—
Majoritarian electoral system	0.51 (0.29)	—
New democracies	1.61 (0.62)	0.67 (0.27)
Log likelihood	−262	−296
Standard dev. of country random intercepts	0.25	0.41
First level N (MPs)	728	1028
Second level N (countries)	15	9
Modal category	87%	91%
Percent correctly predicted	87%	91%
Proportional reduction in error	0%	0%

Results are based on Stata's xtmelogit procedure, using maximum likelihood estimation and unstructured
     variances and covariances.
Notes: Coefficients shown are odds ratios with standard errors given in parentheses. Asterisks indicate statis-
     tical significance at the 0.01***, 0.05**, or 0.10* level.

results remain unsatisfying as none of the odds ratios is particularly large
or small which means that the covariates do not discriminate strongly. The
largest odds ratios were estimated for two political system attributes: the
share of female MPs in parliament and the relative amount of time a country has been ruled by coalition governments in the last two decades. Given
the huge country differences reported in Table 7.1 it is not surprising that
system-level variables take precedence. Our strongest result is for the share
of female MPs in parliament, our proxy for parliamentary culture. Individual role orientation shows the third largest odds ratio: MPs who want
to influence government policy have a higher probability of reporting good
cross-party contacts.

For regional MPs we had to estimate a model with fewer political system variables. The positive relationship between seniority and having good

cross-party contacts is the only noticeable odds ratio of this model, which, again, is not too surprising as variation among regional MPs both across and within countries is much smaller than among national MPs. As 91 per cent of regional MPs and 87 per cent of national MPs reported having good contacts the hard part is identifying the minority of MPs without such contacts. Indicators of model fit are reported in the last three rows of Table 7.4. The covariates produce some spread of predicted probabilities, but overall the model provides no proportional reduction in error. The model as presented here either misses an important variable or having good contacts is simply an idiosyncratic feature.

The models shown in Table 7.5 attempt to predict the reasons for variation among MPs in the breadth of use of good cross-party contacts. They are based on the subsets of MPs at the national and regional level who have such

TABLE 7.5 *Multilevel linear regression models of overall 'breadth of use' of contacts*

Covariates	National MPs	Regional MPs
Individual attributes		
Most important task: influence government policy	0.32 (0.21)	0.04 (0.17)
Speaker of Parliament	0.92 (0.80)	–0.13 (0.48)
Parliamentary party group leader	0.45 (0.74)	1.21 (0.32) ***
Committee chair	0.24 (0.34)	0.40 (0.27)
Seniority	0.33 (0.20)	0.38 (0.17) **
Female	0.15 (0.21)	0.25 (0.18)
Party attributes		
Government party	–0.10 (0.22)	–0.35 (0.18) *
Party left–right extremeness	–0.33 (0.30)	–0.09 (0.21)
Party nicheness	0.28 (0.26)	—
Political system attributes		
% female MPs in parliament	1.37 (0.60) **	0.22 (0.25)
% rule by coalition government in last 20 years	0.89 (0.78)	—
% rule by minority government in last 20 years	–0.95 (0.80)	—
Mean number of parliamentary parties in last 20 years	0.70 (1.10)	—
Mean number of government parties in last 20 years	–2.57 (1.68)	—
Majoritarian electoral system	–2.33 (1.08)	—
New democracies	–0.98 (0.68)	–0.80 (0.68)
Constant	4.54 (0.29) ***	4.96 (0.40) ***
Restricted log likelihood	–1458	–2198
Standard deviation of country random intercepts	0.86	0.90
Standard deviation of individual residuals	2.35	2.50
First level N (MPs)	640	938
Second level N (countries)	15	9

Results are based on Stata's xtmixed procedure, using maximum restricted likelihood and unstructured variances and covariances.

Notes: Standard errors are given in parentheses. Asterisks indicate statistical significance at the 0.01***, 0.05**, or 0.10* level of confidence.

contacts. The dependent variable is continuous with a theoretical range of zero to twelve points. Overall, national MPs typically reported four different uses to which they put their cross-party contacts, regional MPs about five. In the model for national MPs the share of female MPs again has a moderately positive effect on the breadth of use of cross-party contacts. At the regional level parliamentary party group leaders stand out with on average one additional use of their cross-party contacts. Also seasoned MPs put their contacts to more different uses while membership of a government party has a slight depressing effect.

Although there are country differences in the breadth of the use of contacts (see Table 7.2 above), the individual patterns remain largely unaccounted for: reductions in likelihood values in the multivariate models are minor. The standard deviation of the country random intercepts drops from 1.11 to 0.86 in the multivariate model at the national level. At the regional level it is 0.90 for both the null model and the model with covariates.

The final model uses individual party dyads instead of MPs as units of analysis and introduces dyad attributes as new covariates (see Table 7.6). The number of cases increases considerably as individuals may be included several times in the dataset depending on the number of parties covered by their good contacts. We employ a three-level model to represent the nestedness of the data at the level of MPs and country. The dependent variable is the same as in the previous model, but disaggregated to the level of individual party contact dyads.

Looking at individual attributes as before we find first that parliamentary party group leaders tend to gain more instrumental value from their good cross-party contacts than other MPs. Party group leaders are wheelers and dealers in parliament which requires them to stay in contact with other PPGs and make maximum use of such ties. Speakers in parliaments have good contacts with other parties (see Table 7.4), but their usage of these contacts for political purposes is much narrower. Committee chairs are no different from ordinary MPs; nor do senior MPs and less experienced MPs differ a lot. We find a small significant effect for gender at the regional level, but its robustness under different specifications is doubtful. The small positive effect for the role orientation as policy advocate at the national level is a bit more robust.

The effects of the relational covariates are interesting. The usage of contacts among MPs from different government parties tends to be somewhat more varied than that of contacts connecting MPs from different opposition parties. At the same time, opposition MPs addressing government MPs report a wider range of use than government MPs addressing opposition MPs, especially in regional parliaments. Legislature-specific formats of party competition will obviously affect these numbers. Ideological divergence is inimical to broad usage. The further the left–right distance between two parties the less diverse is the use of contacts between them. Majoritarian

TABLE 7.6 *Multilevel regression models of contact 'breadth of use' for party dyads*

Covariates	National MPs	Regional MPs
Individual attributes		
Most important task: influence government policy	0.36 (0.16)**	0.21 (0.14)
Speaker of Parliament	0.09 (0.54)	0.10 (0.39)
Parliamentary party group leader	0.81 (0.52)	1.07 (0.27)***
Committee chair	0.12 (0.25)	0.14 (0.23)
Seniority	0.13 (0.15)	0.15 (0.15)
Female	0.15 (0.16)	0.25 (0.15)*
Party dyad attributes[1]		
Government party MP to government party	0.66 (0.18)***	0.23 (0.17)
Government party MP to opposition party	−0.20 (0.16)	−0.44 (0.17)***
Opposition party MP to government party	0.25 (0.11)**	0.25 (0.12)*
Left–right distance between parties	−0.36 (0.08)***	−0.71 (0.06)***
Political system attributes		
% female MPs in parliament	0.49 (0.41)	0.02 (0.21)
% rule by coalition government in last 20 years	0.85 (0.54)	—
% rule by minority government in last 20 years	−0.09 (0.56)	—
Mean number of parliamentary parties in last 20 years	−0.49 (0.78)	—
Mean number of government parties in last 20 years	−1.87 (1.19)	—
Majoritarian electoral system	−1.48 (0.79)**	—
New democracies	−0.87 (0.46)*	−0.53 (0.50)
Constant	4.10 (0.25)***	4.07 (0.30)***
Restricted log likelihood	−3798	−4843
Standard deviation of country random intercepts	0.58	0.65
Standard deviation of party random intercepts	1.64	1.87
Standard deviation of individual residuals	1.39	1.40
First level N (Party dyads)	1,868	2,336
Second level N (MPs)	688	924
Third level level N (Countries)	15	9

[1]Base category is a contact between MPs from two opposition parties.

Results are based on Stata's xtmixed procedure, using maximum restricted likelihood and unstructured variances and covariances.

Notes: Standard errors are given in parentheses. Asterisks indicate statistical significance at the 0.01***, 0.05**, or 0.10* level of confidence.

electoral systems show a large negative effect that translates into a narrower use of cross-party contacts by French and British MPs. The same applies to the four countries Spain, Portugal, Hungary, and Poland that make up the group of new democracies.

Finally we also tested the 'Strength of Committees' index developed by Martin and Depauw (2011), available for all national parliaments included here except Switzerland. It is excluded from the tables to maintain the maximum number of cases in the PARTIREP survey. Contrary to expectations there is no relationship between the strength of committees in national parliaments and the probability of cross-party contacts or the breadth of the use of these contacts. This could be due to the operationalization of committee strength as the committees' formal rights (Mattson and Strom 1995; Martin and Depauw 2011). An alternative approach would be to use behavioural indicators such as the number of committee sessions per year or the number of amendments to bills passed by committees. It would be premature to cast a verdict on this theoretically interesting variable, given that country experts have repeatedly stipulated a positive effect of committee work on parliamentarians' cross-party ties.

7.6 CONCLUSION

In this chapter we have worked from the realistic assumption that to a large extent political representation is dominated by the party democracy model and therefore we should consider inter-party relations as an issue of key importance to how it works. Yet, research has previously shed very little light on how MPs representing one political party interact with MPs from other parties. The results and analysis presented here reveals that such contacts between MPs are in fact very significant. Across fifteen national parliaments there was a mean average of 79 per cent of MPs who had good, politically helpful contacts with MPs from other parties; on average they had those good contacts with MPs from 2.4 parties, representing 31 per cent of the available parties; and on average these contacts covered 4.8 different types of use. The figures for regional MPs across nine states was virtually the same: 81 per cent of MPs having good contacts with MPs from on average 2.3 parties, representing 35 per cent of the available parties; with those contacts covering 4.9 different uses. Clearly, contacts between MPs at the individual level are a significant aspect of how parties collectively realize the soft information that is essential to processing the hard information on the internal rules, positions, interests, and behaviour of other parties. The very volume, network party penetration, and breadth of types of contacts are testament to their significance to MPs in how they negotiate political representation in both the cross-party and inter-party modes and sometimes in the non-party mode.

At the same time, the PARTIREP survey demonstrated considerable variation across states in all the indicators of MPs' inter-party contacts, though variation was greater at the national than at the regional level. On these bases we placed countries in a comparative index of contacts. In seeking to explain variation we investigated the importance of a wide range of system-, party-, and individual-level variables. This analysis provided some confirmation for a number of hypotheses to explain why MPs have more contacts with MPs from other parties. These are system-level institutional contexts which include the presence of PR, minority or coalition government, a higher share of female representatives (our proxy for a more consensual parliamentary culture) and non-political opportunities (in the single case of Norway); the party-level variable of a high number of parties; and the individual-level variables of parliamentary leadership and of a non-party-based orientation to policy advocacy.

There appeared to be no systematic relationship between the number of parties in a legislature and the number of parties that MPs had significant contacts with, though there was a correlation between the number of parties MPs had contacts with and the number of different purposes for which they had contacts. Here we found that MPs had a greater range of purposes for contacts under coalition and minority governments than in the case of majority governments; in old as opposed to new democracies; and with parties covering a lower ideological distance. The range of purposes for contacts was higher between MPs across government parties in a coalition and between MPs from opposition parties and those of government parties than might be seen of government-party MPs with those of opposition parties. The non-party-based orientation to policy advocacy and at the national level the share of female MPs as a proxy for parliamentary culture, were again important factors. These variables helped to explain variation both among all MPs and in comparing government and opposition party MPs. Nevertheless, these conclusions are tentative, and a number of variables that we expected to be significant appeared not to be. Notably, strength of parliamentary committees (as measured by their formal rights) appeared to have no relationship with the level or breadth of cross-party contacts. Equally, there appeared to be no distinctive regional dimension to inter-party contacts, and at the regional level the individual-level variable of seniority appeared to be the only important factor explaining variation.

It is unquestionable that a key feature of political representation in legislatures remains MPs' loyalty or compliance with their own party and this research shows how it is complemented by quite extensive MP contacts across parties, though this varies across countries and across the government–opposition party divide. We have made some headway in explaining why contacts are so significant and why they vary in ways that we might expect. But it is clear that this is an area of study that requires further research to specify and quantify contacts in the inter-party, cross-party, and non-party modes of MP contact and the parties with which contacts are developed. Equally, we need to better understand the operation of some variables through a combination of quantitative and qualitative research. Notably, these include the role of non-political opportunities for contact, picked out in some previous research; the role of parliamentary culture, which actually emerged as the most significant variable explaining volume of contact in this study; and the role of parliamentary committees, which should repay renewed attention in how to operationalize as a variable. On this basis we may be better able to specify the ways in which inter-party contacts provide evidence of the complexities of political representation per se, or alternatively whether they are symptomatic of party democracy being largely concerned with the more closed world of governing. As the ability of parties to represent people becomes more uncertain and blurred it remains open to question as to whether parties and their MPs seek new ways to represent the public, or whether good working relations between MPs and parties is just a means to maintain rather than dilute the grip of party government.

NOTE

1. We thank Silvia Erzeel for data on the share of female MPs in parliaments and Thomas N. Meyer for providing us with party nicheness scores. Martin Haselmayer und Paul Preuer were a tremendous support in data cleaning and recoding. Jonathan Bradbury acknowledges the Research Institute of Arts and Humanities, Swansea University. Nikolaus Eder, Marcelo Jenny, and Wolfgang C. Müller gratefully acknowledge funding by the Austrian National Bank (Jubiläumsfondsprojekt 13967) and the Austrian Research Fund (FWF) (S10903-G11).

REFERENCES

Andersson, S., T. Bergman, S., and Ersson (2012), The European Representative Democracy Data Project. Main sponsor: Riksbankens Jubileumsfond (In2007-0149:1-E), Principal investigator: Torbjörn Bergman, personal data archive <http://www.erdda.se> accessed 8 November 2013.

Andeweg, R. B. (1992), 'Executive–Legislative Relations in The Netherlands: Consecutive and Coexisting Patterns', *Legislative Studies Quarterly*, 17: 116–82.

—— (1997), 'Role Specialisation or Role Switching? Dutch MPs between Electorate and Executive', in W. C. Müller and T. Saalfeld (eds.), *Members of Parliament in Western Europe: Roles and Behaviour*. London: Frank Cass, 110–27.

—— and L. Nijzink (1995), 'Beyond the Two-Body Image: Relations Between Ministers and MPs', in H. Döring (ed.), *Parliaments and Majority Rule in Western Europe*. Frankfurt: Campus, 152–78.

Arnold, L. W., R. E. Deen, and S. C. Patterson (2000), 'Friendship and Votes: The Impact of Interpersonal Ties on Legislative Decision-making', *State & Local Government Review*, 32: 142–7.

Baker, R. K. (1980), *Friend and Foe in the US Senate*. New York: Free Press.

Benoit, K. and M. Laver (2006), *Party Policy in Modern Democracies*. London: Routledge.

Bielasiak, J. (1997), 'Substance and Process in the Development of Party Systems in East Central Europe', *Communist and Post-Communist Studies*, 30 (1): 23–44.

Bratton, K. A. (2005), 'Critical Mass Theory Revisited: The Behavior and Success of Token Women in State Legislatures', *Politics & Gender*, 1: 97–125.

Caldeira, G. A. and S. C. Patterson (1987), 'Political Friendship in the Legislature', *Journal of Politics*, 49: 953–75.

—— (1988), 'Contours of Friendship and Respect in the Legislature', *American Politics Quarterly*, 16: 466–85.

—— J. A. Clark, and S. C. Patterson (1993), 'Political Respect in the Legislature', *Legislative Studies Quarterly*, 18: 3–28.

Cho, W. T. and J. H. Fowler (2010), 'Legislative Success in a Small World: Social Network Analysis and the Dynamics of Congressional Legislation', *Journal of Politics*, 72: 124–35.

Dahlerup, D. (1988), 'From a Small to a Large Minority: Women in Scandinavian Politics', *Scandinavian Political Studies* 11: 275–98.

Dalton, R. J. and W. Jou (2010), 'Is there a Single German Party System?' *German Politics & Society*, 28: 34–52.

Enyedi, Z. and F. Casal-Bértoa (2011), 'Patterns of Party Competition 1990–2009', in P. Lewis and R. Markowski (eds.), *Europeanizing Party Politics? Comparative Perspectives in Central and Eastern Europe after Enlargement*. Manchester: Manchester University Press, 147–68.

Esaiason, P. and S. Holmberg (1996), *Representation from Above: Members of Parliament and Representative Democracy in Sweden*. Dartmouth: Aldershot.

Gelman, A. (2008), 'Scaling Regression Inputs by Dividing by Two Standard Deviations', *Statistics in Medicine* 27: 2865–73.

Heidar, K. (1997), 'Rules, Structures and Behaviour: Norwegian Parliamentarians in the Nineties', in W. C. Müller and T. Saalfeld (eds.), *Members of Parliament in Western Europe: Roles and Behaviour*. London: Frank Cass, 91–109.

Jenny, M. and W. C. Müller (1995), 'Presidents of Parliament: Neutral Chairmen or Assets of the Majority', in. H. Döring (ed.), *Parliaments and Majority Rule in Western Europe*. Frankfurt: Campus, 326–64.

Jensen, T. K. (2000), 'Party Cohesion', in P. Esaiasson and K. Heider (eds.), *Beyond Westminster and Congress: The Nordic Experience*. Columbus: Ohio State University Press, 210–36.

King, A. (1976), 'Modes of Executive-legislative Relations: Great Britain, France, and West Germany', *Legislative Studies Quarterly* 1: 11–36.

Kingdon, J. W. (1973), *Congressmen's Voting Decisions*. 3rd edn. New York: Harper and Row.

Kitschelt, H., Z. Mansfeldova, R. Markowski et al. (1999), *Post-Communist Party Systems: Competition, Representation, and Inter-party Cooperation*. Cambridge: Cambridge University Press.

Kostadinova, T. (2003), 'Voter Turnout Dynamics in Post-Communist Europe', *European Journal of Political Research*, 42 (6): 741–59.

Laver, M. and N. Schofield (1990), *Multiparty Government: The Politics of Coalition in Europe*. Oxford: Oxford University Press.

Mair, P. (1997), *Party System Change: Approaches and Interpretations*. Oxford: Oxford University Press.

Martin, S. and S. Depauw (2011), 'The Impact of Multiparty Government on the Internal Organization of Legislatures', paper prepared for presentation at the 69th Annual National Conference of the Midwest Political Science Association, Chicago, 31 March–3 April 2011.

Matthews, D. R. and H. Valen (1999), *Parliamentary Representation: The Case of the Norwegian Storting*. Columbus: Ohio State University Press.

Mattson, I. and K. Strøm (1995), 'Parliamentary Committees', in H. Döring (ed.), *Parliaments and Majority Rule in Western Europe*. Frankfurt: Campus, 249–325.

Meguid, B. M. (2008), *Party Competition Between Unequals: Strategies and Electoral Fortunes in Western Europe*. Cambridge: Cambridge University Press.

Meyer, T. and M. Miller (forthcoming), 'The Niche Party Concept and its Measurement', *Party Politics*.

Müller, W. C. (1993), 'Executive–Legislative Relations in Austria: 1945–1992', *Legislative Studies Quarterly*, 18: 467–94.

Patterson, S. C. (1959), 'Patterns of Interpersonal Relations in a State Legislative Group: The Wisconsin Assembly', *Public Opinion Quarterly*, 23: 101–9.

—— (1972), 'Party Opposition in the Legislature: The Ecology of Legislative Institutionalization', *Polity*, 4: 344–66.

Rommetvedt, H. (1992), 'The Norwegian Storting: The Central Assembly of the Periphery', *Scandinavian Political Studies*, 15: 79–97.

Routt, G. C. (1938), 'Interpersonal Relationships and the Legislative Process', *Annals of the American Academy of Political and Social Science*, 195: 129–36.

Sartori, G. (1976), *Parties and Party Systems: A Framework for Analysis*. Cambridge: Cambridge University Press.

Sawer, M., M. Tremblay, and L. Trimble (eds.) (2006), *Representing Women in Parliament: A Comparative Study*. London: Routledge.

Searing, D. S. (1994), *Westminster's World: Understanding Political Roles*. Cambridge, MA: Harvard University Press.

Shaw, M. (1979), 'Conclusion', in J. D. Lees and M. Shaw (eds.), *Committees in Legislatures*. Oxford: Martin Robertson, 361–434.

—— (1998), 'Parliamentary Committees: A Global Perspective', *Journal of Legislative Studies*, 4: 225–51.

Sikk, A. (2005), 'How Unstable: Volatility and the Genuinely New Parties in Eastern Europe', *European Journal of Political Research*, 44 (3): 391–412.

Steenbergen, M. R. and B. S. Jones (2002), 'Modeling Multilevel Data Structures', *American Journal of Political Science*, 46: 218–37.

Strøm, K. (1990), *Minority Government and Majority Rule*. Cambridge: Cambridge University Press.

—— (2012), 'Roles as Strategies: Towards a Logic of Legislative Behavior', in M. Blomgren and O. Rozenberg (eds.), *Parliamentary Roles in Modern Legislatures*. London: Frank Cass, 85–100.

—— W. C. Müller, and T. Bergman (eds.) (2008), *Cabinets and Coalition Bargaining*. Oxford: Oxford University Press.

Studlar, D. and I. McAllister (2002), 'Does a Critical Mass Exist? A Comparative Analysis of Women's Legislative Representation since 1950', *European Journal of Political Research*, 41: 233–53.

Tavits, M. (2005), 'The Development of Stable Party Support: Electoral Dynamics in Post-communist Europe', *American Journal of Political Science*, 49 (2): 283–98.

Thomassen, J. and R. Andeweg (2004), 'Beyond Collective Representation: Individual Members of Parliament and Interest Representation in the Netherlands', *Journal of Legislative Studies*, 10: 47–69.

Tóka, G. (1998), 'Party Appeals and Voter Loyalty in New Democracies', *Political Studies*, 46 (3): 589–610.

Wängnerud, L. (2009), 'Women in Parliaments: Descriptive and Substantive Representation', *Annual Review of Political Science*, 12: 51–69.

Wahlke, J. C., H. Eulau, W. Buchanan et al. (1962), *The Legislative System: Explorations in Legislative Behavior*. New York: John Wiley.

Zorn, C. (2005), 'A Solution to Separation in Binary Response Models', *Political Analysis*, 13: 157–70.

8

Legislators' Constituency Orientation

Audrey André, Michael Gallagher, and Giulia Sandri

8.1 INTRODUCTION

Much of the research on the degree of representation provided by MPs, parties, and parliaments focuses on policy congruence, socio-demographic representation or interest representation. But whether an ordinary European feels 'represented' by his or her MP may depend less on the views that the MP expresses on the floor of parliament or in a committee than on what the MP does at a more local level: whether the MP seems to be active and successful at securing the spending of public money in the constituency; at 'selling' the constituency to companies looking for a location to establish a factory or a corporate headquarters; at fighting to prevent a workplace closing as a company ceases business or plans to relocate; or at a more individual level whether he or she will take up a matter of personal concern, or will help secure some redress of a grievance. There is a widespread awareness that the strength of MPs' constituency orientation differs across countries, yet the phenomenon is somewhat under-researched comparatively (Mezey 2008 provides a useful overview).

This chapter will therefore examine MPs' constituency representation— that is, their commitment to promoting and defending the interests of their geographical constituency or of individual constituents. The argument will proceed in four steps. The first section discusses the theoretical background from which we derive a set of testable hypotheses. In the second section, we operationalize the dependent variable and map differences in the constituency orientation of elected representatives in the fifteen countries included in the PARTIREP cross-national survey. We furthermore demonstrate that cultural repertoires of constituency-oriented actions exist that legislators can successfully pursue in these countries. We then present the results of the analysis in the third section. Multilevel logit models demonstrate that legislators' commitment to constituency representation is to an important extent shaped by contextual, party-level, and individual-level factors. The findings, finally, will be summarized and discussed in the conclusion of this chapter. They will enable us to assess whether citizens are better represented in this sense under certain institutional arrangements than others—or, to put it another way, what kind of institutional architecture is most likely to promote this kind of representation.

8.2 THEORETICAL FRAMEWORK

Rather than seeing constituency work as an undifferentiated set of activities, we can usefully disaggregate it into what are sometimes termed the local promoter role (in US terms, obtaining 'pork' for the constituency) and the welfare officer role (dealing with grievances or requests from individuals or local groups). As defined by Donald Searing (1994: 124):

> Welfare Officers are those whose primary focus falls on individual constituents and their difficulties with housing, pensions, or whatever problems they may bring to the surgery. By contrast, Local Promoters concentrate primarily on collective concerns of the constituency as a whole, or of sectors within it, on matters such as industrial development, unemployment, or securing a road bypass.

In Searing's study of Westminster MPs (published in the mid 1990s but based on in-depth interviews conducted in the 1970s), the constituency role was regarded as a preference role: one that MPs typically chose to fill or not to fill. Given the years that have passed since this research, things might have changed—it could be that, concomitant with the professionalization of parliaments and the increased career-orientation of parliamentarians, MPs nearly everywhere regard constituency representation as an unavoidable aspect of their work (King 1981; Norton and Wood 1993). In this chapter, we will show that in fact there is considerable variation in the attitudes of MPs towards constituency representation, and we will then explore the causes of this variation. Based on an extensive review of the existing literature on constituency representation, three categories of explanatory variables could be identified: factors relating to the political system (contextual variation), factors relating to a legislator's party (party-level variation), and factors relating to a legislator's individual characteristics (individual-level variation). We will deal with these in sequence.

8.2.1 Contextual Variation

Previous studies have underlined the importance of institutional and social context variables in shaping legislators' role perception.

First, when the electoral system encourages candidates to seek personal support over and above, or within, the support for their party, candidates and incumbent MPs have to build a personal reputation. Constituency work is one way of achieving this, and, unlike the adoption of a distinctive policy stance, it has the advantage that it is unlikely to alienate any voters—it has 'the virtue of making friends without simultaneously making enemies' (Lee 2005: 284; see Kam 2009 for a similar argument). Thus we would expect to find that, other things being equal, in countries that employ open-list PR systems or PR-STV, that is, electoral systems that provide voters with the opportunity to express intra-party preferences, members will be more constituency-oriented than in those countries that employ closed-list systems, under which voters have no power to determine which individual candidates win seats. Nurturing the constituency is electorally more valuable to legislators when voters can make a choice among candidates of their favoured party instead of simply endorsing the list as a whole. We already know that under open-list PR and PR-STV systems, MPs are more likely than elsewhere to have local roots (Shugart, Valdini, and Suominen 2005), so they may be more locally oriented generally. This tendency is likely to be heightened in parliamentary systems where MPs cannot make a name for themselves by promoting bills and piloting them through the legislature in the manner of members of the US Congress (see e.g. Mayhew 1974). It has been hypothesized (Carey and Shugart 1995: 430–2), however, the ballot structure affects the relationship between district magnitude and constituency orientation. Specifically, when the electoral system allows voters to exercise meaningful intra-party choice, then candidates have a greater incentive to distinguish themselves from their co-partisans as district magnitude increases, because the number of co-partisans is likely to increase concomitantly and each has more intra-party rivals. When there is no opportunity for voters to exercise meaningful intra-party choice, however, an increase in district magnitude is likely to be associated with less effort by candidates (and MPs) to cultivate a personal reputation among the voters, because all that matters is their reputation among the candidate selectors.

> Hypothesis 1a: Legislators' constituency orientation will be stronger under conditions of intra-party electoral competition than in the absence of such competition;

> Hypothesis 1b: Legislators' constituency orientation will strengthen with district magnitude when voters have the power to exercise meaningful intra-party choice and decrease with magnitude when voters do not have this power.

Second, the extent to which the decision-making process is decentralized can be expected to affect the strength of legislators' commitment to constituency representation. Where there is a regional level of government, the number of contact points voters can turn to in order to talk about their personal grievances multiplies, thereby relieving national legislators of part of their caseload. Where there is no significant tier of government below the national level, members of the national parliament will inevitably be the recipients of the overwhelming majority of requests for assistance. In Belgium, for example, the volume of national MPs' constituency work declined greatly in the 1990s because the introduction of significant regional parliaments meant that voters now had other representatives to take their requests and problems to (De Winter 2002: 100). In a similar vein, Patzelt (2007) observed that members of the German *Bundestag* are less attentive to their constituency than *Landtag* members. He puts forward two mechanisms underlying this finding. Regional legislators are elected in districts with smaller constituent–representative ratios, on the one hand. The jurisdictions of regional parliaments, on the other hand, are by definition mainly restricted to issues of regional and local interest. The strength of regional legislators' constituency focus, it be added however, will depend on the powers of the legislature. We would expect that the less power a regional parliament has, the less input its members have into major decisions, and the more emotionally gratifying the constituency role becomes.

> Hypothesis 2a: The more decentralized the country, the weaker national legislators' constituency orientation;

> Hypothesis 2b: The higher a state's regional authority, the weaker regional legislators' constituency orientation.

8.2.2 Party-level Variation

If the role of constituency member is by and large a preference role, we would not expect party to be a strong predictor of legislators' constituency orientation. Yet, there are two ways in which we might find variation within parliaments that is related to the party affiliation of legislators, in particular the party's seat share and ideology.

First, legislators' probability of adopting a constituency focus might be affected by the size of the parliamentary party they are in. Constituency members are expected to be more common in large parties than in small ones (Patzelt 2007). Where performance of parliamentary duties is seen as being of prime importance, the representatives of a small party may have to concentrate on their parliamentary role. Only in large parties is a division of labour possible: some legislators can afford to pay little attention to parliamentary responsibilities and concentrate on their constituency instead.

> Hypothesis 3: The higher a party's share of seats in parliament, the stronger legislators' constituency orientation will be.

Second, a legislator's role orientation might be influenced by the party's ideological position on the left–right dimension. Democratic Congressmen and Labour MPs, Cain et al. (1987) found, put significantly more effort into constituency service than representatives from right-wing parties. They traced the effect back to theories of class voting arguing that the 'natural constituencies of the left' are more likely to feel the need to call upon a politician for help in dealing with public authorities to obtain social housing or other social security benefits. As proponents of the welfare state, leftist legislators should be more inclined to regard the redress of constituents' grievances as an important part of their task as elected representatives.

> Hypothesis 4: Legislators of left-wing parties are more constituency-oriented than those of right-wing parties.

8.2.3 Individual-level Variation

Although there are reasons for expecting systematic system- and party-level differences, it may be that a certain amount of variation results from characteristics of individual legislators. These characteristics might relate to their perceptions of the representative process and their seniority in parliament.

First, legislators' constituency orientation might be related to their conception of the process of political representation. Following Wahlke et al.'s (1962) study of US state legislators, previous research has focused strongly on the distinction between trustees and delegates. But efforts to link the preferences of trustees and delegates to the conditions they compete under for re-election or their behaviour have been largely unsuccessful (Jewell 1970; Friesema and Hedlund 1974; Thomassen 1994). Legislators, Andeweg and Thomassen (2005) argued, think about the representative process as a top-down or a bottom-up process (see also Esaiasson and Holmberg 1996). Legislators holding a representation-from-above view feel that it is their responsibility to lead and try to persuade citizens to follow them. Those who consider it their task to translate the political views of citizens as accurately as possible into policy, by contrast, look at representation as a process initialized by the represented rather than by the representative. *Ceteris paribus*, we might expect those holding the latter view to be predisposed to be closer to citizens and, hence, to put greater emphasis on nurturing the constituency. Legislators holding a top-down conception of representation, on the other hand, are less directly concerned with the views and wishes of individual constituents.

> Hypothesis 5: Legislators who conceive of representation as a bottom-up process will be more constituency-oriented than those who conceive of it in top-down terms.

Second, the tendency to concentrate on constituency work may be related to a legislator's career stage. Junior MPs can be expected to undertake the most constituency work, not simply out of youthful enthusiasm but also because they have no other method of establishing a personal reputation and measure of electoral support. As legislators establish seniority in the legislature, they typically rise up the political greasy pole. Veteran legislators move into government, party, or parliamentary positions that provide them with a profile and perhaps some opportunity to claim credit for some impact on policy or legislation, so the need to maintain a high level of constituency work, as well as the energy to sustain this when faced with many other demands on their time, may diminish. Moreover, constituency work may bring a sense of gratification, a feeling that one has actually achieved something for someone (Norris and Lovenduski 1995; Norris 1997), in contrast to the futility of work as a junior parliamentarian, given that all legislators are aware that an individual legislator's chances of amending a piece of legislation are low. Previous work comparing legislators in a number of Westminster systems found that length of time served in parliament was strongly and negatively related to the level of constituency focus of MPs (Heitshusen, Young, and Wood 2005: 41).

> Hypothesis 6: First-term legislators are more constituency-oriented compared to more senior legislators.

8.3 LEGISLATORS' CONSTITUENCY ORIENTATION IN FIFTEEN EUROPEAN COUNTRIES

The cross-national PARTIREP survey captures MPs general orientation toward the constituency as well as the particular ways in which they seek to connect to constituents. Inspired by Searing's (1994) seminal work, a task prioritization question is used to gauge legislators' constituency orientation—separating 'Constituency Members' from 'Policy Advocates' and 'Parliament Men'.[1] As indicated above, two types of constituency members are further distinguished: 'Welfare Officers' act on behalf of *individual* constituents, whereas 'Local Promoters' advocate the constituency's *collective* interests. That is, legislators were asked to weigh up the importance of 'providing assistance to individual voters in their dealings with public authorities', 'looking after the collective social and economic needs of the local area', 'influencing government policy', and 'liaising between members of the parliamentary party and the party leadership and managing Parliament's business'.

Representing the People

TABLE 8.1 *Legislators' constituency orientation in fifteen countries*

	Constituency members (%)		
	Welfare officers	Local promoters	Total
Austria	9.3	33.2	42.5
Belgium	4.2	13.1	17.3
France	12.3	19.5	31.8
Germany	4.4	35.7	40.1
Hungary	12.2	25.2	37.3
Ireland	13.0	20.2	33.2
Israel	22.3	5.1	27.4
Italy	16.8	45.7	62.5
Netherlands	0.0	2.5	2.5
Norway	12.1	0.0	12.1
Poland	5.3	11.0	16.3
Portugal	1.4	24.8	26.2
Spain	7.7	46.6	54.3
Switzerland	4.3	20.1	24.4
United Kingdom	30.7	33.8	64.5
All	9.0	28.9	37.9

Policy advocates by far outnumber the parliament men: only a very small minority of legislators in the selection report that they focus first and foremost on parliament as an institution. Yet, two in five legislators on average consider constituency representation the single most important task they fulfil as elected representatives.[2] As indicated in Table 8.1, more constituency members prioritize the promotion of collective interests (29 per cent) over the address of individual grievances (9 per cent). This finding contrasts with Searing's (1994) earlier observations in the UK House of Commons: 75 per cent of the constituency members he interviewed strongly favoured the welfare officer role, whereas only 15 per cent clearly preferred the role of local promoter. It further takes the edge off the claim that legislators in parliamentary systems are more likely to focus on casework than on local promoter activities, simply because the ordinary MP is unable to determine the allocation of public funds in the way that US representatives can (Mezey 2008: 110). Bills in parliamentary systems do not usually emerge from the legislative process adorned with the 'earmarks' that characterize US legislation, specifying expenditure on specific projects, because government in European parliamentary systems is fundamentally party government in a way that government in the US is not. As Cox (1987: 133–4) puts it in the context of the British House of Commons, 'the mainstays of the US Congressman's particularistic usefulness to his constituents'—primarily civil service patronage and 'local improvement' bills securing public expenditure on rivers and harbours, railways, roads, dams, canals, and so on—were all largely removed from the influence of the backbench MP from the middle of the nineteenth century onwards. More importantly, however, we find considerable cross-national differences in legislators' commitment to constituency representation. Constituency members are all but absent in the Netherlands and Norway, while their number exceeds 60 per cent in Italy and the UK. Because local promoters far outnumber welfare officers in almost every country, no distinction between these subtypes can be made in the subsequent multivariate analysis.

But does a legislator's stated focus on the constituency translate into actual behaviour? The PARTIREP data reveals that legislators prioritizing constituency representation are indeed more active on behalf of their constituents than those favouring other role orientations. Constituency representation has two components: legislators may act on behalf of their constituents (1) in the parliamentary arena and (2) in the constituency (e.g. Norton and Wood 1993; Searing 1994). Constituency members, on the one hand, are significantly more likely to take up constituents' concerns in their parliamentary work ($\eta = 0.088$; $p \leq 0.001$). With 23 per cent, the proportion of legislative initiatives (bills, written and oral questions, etc.) raised in parliament that derive from meeting with individual citizens is higher among constituency members than among policy advocates and parliament men (average of 20 per cent). Constituency members also spend significantly more time among constituents than those prioritizing parliamentary duties. Whereas the average constituency member is approximately 115 hours per month physically present in the constituency, the average policy advocate devotes only up to 87 hours per month among constituents ($\eta = 0.172$; $p \leq 0.001$). But elected representatives differ greatly in the manner in which they interact with constituents between elections.

In seeking to connect to and communicate with constituents, legislators can choose from a myriad of constituency-oriented actions (see Cain, Ferejohn, and Fiorina 1987; Studlar and McAllister 1996). They will trade off the different options and engage in those patterns of behaviour that they believe to be most effective in their given re-election environment and cultural context (Saward 2010). Legislators need to take into account the cultural repertoires of behaviours to which constituents pay heed. In some countries, voters expect constituency-related activity of their legislators; in others, they do not. Culture has, for instance, been identified as a significant factor in the United Kingdom. A survey of Members of the European Parliament found that British MEPs, elected under a closed-list system, did more constituency work than many MEPs from other countries elected under open-list PR (Scully and Farrell 2003). British MPs have been reported as sharing 'a general sense that casework is an important public duty of representatives' (Norris 1997: 47). Even without an electoral incentive to build a personal reputation, such MPs would not necessarily shirk doing constituency work. We have further explored cross-national patterns in legislators' action-repertoires.

TABLE 8.2 *Constituency activities in fifteen countries*

	Wedding	Coffee	Surgery	Pork	Any of these
Austria	25.2	12.6	43.6	7.2	53.6
Belgium	31.2	12.8	49.5	8.4	62.6
France	18.0	10.1	60.8	19.5	73.7
Germany	29.0	9.3	33.9	12.9	56.2
Hungary	3.2	24.7	28.0	13.1	50.2
Ireland	72.5	24.9	83.1	21.5	93.7
Israel	43.9	29.0	42.6	7.8	80.0
Italy	18.5	18.4	72.2	10.6	73.2
Netherlands	3.4	15.6	3.2	8.6	23.2
Norway	0.0	18.4	0.0	13.5	25.1
Poland	0.4	8.0	89.8	8.4	88.8
Portugal	5.6	10.5	47.2	7.3	54.6
Spain	11.1	10.3	42.2	14.0	50.9
Switzerland	5.2	3.7	3.4	0.8	9.8
United Kingdom	6.7	12.6	74.0	21.8	80.7
Total	17.9	12.8	42.7	11.3	55.5

Note: Entries display the percentage of legislators engaging at least once a fortnight in a particular constituency-oriented action outside election campaign periods. The actions include attending (or sending out letters on the occasion of weddings), wedding anniversaries, and funerals in your local area (WEDDING); meeting with (small parties of) constituents in their private home to talk about their wants and needs (COFFEE); holding surgeries (SURGERY); publicizing your successes in attracting business and obtaining government grants for the local area (PORK). The last column indicates the percentage of legislators engaging in any of these four activities at least once a fortnight.

Table 8.2 demonstrates that there exists considerable cross-country variation in the extent of constituency work. More than nine in ten Irish TDs engage in at least one constituency-oriented action every fortnight. Swiss part-time legislators (10 per cent), Dutch members of the Second Chamber (23 per cent) and Norwegian members of the Storting (25 per cent), by contrast, are far less active in their district. Unlike in the US, organizing coffee mornings in constituents' private homes is quite uncommon in Europe (Fenno 1978): discussing issues with small groups of constituents is almost absent among French and Swiss elected representatives, while it is a bit more frequent among Irish TDs and Hungarian and Israeli legislators. In Israel and Ireland, it is common for elected representatives to interact with constituents, for example by frequently attending weddings, wedding anniversaries, and funerals. Similar assertions have been made by previous studies: UK MPs and Irish TDs are known to be more likely to engage in casework and especially in surgeries (Cain, Ferejohn, and Fiorina 1987; Searing 1994; Gallagher and Komito 2010), whereas constituents' concerns do not loom large in the minds of Dutch MPs.

The number of legislators regularly holding surgeries (known in Ireland as 'clinics') in their constituency exceeds 60 per cent in Italy, Ireland, Poland,

and the United Kingdom, while this activity is less frequent but overall quite common among Belgian, French, Israeli, and Portuguese MPs. In contrast, in the Netherlands, Norway, and Switzerland elected representative never hold surgeries. Casework activities such as holding surgeries or dealing with individual constituents' inquiries are way more common in countries that are either culturally characterized by strong localism, such as Ireland or Italy, or where candidates are usually selected locally, such as the UK, as could be expected on the basis of the literature (Norris 1997). A favourable attitude towards pork barrelling, and thus to those home-style activities which concern the distribution of public works projects is most common in France, Germany, and the UK. All three countries employ single-member district systems, which facilitate uncontested credit-claiming by MPs as each can claim full responsibility for benefits received by their own constituency.

Because one particular action may be offset by another, the explanatory part of this chapter will concentrate on legislators' self-reported role orientation. Our data indicate that there are significant cultural differences in the specific actions legislators choose to engage in to connect and interact with their constituents. For instance, French and Italian legislators rarely attend weddings or funerals in their constituency and rarely meet with constituents in their private home, but they appear to be overall quite locally oriented in their behaviour given the high number of them regularly holding surgeries. Cultural differences in legislators' action repertoires hinder cross-national comparability and as a result no strong effects can be expected when looking at any single behaviour. Therefore, MPs' self-reported role orientation, we argue, may represent the most reliable indicator of constituency representation.

8.4 EXPLAINING LEGISLATORS' CONSTITUENCY ORIENTATION

To fully explore the main and combined effects of the above-mentioned explanatory variables we need to take into account the binary nature of the dependent variable. As a result the analysis relies on logit regression models. Recall that constituency members are those legislators who believe casework or project work to be the single most important task they perform as elected representatives. Those prioritizing other aspects of the job make up the reference category. The analysis further acknowledges the hierarchical structure of the data. The assumption that observations are independent of one another cannot be maintained and, when disregarded, we risk overestimating the standard errors (Steenbergen and Jones 2002). Legislators are grouped in political parties. Each parliament is composed of several party groups. And parliaments are nested within countries. In unitary political systems, however, the levels of the parliament and the country coincide. To address this asymmetry in the selection and control for alternative country-specific— possibly cultural—effects, the parliament-level is not retained in the model specification. Three-level random intercept logit models are fitted to the data and penalized quasi-likelihood (PQL) iterative estimation techniques with a second-order linearization are used to improve the parameter estimates.[3] Likelihood ratio tests comparing multilevel models to a non-hierarchical model confirm that the variance at both the party-level and the country-level differs from zero at the 1 per cent level of statistical significance. The null model further reveals that 6 per cent of the variance in legislators' constituency orientation is due to differences between parties and 18 per cent due to differences between countries.

Electoral incentives are commonly considered to be a key factor in explaining legislators' constituency orientation and efforts. The assumption that intra-party competition increases constituency attentiveness (hypothesis 1a) is tested in the first model. Variation in ballot structure is reduced to a dichotomous indicator coded '1' for open-list systems in which preference votes effectively determine which individual candidates are elected (Belgium, Ireland, Poland, and Switzerland) and '0' for closed-list systems in which preference votes do not (Israel, the Netherlands, Norway, Portugal, and Spain). In all other countries, the coding of ballot structure varies across parliaments or across tiers within parliaments. Within Italy's boundaries, for instance, some parliaments use fixed party lists (*Camera dei Deputati* and Tuscany), others let voters determine the order in which candidates are elected (Campania and Aosta Valley), and still others combine both ballot types in a two-tiered PR system (Calabria, Lazio, and Lombardy). In Austria too parliaments adopted multi-tiered PR systems in which voters can affect the allocation of seats to candidates in the lowest tier but this is not the case in the higher tiers (or only under very exceptional conditions). The electoral institutions used in France and the UK vary across levels of government. The members of the French National Assembly and the UK House of Commons are elected in single-seat districts with a two-round majority or plurality of the vote respectively. By contrast, a closed-list system with a majority bonus governs elections to the regional councils in France, whereas mixed-member proportional systems are the rule in Wales and Scotland. Germany and Hungary use mixed systems that combine a nominal and proportional tier of seat allocation as well. In these cases, ballot structure is invariably coded '0'. Table 8.3 summarizes the coding decisions.

The ballot structure is moreover expected to condition the effect of district magnitude (hypothesis 1b) and therefore both components of electoral system design enter the equation in a multiplicative interaction in model 2. The

TABLE 8.3 *Summary statistics of the main independent variables*

	Ballot structure		District magnitude		Top-down conceptions of representation		Regional Authority Index score	
	Open-list		Range		Mean	S.D.	National	Regional
Austria	0 —	1	1 —	36	3.05	1.26	18	18
Belgium	1		2 —	72	3.16	1.04	29	16–20
France	0		1 —	25	3.40	0.98	16	8
Germany	0		1 —	65	3.49	0.95	29.3	21
Hungary	0		1 —	64	2.65	1.15	10	
Ireland	1		3 —	5	3.10	1.40	6	
Israel	0		120		3.51	1.19	0	
Italy	0 —	1	1 —	44	2.41	1.04	22.7	14–18
Netherlands	0		150		3.70	0.91	14.5	
Norway	0		4 —	17	3.53	0.95	10	
Poland	1		7 —	19	3.31	1.21	10	
Portugal	0		2 —	47	2.64	1.15	3.7	15.5
Spain	0		1 —	85	2.51	1.11	22.1	14.5–15.5
Switzerland	1		1 —	34	3.03	1.23	19.5	19.5
United Kingdom	0		1 —	7	3.64	0.82	9.6	11.5–16.5

selection displays wide within- and cross-country variation in district magnitude ranging from single-seat districts to nationwide or region-wide districts (see Table 8.2). The strength of the electoral incentive, however, is not expected to increase or decrease in a linear fashion with the number of seats to be allocated in the district. To account for the idea that an increase in magnitude from two to three seats will be more influential than an increase from forty-two to forty-three seats, we take the decimal logarithm of district magnitude.

Table 8.4 reports the estimated logit coefficients and robust standard errors. The first and second models demonstrate that electoral considerations are what motivate constituency members. They provide strong evidence for the assumption that the formal properties of electoral institutions shape a legislator's strategic choice as to whether to prioritize his work in parliament or his work in the constituency. The first model corroborates hypothesis 1a: legislators competing for re-election in systems that allow voters to determine which individual candidates of a party are elected are more likely to adopt the role of constituency member compared to those competing in closed-list systems. More specifically, in line with hypothesis 1b, it is the interplay between the ballot structure and the district's magnitude that determines his likelihood of favouring the constituency component. We find district magnitude to have a clear differential effect in open-list and closed-list systems. Where candidates are elected in the order of the list as predetermined by the

TABLE 8.4 *Explaining legislators' constituency orientation in fifteen European countries*

	Model 0 b	Model 0 s.e.	Model 1 b	Model 1 s.e.	Model 2 b	Model 2 s.e.	Model 3 b	Model 3 s.e.	Model 4 b	Model 4 s.e.	Model 5 b	Model 5 s.e.
Open-list			0.653	(0.270)**	-0.531	(0.293)*	-0.795	(0.273)***	-0.194	(0.745)	-0.836	(0.253)***
District magnitude (log)			-0.411	(0.129)***	-0.563	(0.137)***	-0.612	(0.147)***	-1.066	(0.310)***	-0.626	(0.148)***
— * open-list					1.179	(0.360)***	1.026	(0.351)***	0.752	(0.875)	1.055	(0.344)***
Top-down conception of representation							-0.268	(0.052)***	-0.370	(0.123)***	-0.269	(0.054)***
— * district magnitude									0.142	(0.106)		
— * open-list									-0.250	(0.253)		
— * district magnitude * open-list									0.140	(0.242)		
Regional parliament							0.712	(0.196)***	0.698	(0.191)***	2.115	(0.378)***
Regional Authority Index (RAI)											0.013	(0.015)
— * regional parliament											-0.083	(0.024)***
Country's unemployment rate			0.138	(0.036)***	0.149	(0.029)***	0.111	(0.028)**	0.117	(0.030)***	0.097	(0.030)**
Party's left–right position			0.059	(0.041)	0.057	(0.042)	0.073	(0.047)	0.071	(0.049)	0.079	(0.048)
Party's seat share			1.149	(0.356)***	1.092	(0.374)***	0.798	(0.348)**	0.821	(0.357)**	0.923	(0.397)**
Rookie			0.494	(0.117)***	0.512	(0.118)***	0.465	(0.121)***	0.468	(0.118)***	0.458	(0.118)***
Constant	-0.860	(0.255)***	-2.652	(0.551)***	-2.572	(0.615)***	-1.477	(0.545)***	-1.186	(0.541)***	-1.594	(0.556)***
σ^2(country)	0.805	(0.348)	0.622	(0.228)	0.612	(0.217)	0.426	(0.166)	0.436	(0.171)	0.427	(0.155)
σ^2(party)	0.278	(0.089)	0.167	(0.057)	0.156	(0.066)	0.097	(0.096)	0.091	(0.095)	0.085	(0.080)
Pseudo log-likelihood	-1420.76		-1376.71		-1371.91		-1344.14		-1337.47		-1340.26	
LR(df)			88.10	(6)***	97.7	(7)***	153.24	(9)***	166.57	(12)***	160.99	(11)***
Nagelkerke r²			0.07		0.08		0.13		0.14		0.13	

Note: The table displays the parameter estimates and robust standard errors (in parentheses) of three-level random–intercept probit regression models. The dependent variable is whether or not a legislator reports prioritizing the role of constituency member. The number of observations equals 1,942 at the individual level, 289 at the party level, and 15 at the country level. * p ≤ 0.10; ** p ≤ 0.05; *** p ≤ 0.01, using two-tailed t-values.

party candidate selectors, district magnitude has a negative effect. The role of constituency member tends to lose attractiveness as the number of seats to be allocated in the district increases and the extra votes a legislator can bring to the party become negligible compared to the party result. Disseminating one's name among constituents then no longer pays off in terms of improved re-election prospects. Where voters' candidate preferences can alter the order of intra-party seat allocation, by contrast, more legislators tend to focus on defending constituents' individual needs and collective interests as districts grow in magnitude. That is, the constituency will loom larger in the minds of legislators as more co-partisan competitors court constituents' preference votes.

Interaction terms in non-linear models however lack a straightforward understanding—not least because the magnitude of an effect depends on the values of the other explanatory variables included in the equation. Only by simulating the model can we enhance the interpretation of the results. Legislators' predicted probability of adopting the role of constituency member in closed-list and open-list systems was computed across a range of values of district magnitude while keeping all other variables constant.[4] A first difference test between the minimum and maximum observed value of district magnitude is used to ascertain that the slopes of the effect obtain statistical significance under both ballot types. Figure 8.1 plots the simulated predicted values and bold lines indicate that the null hypothesis that district magnitude has no effect can be rejected at the 5 per cent level. The figure clearly demonstrates that we cannot tell apart both list-types in the smallest districts: both lines intersect at a district magnitude of about 3. Only when the number of seats to be allocated in a district exceeds that threshold are legislators in open-list systems systematically more constituency-oriented than legislators in closed-list systems. Changing district magnitude from a single to one hundred seats decreases the predicted probability that a legislator is a constituency member by 19 per cent in closed-list systems, but increases that probability by 24 per cent in open-list systems. The positive effect does not reach conventional levels of statistical significance. But a more thorough analysis demonstrates that the constituency orientation and work of legislators is not merely a pure mechanical response to the incentives and constraints generated by the formal properties of institutions. The effect of the conditions legislators compete under for re-election is indirect. It is conditioned by what they think about the process of political representation.

The views legislators hold about representation guide what aspects of the job they feel strongest about. To measure how they conceive of political representation in a systematic way, the survey presented legislators with the hard choice between representation-from-below and representation-from-above (see Andeweg and Thomassen 2005). The dilemma constitutes a five-point scale. Legislators indicating a value of '1' hold a bottom-up conception of

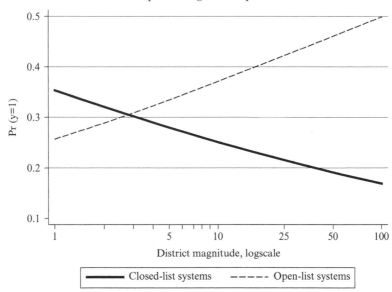

FIGURE 8.1 The effect of district magnitude on legislators' constituency orientation

Note: The lines indicate a legislator's simulated predicted probability of prioritizing the role of constituency
    member. Bold lines are statistically significant at the 5% level.

representation. They believe that politicians should aim to translate the political views of citizens into policy as accurately as possible. Legislators indicating a value of '5', on the other hand, think of representation as a top-down
process in which politicians should stand clearly on their party's platform and
aim to win citizen support for those views. But trading off these alternative
notions proves tough: on average 33 per cent of the respondents give equal
value to both and gravitate towards the middle of the scale. More legislators,
in addition, favour the top-down over the bottom-up perspective of representation (37 per cent) than vice versa (30 per cent). The summary statistics displayed in Table 8.3 underline substantial differences between legislators and
countries. Model 3 looks at the dilemma's main effect. We find strong support for hypothesis 5: representation-from-below conceptions tend to divert
legislators' attention away from their parliamentary duties and increase their
constituency-centredness.

   More importantly, electoral institutions seem to bring legislators to do
what they would otherwise not have done and seem to keep them from doing
what they would otherwise have done. To fully appreciate the way in which
legislators' conceptions of representation condition the effect of electoral
incentives a three-way interaction with ballot structure and district magnitude is added to the model specification. In open-list systems, model 4
demonstrates, the electoral incentive matters only to legislators who hold a

top-down view of representation that keeps them from favouring the constituency role. In closed-list systems, by contrast, the electoral disincentive only matters to legislators who hold a bottom-up view that brings them to prioritize constituency work. This is illustrated by Figure 8.2, that is, the graphical depiction of model 4. The effect of district magnitude in open-list and closed-list systems is plotted for each of the five points on the scale that opposes bottom-up and top-down conceptions of political representation. In systems where preference votes determine legislators' chances of re-election, the figure shows increasing lines, but the increase reaches statistical significance only for the highest values on the scale. Legislators who view political representation as a process that is run from below are very committed to nurturing their constituency, irrespective of the scope of intra-party competition they face. Those who do not already consider it their prime objective to translate citizens' preferences into policy are the ones swayed by electoral calculations. Only they feel the pressure to set aside their bedrock ideas about the representative process to retain their seat in parliament. The exact opposite holds in closed-list systems, on the other hand. District magnitude's decreasing effect grows weaker when moving towards the top-down end of the scale. The more legislators are convinced that representation should be run from above, the less electoral considerations come into play. That the lines in Figure 8.2 converge underlines moreover that legislators' conceptions of representation carry more weight in small districts than in large: the likelihood that a legislator who feels that representation is a bottom-up rather than a top-down process reports being a constituency member grows by 29 per cent in a single-seat district and by 4 per cent in a district of one hundred seats.

Whereas the impact of the electoral rules is closely interlinked with that of legislators' beliefs about representation, the level of government they represent has an independent effect. The impact of electoral institutions remains unaltered when accounting for differences in the constituency orientation of national and regional legislators.[5] Regional legislators, model 3 indicates, are more likely to prioritize constituency casework and project work compared to their national counterparts: their predicted probability of favouring the role of constituency member is 13 per cent higher. This difference in role orientation cannot simply be ascribed to the fact that the constituencies of regional legislators are smaller than those of national legislators though. The median regional legislator in the selection represents 47,500 constituents, whereas the median national legislator represents 76,500. The magnitude and population size of a district are strongly correlated at 0.8 moreover. If differences in professional priorities are generated by differences in the re-election context, then the effect of district magnitude should markedly shrink when the level of government is added to the regression equation and this is not the case. One plausible explanation would pertain to the partition of jurisdictions across levels of parliament (Patzelt 2007). Regional parliaments are charged with

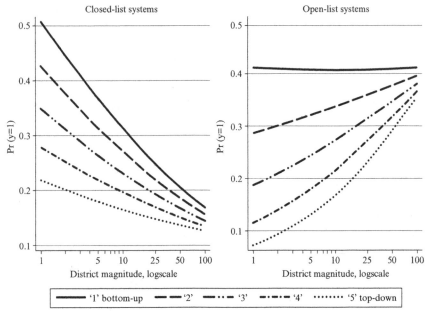

FIGURE 8.2 The effect of district magnitude and conceptions of representation on legislators' constituency orientation

Note: The lines indicate a legislator's simulated predicted probability of prioritizing the role of constituency member. Bold lines are statistically significant at the 5% level.

those jurisdictions and decisions that more directly affect citizens' day-to-day lives including economic, cultural, and social policies. Clearly, these policy domains will yield more constituent cases and are more suited for project work than areas such as foreign aid and external trade.

Not only the nature of the competencies has an impact however. Differences across regions in the scope of regionalization affect legislators' commitment to constituency work. The scope is captured by Hooghe et al.'s (2008) regional authority index (RAI) providing an overall score of the extent of regional self-rule and shared rule for each state. First and foremost the index is used to compare jurisdictions across regions; to account for asymmetries in regionalization these region-level observations are weighted by population for the aggregation to country scores. The index of self-rule and shared rule both constitute an additive scale: the first measuring institutional depth, policy scope, fiscal autonomy, and representation; the second measuring the extent of shared powers over law-making, executive control, fiscal control, and constitutional reform.[6] As indicated in Table 8.3, the country's RAI scores vary widely across the selection. The scope of regional authority is highest in Belgium, Germany, Italy, and Spain and lowest in Hungary,

Ireland, Israel, Norway, Poland, Portugal, and the UK. Austria, France, the Netherlands, and Switzerland cover the spectrum in-between.

Model 5 provides strong support for hypothesis 2b, but hypothesis 2a is not corroborated by the data. We find that regional legislators become less inclined to assume the role of constituency member as the extent of regional self-rule and shared rule measured in RAI scores expands. Increasing the Regional Authority Index from a low value of ten to a high value of twenty-five decreases the predicted probability that the average regional legislator focuses on the constituency from 47 to 26 per cent. A similar increase in the scope of regionalization does not affect the constituency attentiveness of the average national legislator however. Only the role orientation of regional legislators, it seems, shifts from the constituency to parliament as the region gains authority in terms of the scope of powers as well as co-decision-making at the national level. Scrutinizing government and managing parliament's business will only be emotionally gratifying if legislators can influence legislation and the institution has a certain standing. For members of regional parliaments that are strongly constrained in their ability to shape policy, providing services to constituents and looking after their social and economic well-being may well be the most rewarding part of the job. In this respect, feelings of powerlessness may also provide an explanation for the positive effect of seniority in parliament.[7] Newly elected legislators tend to turn their attention away from parliamentary responsibilities towards the constituency (hypothesis 6). Only after going through a period of apprenticeship can legislators take up more prominent positions in parliament and leave a mark on the legislative process.

Confidence in our findings is further enhanced by adding a number of alternative country- and party-level explanations to the regression models. None of these factors detracts from the effect that electoral institutions, conceptions of representation and regionalism have on the constituency orientation of legislators in fifteen advanced industrial democracies. We do, however, find evidence that controlling for demand on the part of constituents might be important: in countries with large unemployed populations constituency members tend to be more common.[8] It is not only that constituent demands for assistance in obtaining social benefits comprise the bulk of a legislator's caseload. Under conditions of economic hardship, moreover, constituents will put more pressure on their representatives to funnel public expenditures to the constituency and stimulate business (Young, Heitshusen, and Wood 2005). Political parties further constrain their members' role choice. While the party's position on the left–right dimension hardly impacts legislators' constituency orientation (hypothesis 4), the number of seats a party holds in parliament does have the expected effect (hypothesis 3): as a party's seat share increases, so does legislators' likelihood of defining their role in terms of constituency work.[9] A division of labour among co-partisan representatives develops as the size of the parliamentary party group crosses a certain threshold. Not all legislators then have to share the burden of legislative work: some will prioritize parliamentary responsibilities and thereby open up the opportunity for others to concentrate on their constituency. First-time legislators, in particular, have a stronger focus on the constituency.

8.5 CONCLUSION

The existence of a relationship between the represented and those acting on their behalf is one fundamental requirement of representative government. Previous research has demonstrated that legislators across the globe return home to their district to mix and mingle with constituents. We have demonstrated that there are cultural repertoires of actions that elected representatives can tap into to keep in touch with constituents. But what explains variation in the strength of legislators' commitment to constituency representation? In this chapter we have developed an explanatory model including contextual, party-level, and individual-level factors and put it to the test.

Our results provide strong evidence for the assumption that electoral incentives shape legislators' constituency orientation: the probability of prioritizing casework and local promoter activities increases with district magnitude in open-list systems and decreases with magnitude in closed-list systems. But the impact that electoral incentives have on legislators' role choice is conditioned by the conception of political representation they hold. Electoral incentives impact only on those legislators whose views on representation conflict with these incentives. That is, the effect of district magnitude in open-list systems is statistically significant only for those perceiving representation as a top-down process, whereas in closed-list systems this is the case only for those holding a bottom-up perception. One implication for the broader subject of representation is that MPs' own policy preferences might matter most in closed-list systems that use large district magnitudes, because it is there that MPs are least likely to be 'distracted' by any perceived need to be active constituency representatives and are thus freest to promote their policy goals. In addition, the level of government seems to matter. Regional legislators tend to prioritize constituency casework and project work more compared to their national counterparts, while the degree of regional authority negatively affects the strength of regional legislators' constituency focus (but has no significant effect on the orientation of the average national legislator). Finally, we also found that the country's unemployment rate, the party size (but not the party ideology), and seniority in parliament significantly impact the strength of legislators' constituency orientation.

In conclusion, our exploration has laid the grounds for further analysis of contextual, party-level, and individual-level factors on the activities legislators choose to prioritize and their role conception. In particular, more research is needed to assess the independent effect of the level of government and the degree of regional authority. It is unclear whether our observations derive from the presence of different 'models of democracy' at the regional and national level with regard to the representative relation. In other words, is this difference in the shape of the territorial link with voters mainly due to the assimilation of the different conditions and incentives present at different levels of government or is it related to more in-depth cleavages between the two political classes?

NOTES

1. We retain Searing's terminology, though of course parliaments today are not quite as male-dominated as when Searing conducted his research. Although Searing (1994) also distinguished 'Ministerial Aspirants', this category was excluded from the survey. Few MPs, Searing concluded, make this role the principal focus of their work and closed-ended questionnaires plausibly only increase the likelihood of socially desirable answer patterns.
2. To correct for the under- or overrepresentation of political parties survey responses are weighted by the size of the parliamentary party in each parliament. In addition, the large number of observations at the Swiss cantonal level is down-weighted in order not to skew the analysis.
3. This hierarchical structure implies that only parliamentary party groups of which at least two members have responded to the questionnaire are included in the analyses.
4. To compute predicted probabilities, continuous variables were set to their mean values and dichotomous variables were fixed at zero.
5. The level of government is operationalized as a dichotomous variable taking the value of '1' for members of regional parliaments and the value of '0' for members of national parliaments.
6. The RAI scores of regional parliaments cannot exceed 24: the maximum self-rule score is 15 and the maximum shared-rule score is 9. To obtain country scores, a score for each regional tier is first calculated and then aggregated. Countries with more regional tiers of government, that is, receive higher scores. In addition, scores are weighted by population to account for horizontal (i.e. the regions of one tier have different scores) and vertical (i.e. lower levels of government exists only in some higher-level regions or their scores differ across higher-level regions) asymmetries in the process of decentralization (for more details on the coding and calculation of RAI scores, see Hooghe, Marks, and Schakel 2008). Because the analysis includes the RAI index only in interaction with the level of government,

we compare like with like, and differences in the range of the index among national and regional legislators do not skew the analysis.

7. Seniority is dichotomized in order to separate first-time legislators from those who have served in parliament for one or more terms. First-term legislators are coded as '1' and veterans as '0'.
8. Countries differ as to the percentage of unemployed persons in the economically active population. Unemployment rates range from up to 18 per cent in Spain down to 3 per cent in Norway (EUROSTAT).
9. Ideology reflects a party's position on an eleven-point left–right scale. To estimate this position as accurately as possible, we have calculated the party-level average of the scores respondents have assigned their party. The size of the parliamentary party group is expressed in relative terms to assure optimal comparability: the number of seats a party has obtained is divided by the total number of seats in the parliament.

REFERENCES

Andeweg, R. B. and J. A. Thomassen (2005), 'Modes of Political Representation: Toward a New Typology', *Legislative Studies Quarterly*, 30 (4): 507–28.

Cain, B., J. Ferejohn, and M. Fiorina (1987), *The Personal Vote: Constituency Service and Electoral Independence*. Cambridge, MA: Harvard University Press.

Carey, J. M. and M. S. Shugart (1995), 'Incentives to Cultivate a Personal Vote: A Rank Ordering of Electoral Formulas', *Electoral Studies*, 14 (4): 417–39.

Cox, G. W. (1987), *The Efficient Secret: The Cabinet and the Development of Political Parties in Victorian England*. Cambridge: Cambridge University Press.

De Winter, L. (2002), 'Belgian MPs: Between Omnipotent Parties and Disenchanted Citizen-Clients', in P. Norton (ed.), *Parliaments in Contemporary Western Europe*. London: Frank Cass, 89–110.

Esaiasson, P. and S. Holmberg (1996), *Representation from Above: Members of Parliament and Representative Democracy in Sweden*. Ashgate: Dartmouth.

Fenno, R. F. (1978), *Home Style: House Members in Their Districts*. Boston: Longman.

Friesema, P. H. and R. D. Hedlund (1974), 'The Reality of Representational Roles', in N. R. Luttbeg (ed.), *Public Opinion and Public Policy: Models of Political Linkage*. Homewood: Dorsey, 413–17.

Gallagher, M. and L. Komito (2010), 'The Constituency Role of Dáil Deputies', in J. Coakley and M. Gallagher (eds.), *Politics in the Republic of Ireland*. London: Routledge, 230–62.

Heitshusen, V., G. Young, and D. M. Wood (2005), 'Electoral Context and MP Constituency Focus in Australia, Canada, Ireland, New Zealand, and the United Kingdom', *American Journal of Political Science*, 49 (1): 32–45.

Hooghe, L., G. Marks, and A. H. Schakel (2008), 'Operationalizing Regional Authority: A Coding Scheme for 42 Countries, 1950–2006', *Regional & Federal Studies*, 18 (2–3): 123–42.

Jewell, M. E. (1970), 'Attitudinal Determinants of Legislative Behavior: The Utility of Role Analysis', in A. Komberg and L. D. Musolf (eds.), *Legislatures in Developmental Perspective*. Durham: Duke University Press, 460–500.

Kam, C. J. (2009), *Party Discipline and Parliamentary Politics*. Cambridge: Cambridge University Press.

King, A. (1981), 'The Rise of the Career Politician in Britain—And Its Consequences', *British Journal of Political Science*, 11 (3): 249–85.

Lee, F. E. (2005), 'Interests, Constituencies, and Policy Making', in P. J. Quirk and S. A. Binder (eds.), *The Legislative Branch*. Oxford: Oxford University Press, 281–313.

Mayhew, D. R. (1974), *Congress: The Electoral Connection*. New Haven, CT: Yale University Press.

Mezey, M. L. (2008), *Representative Democracy: Legislators and Their Constituents*. Lanham, MD: Rowman & Littlefield.

Norris, P. (1997), 'The Puzzle of Constituency Service', *Journal of Legislative Studies*, 3 (2): 29–49.

—— and J. Lovenduski (1995), *Political Recruitment: Gender, Race, and Class in the British Parliament*. Cambridge: Cambridge University Press.

Norton, P. and D. M. Wood (1993), *Back from Westminster: British Members of Parliament and Their Constituents*. Lexington, KY: University Press of Kentucky.

Patzelt, W. J. (2007), 'The Constituency Roles of MPs at the Federal and Länder Levels in Germany', *Regional & Federal Studies*, 17 (1): 47–70.

Saward, M. (2010), *The Representative Claim*. Oxford: Oxford University Press.

Scully, R. and D. M. Farrell (2003), 'MEPs as Representatives: Individual and Institutional Roles', *JCMS: Journal of Common Market Studies*, 41 (2): 269–88.

Searing, D. (1994), *Westminster's World: Understanding Political Roles*. Cambridge, MA: Harvard University Press.

Shugart, M. S., M. E. Valdini, and K. Suominen (2005), 'Looking for Locals: Voter Information Demands and Personal Vote-earning Attributes of Legislators Under Proportional Representation', *American Journal of Political Science*, 49 (2): 437–49.

Steenbergen, M. R. and B. S. Jones (2002), 'Modeling Multilevel Data Structures', *American Journal of Political Science*, 46 (1): 218–37.

Studlar, D. T. and I. McAllister (1996), 'Constituency Activity and Representational Roles among Australian Legislators', *Journal of Politics*, 58 (1): 69–90.

Thomassen, J. (1994), 'Empirical Research into Political Representation: Failing Democracy or Failing Models?' in W. E. Miller, M. Kent Jennings, and T. E. Mann (eds.), *Elections at Home and Abroad: Essays in Honor of Warren E. Miller*. Ann Arbor, MI: University of Michigan Press, 237–64.

Wahlke, J. C., H. Eulau, W. Buchanan et al. (1962), *The Legislative System: Explorations in Legislative Behavior*. New York, NY: Wiley.

Young, G., V. Heitshusen, and D. M. Wood (2005), 'Home Style from the Demand Side: A Comparative Look at the Westminster Systems', paper presented at the APSA annual meeting, 1–4 September, Washington, DC.

Do the Media Set the Agenda of Parliament or Is It the Other Way Around? Agenda Interactions between MPs and Mass Media

Tor Midtbø, Stefaan Walgrave, Peter Van Aelst, and Dag Arne Christensen

9.1 INTRODUCTION

How do European Members of Parliament (MPs) interact with the media? Scholars agree that the mass media have become some kind of political institution (Cook 2005). Longitudinal studies show that there is an ongoing process of mediatization of politics. Political institutions and actors are increasingly affected by mass media coverage, mass media formats, and mass media rules (Altheide and Snow 1979; Strömback 2008). Over time, the impact of the mass media on politics seems to have increased in a measurable way (see, for example, Vliegenthart and Walgrave 2008). Starting from the idea that for many MPs the mass media have become a significant actor, this chapter zooms in on just one aspect of the conjoint dealings of MPs and the media: how they mutually affect each other's agenda. Are MPs' parliamentary actions inspired by the media or is media coverage driven by MPs' activities in parliament?

Our goal in this chapter is not only to offer a systematic description of the agenda interactions—the mutual influences regarding their priorities—between MPs and the media but also to provide some explanation. In fact, as we will see, there are significant differences amongst MPs in the fifteen countries under study here. Some MPs' work is largely inspired by media coverage, other MPs manage to exert influence on the media agenda, still other MPs are both inspired by and actively driving media coverage, while yet another group appears to be entirely disconnected from media as they are not affected by nor actively affect media coverage. These differences between MPs in their dealings with the media are patterned, not random. The second aim of this chapter therefore is to account for the differences in agenda interactions amongst MPs in the fifteen countries under scrutiny. Which features of individual MPs, of their party, of the assembly they are member of, and of the country in which they are elected affect MPs' agenda interactions with the media?

In fact, in line with the main thrust of this book, we expect that MPs' representational behaviour—here, their behaviour vis-à-vis the media—is determined not only by their own personal features, but also by the institutions in which they operate. With institutions we refer here to the type of parliament the MPs are member of, the party they represent, and the country (and its political system) in which they are elected. The PARTIREP survey contains two questions on the perceptions of MPs on their own agenda interactions with the media: one about the extent to which MPs' actions react on preceding media coverage; the other about how successful they are in gaining media attention for their parliamentary work. The information gathered via our survey does certainly not reflect the entire reality (for a discussion about the relative value of survey data compared to behavioural data see: Van Aelst and Walgrave 2011). But our survey produced unique data that are especially suited for comparing among MPs, parties, parliaments, and countries.

9.2 AGENDA INTERACTIONS BETWEEN MPS AND MASS MEDIA

In any democratic system, political elites and mass media interact. Not only do elites and media exchange information, they are often entangled in an uneasy struggle to gain the upper hand. Extant work has analysed this give-and-take relationship (see for example, Althaus 2003; Brants, de Vreese, Möller, and van Praag 2010; Cook 2005; Entman 2003; Norris, Curtice, Sanders, Scammell, and Semetko 1999). This chapter focuses on what we call the 'agenda interactions' between political elites and the media. We adopt the perspective of an individual MP: how does he/she describe his/her dealings with the media and how do these descriptions vary amongst MPs? We are interested in how MPs give information to the media and use information from the media. The former interaction we label *media access*; the latter denotes *media reaction*. We build on the simple notion that MPs prefer and seek media coverage since this is one—perhaps *the*—way to heighten their public visibility and to get their stories out. In fact, there is evidence suggesting that the more MPs get into the news, the more votes they get (Van Aelst, Maddens, Noppe, and Fiers 2008). Similarly, Cook (2005: 124) observes that making the news is instrumental to policymaking, as it is a way for MPs to get the issues they care about on the agenda, to build a reputation, and to persuade others to support their point of view (see also Sellers 2010). Therefore, for both electoral and policy reasons, attracting journalists' attention is a major challenge for any modern politician. MPs respond to media issues and surf on highly mediatized issues so as to demonstrate that they care and are on top of things (Wolfsfeld and Sheafer 2006). Dealing with issues that are already high on the media agenda is therefore a preferred strategy politicians use to connect to the public (Walgrave and Van Aelst 2006).

Agenda interactions between political actors and journalists are hardly a new topic in political science. A substantial body of literature analyses the political agenda-setting power of the mass media, scrutinizing the inter-relation between media attention and political attention. Drawing on behav-ioural data—mostly parliamentary questions but sometimes also other governmental outputs—this research finds that political elites tend to adopt mediatized issues on a regular basis (e.g. Green-Pedersen and Stubager 2010; Soroka 2002a; Thesen 2011; Van Noije, Kleinnijenhuis, and Oegema 2008; Vliegenthart and Walgrave 2011; Walgrave, Soroka, and Nuytemans 2008). With only a few exceptions (see, for example, Van Noije et al. 2008), this work deals with single countries. As a consequence, we do not really know whether, agenda-wise, media matter more for political elites in some countries than in others. Nor is there much systematic evidence as to the moderating role played by institutions—parties and parliaments—on agenda interactions.

In an attempt to deal with these shortcomings, some students of media and politics have recently started gathering survey data among politicians and journalists in several countries (see, for example, Maurer 2011). Typi-cally, these surveys ask MPs about their general perception of the mass media's political agenda-setting power without asking specific questions with regard to their actual behaviour. The results of extant studies suggest that the general agenda-setting influence of the mass media is perceived to be high by MPs and varies across nations (Van Aelst and Walgrave 2011; Van Dalen and Van Aelst 2013).

Building on these recent developments, the present study deals with the challenge of using comparative designs to gauge agenda interactions. It con-tributes in several ways. First, the evidence we use is not based on unchecked questions regarding the agenda power of the media in general but results from constraining and precise questions about MPs own quantifiable behav-iour. Second, the evidence relates to both directions of influence: from media to MPs but also from MPs to the media. This yields a more complete and realistic picture of how political elites and media interact. Third, and most importantly, the scope of our evidence largely exceeds that of previous work. We present evidence for fifteen countries, seventy-three assemblies, 162 par-ties, and 1,898 MPs. This is by far the largest comparative effort to date. This allows us to deal with determinants on higher levels of aggregation (parties, assemblies, and countries) which, as we will show, effectively shape the agenda interactions between MPs and the media.

9.3 MODERATING AGENDA INTERACTIONS: THE IMPACT OF MPS, PARTIES, AND ASSEMBLIES

We first focus on the level of the *individual* MPs. Which of MPs' personal features affect how they deal with the media? The literature on the newsworthiness of politicians has clearly identified political status as the key explanatory variable. The more political power an actor has the higher the chance (s)he will receive frequent media coverage (Midtbø 2011; Sellers and Schaffner 2007; Tresch 2009). In the case of MPs we can identify two key status indicators that explain why journalists are attracted to particular MPs: their political experience and their parliamentary position (Van Aelst, Shehata, and Van Dalen 2010: 314–15). Position is perhaps the most obvious factor. Not all MPs are of interest to the media. Not only politicians but also journalists seek power: high-ranking politicians are seen as holders of exclusive information as well as having the authority to act upon that information. As for experienced MPs, they may be seen by journalists as particularly good sources for inside information leading to more media access. Long service could also provide politicians with a better understanding of how journalists think and operate (see, for example, Elmelund-Præstekær, Hopman, and Nørgaard 2011: 387–8) leading to behaviour that is more tailored to the media's needs. Added to that, experienced politicians have also learned that surfing on the media waves is a good strategy to become part of the story. Therefore, we expect them to display higher levels of media reactivity as well. In sum, position and experience should strengthen media interactions, both media access and reactivity.

Media interactions could be affected by the behaviour of MPs as well. According to the famous distinction made by Tetlock (2005), some MPs can be defined as 'hedgehogs' while others are 'foxes'. Foxes eclectically utilize a broad range of sources of information; they know a little about a lot. Hedgehogs, by contrast, are devoted to a few sources of information; they know a lot about the issues they specialize in. Foxes rely more on the general media as a source of information than hedgehogs. And, thus, we expect them to be more reactive to media stories than hedgehogs. So, we expect specialized MPs to be less reactive to media cues. Since foxes try to please the general public while hedgehogs are only catering to specific segments of the public, we also anticipate specialized politicians to undertake less effort to get into the general media and, as a consequence, to have less access to the media. A similar logic of specialization and using the media as a source of inspiration has been suggested by Kingdon (1984: 64).

While every MP's primary goal probably is re-election (Carey and Shugart 1995), the ways in which this goal is pursued, may differ. Some MPs mainly target their existing constituency and primarily want to keep these voters on board, they preach to the (previously) converted. Other MPs, in contrast, try to reach out beyond their supporters and connect to a larger audience. These two different strategies, we expect, have a bearing on how MPs interact with the mass media. Since the mass media are the chief channel to connect to the population at large, we expect the 'expansionist' MPs who seek out voters that have not voted for them in the past to be more reactive to media stories than their colleagues who target a more confined and well-defined audience. Also, going beyond the more narrow preferences of their existing voters, expansionist MPs are on the lookout for new issues and policies. To compensate for insufficient information these MPs use the media more as a source of information than their colleagues. We do not expect expansionists to be per se more successful in getting coverage in the media (media access) but to try harder by displaying more responsiveness (media reaction).

To what extent could the ideological position of an MP be affecting his/her media access and media reactivity? Here we expect there to be differences between access and reactivity. In terms of access, getting covered by the media, we expect journalists to prefer to give airplay to those politicians who share their ideological position. We know from surveys among journalists that most of them place themselves on the left side of the ideological left–right spectrum (while they consider their medium to be more right-wing) (Van Dalen and Van Aelst 2012). This leads to the expectation that left-of-centre MPs would be met with more frequent coverage. Added to that, in many European countries there is an ongoing debate of how the media deals and should deal with the radical-right populist parties (see, for example, Walgrave and De Swert 2002). There is some evidence that radical-right populist parties have less frequent contacts with journalists and are treated differently in the media compared to other parties (Van Aelst et al. 2010; Viegenthart, Boomgaarden, and Van Spanje 2012). So this literature suggests that radical right-wing parties are covered less (less media access) than the other, more left-wing parties. For the media reactivity, we do not have firm expectations about differences between left- and right-wing MPs. We do not see why they would be differently inspired by media coverage.

Still on the level of individual MPs, two control variables are worth including in the models. There have been reports of an 'anti-feminist' element in the media (Gidengil and Everitt 2003: 214) which makes it useful to control for gender. As for age, it can be argued that older MPs have been brought up in a time with strong party organizations and a media situation quite different from the present. This may cause both media reactivity and media access to decline with age.

A second level of explanation is the *party* an MP belongs to. Some parties are more attractive sources for the media; they have higher media access. Other parties' MPs may on average react more to media coverage—having higher media reactivity. The key variable on the party level is the incumbency of the party the MP belongs to. Recent studies suggest that opposition MPs are more prone to follow media cues than government MPs (Green-Pedersen and Stubager 2010; Vliegenthart and Walgrave 2011). This is really not that surprising, considering that both the media and the opposition share a common goal, namely to control the government (Midtbø 2011). This often implies criticizing government actions. Negativity is an essential part of journalistic framing (Soroka 2006) and it certainly plays a key role for an effective and critical opposition too (Thesen 2011). Added to that, opposition parties are not bound by any agreements made in government and can use media coverage as ammunition to attack the government. In sum, we think government MPs display a higher level of media reactivity.

The story regarding media access of incumbents and challengers is less straightforward, though. On the one hand, considering journalists' aforementioned attraction to power, we expect MPs representing the government to get media access more easily. After all, these MPs are in a position to actually influence policies and impact the daily lives of media consumers and voters. On the other hand, increased media access may only hold for politicians actually having a cabinet position and not for government backbenchers. Previous studies show that government backbenchers receive even less media attention than MPs from major opposition parties (De Swert and Walgrave 2002; Van Aelst et al. 2008). Hence, we cannot formulate a clear expectation as to the media access of incumbents versus the opposition.

On the party level we control for the ideology of the party of the MP. As mentioned above, we think there are reasons to expect that individual right-wing MPs are less successful in gaining access to the media. To make sure that we are dealing with an effect on the level of the individual politician, we control for the party family the surveyed MPs are a member of.

Shifting focus to a possible third explanatory level, the *assembly* MPs are members of, we introduce two explanatory variables. The first simply is the size of the parliament at stake. Individual MPs, purely statistically speaking, play on average a less prominent role in large parliaments. Therefore they are expected to have less media access compared to MPs of small parliaments. For instance, Van Aelst and colleagues (2010) showed that members of larger parliaments (e.g. Sweden) have less contact with journalists than MPs that operate in smaller parliaments (e.g. Norway). We do not expect parliamentary size to affect media reactivity.

The second explanation at this level—and a quite obvious one given the structure of our data—builds on the distinction between regional and national parliaments. The dataset includes seventy-three parliaments—fifty-eight of which are regional. Given the larger attention in the general media for the activities of the national as compared to those of the regional parliaments (for the Belgian case, see, for example: De Swert and Walgrave 2002) we expect the average media access for national MPs to be higher than for regional MPs. Added to that, research has shown that the media are a more important political agenda-setter for some issues than for others (Soroka 2002b). Crime and justice and foreign affairs are amongst the issues for which earlier work has indicated a particularly large media effect (Van Noije et al. 2008; Walgrave et al. 2008; Wood and Peake 1998). Knowing that these two issues, in most countries, are dealt with at the national level, we also expect that media reactivity amongst national MPs is on average higher than amongst regional MPs.

There is, of course, yet another, fourth, explanatory level—the *country* level. As already pointed out, with only a limited number of countries (fifteen) and a large number of potential explanations at this level, it would be unwise to attempt to test country-level hypotheses in this chapter. Such a model would definitely be underspecified and contain biased estimates. So, for the time being, we leave the country level aside and we will just control for cross-national variation by including country dummies.

9.4 DATA AND METHODS

Details about the survey are provided in the introductory chapter of this volume. Note again, though, that we only study MPs' perception of media reactivity and media access as opposed to objective, direct behavioural measures (see Midtbø 2011). The dependent variables are based on the following two questions in the survey:

(1) Of the initiatives (e.g. bills, written and oral questions) which you personally raised in Parliament in the last year, roughly what proportions of these did you respectively derive from the media, from interest groups, from within the party, from meeting with individual citizens, and from your personal experience? Could you please give a rough estimate in percentages?
(2) And how often have these initiatives that you raised actually been covered by the media? Again a rough estimate in percentages is sufficient.

As we will see momentarily, the two dependent variables, which are defined by scales from 0 to 100, are anything but normally distributed. Nevertheless, we have chosen to work with standard linear models, compensating for non-normality by $\log(Y+1)$-transforming the dependent variables.[1] Table 9.1 presents the independent variables together with their operationalizations.[2]

Since we expect variation in media interaction at more than one level, we adopt a multilevel modelling (MLM) approach which accounts for variation at the MP, party, assembly, and country level (the latter only in terms of dummies). We include both national and regional assemblies, wherever the latter exist. Note that parties and assembly levels are not nested. MPs from the same party can belong to different parliaments. For example, the German

TABLE 9.1 *Independent variables and description*

Independent variable	Description
MP level	
Female	Man = 0, Woman = 1
Age	2011 minus year of birth
Elite	Party leader, speaker, mayor or committee chair = 1, others = 0
Experience	2011 minus year first elected
Generalist	MP deals with a wide range of issues = 1, only one or two issues = 0
Expansionist	MP seeks out groups in society that have (= 0)/have not (= 1) supported them in the past
Right wing	Self-placement on an 11 point left–right scale
Right wing^2	Self-placement on an 11 point left–right scale, squared
Party level	
Party family	Parties divided into 13 ideological families
Incumbent	MP from the opposition = 0; MP representing government = 1
Assembly level	
Size	Number of representatives in assembly
Regional	MP member of national parliament = 0, of regional parliament = 1

CDU appears in five parliaments one of which is national, the other regional. Inasmuch as parties can appear in several assemblies, the structure of our model will be cross-classified. After having distinguished between variation at the various levels, the next step is to estimate models that include explanatory variables at the MP level. We then add explanatory variables from higher levels. Throughout the analysis we include country dummies to see if there is any leftover cross-national variation.

We employ a Bayesian modelling approach—an approach that since the advent of Markov Chain Monte Carlo methods and modern computers, has become increasingly more popular in statistical modelling in general and multilevel modelling in particular (e.g. Gelman and Hill 2007; Hamaker and Klugist 2011; Jackman 2007). This popularity stems from, among other things, a tremendous flexibility in handling complex multilevel structures even with a small number of groups, the ability to cope with data missing at random through the Gibbs sampler, and also not having to rely on normality assumptions and asymptotic results as in the classical setting.[3]

9.5 DESCRIPTIVE ANALYSIS

We start by looking at our original dependent variables (before transformation). Although Figure 9.1 is simple, it is still informative: the mean value on the scales from 0 to 100 is much lower for media reaction than for media access. The relationship with the media is clearly portrayed by the MPs as

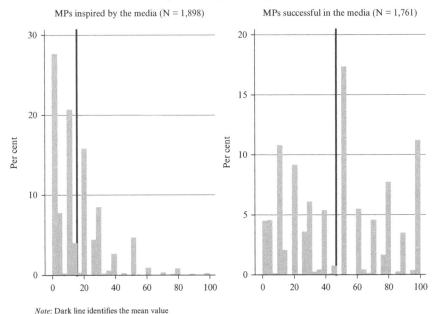

FIGURE 9.1   Frequency (%) of agenda interactions: media reaction and media access

being asymmetric. According to the MPs themselves, they get their actions much more often in the media than that the media inspire their own actions. The average legislator estimates that 47 per cent of their initiatives are covered by the media, whereas 16 per cent of these initiatives had been inspired by media stories. Agendas emanate from politics, not from the media, the results suggest. Note also that media reaction and media access are only weakly correlated, with a Pearsons R of 0.06.[4] This may indicate that the two types of agenda interaction are not mutually reinforcing.

The fact that MPs indicate that they are mastering their own agendas and that they are successful in attracting media attention for their actions, directly contradicts the already mentioned extant research—although based on similar evidence—in which MPs were asked about their assessment of the political agenda-setting power of the mass media in general. In these studies, the mass media's political agenda-setting power was invariably estimated as being exceedingly high and stronger than their own agenda-setting power (Van Aelst and Walgrave 2011; Walgrave 2008). It appears that if MPs are asked very concretely about their own concrete legislative behaviour and not just about media and politics in general, and if they are given the chance to ascribe their activities not just to the media but to a whole series of alternative sources of inspiration (e.g. interest groups, party, citizens), that they come to a maybe more realistic assessment of the role of the media in their daily activities. The media obviously matter, but they are not all-powerful agenda-setters.

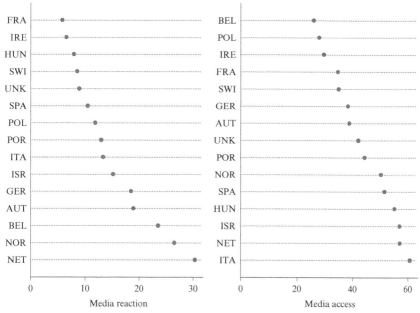

FIGURE 9.2 Cross-national differences in agenda interactions

Despite the global picture of low media reaction and high media access, cross-national divergences can still be detected. Figure 9.2 shows that the mean value for media reaction varies from less than 6 to more than 30 between the fifteen countries, the range for media access goes from 26 to 57. We see that countries such as the Netherlands, score high on both reactivity and access while others—such as France, Ireland, and Poland—appear to have only a modest number of media interactions (both reaction and access are low). Media reaction and media access are positively related on the country level (Pearson's R is 0.29), implying that in countries where MPs, in their legislative activities, take more media issues into account they also display higher success rates in getting coverage for their initiatives. That said, we also find countries such as Belgium that score comparatively highly on one variable (in this case media reaction) but low on the other (in this case media access).

9.6 EXPLANATORY ANALYSES

The next step is to find out whether these cross-national differences can be attributed to country characteristics as such, or whether they reflect differences located at lower levels (MP, party, and assembly). We first identify the sources of variation for our two dependent variables across the multiple levels. This amounts to comparing so-called empty models (i.e. models without explanatory variables) in a sequential manner, starting out with a single-level model with an intercept only, proceeding to a pair of two-level models (one with parties and another with parliament at the second level), before introducing models with crossed effects with and without country dummies.

Tables 9.2 and 9.3 contain the mean of the MCMC (Markov Chain Monte Carlo) results for all parameters, the standard deviation, and their 95 per cent posterior interval. As is usual for such data, most of the variation appears to be located at the lowest level, that is, at the MP level. The MP-level variance in the single-level model for media reaction in the first column is 1.95, while the corresponding figures are 1.67 in a two-level assembly model and 1.71 in a two-level party model (the second and third column). To get an idea of how much of the overall variance can be attributed to the different levels, intraclass correlations (ICC) are calculated. The ICC measures the distribution of the variance for the dependent variables between MPs, parties, and assemblies. By moving on to models with varying intercepts at both the party and assembly levels in the last two columns, we find sizeable intraclass correlations (and variance components) for both variables, especially for media reaction. The proportion of the variance in MPs' reaction to the media is around 6 per cent at the party level in the two cross-classified models, while the ICC scores at the assembly level is affected by introducing the country dummies (the ICC has been reduced from 27 to 11 per cent). In other words, agenda interactions do vary systematically between parties and across assemblies. However, both parties and assemblies seem to be more important for media reaction than for media access. The size of the Bayesian DIC's at the bottom of the tables suggest that models with crossed effects provide a better fit to the data in both cases. For media reaction we see that these figures are getting lower at each stage of the modelling process. Finally, according to the country dummies, even after including party and assembly variables, some additional national source of variation remains for media reaction, but not for media access (DIC 5009 with country dummies and 5007 without).

Having identified variation at the different levels, we now move on to explain this variation. Table 9.4 contains two columns for each dependent variable, one with explanatory variables at the MP level only; the other including explanatory variables at all levels (party, assembly, and country). Starting with the level of the individual MPs and both control variables, we do not see an effect from sex. There is a slight tendency for *female* MPs to feel less successful in getting access to the media than their male colleagues. The posterior density is centred near 13 per cent in the final model (see the '–0.13' in the final column of the age line), and has a 95 per cent interval that does not overlap zero. This means that women MPs, all other things being equal, report that their legislative actions were covered 13 per cent less than male MPs.[5]

TABLE 9.2 *Empty Bayesian models: media reaction (posterior mean, standard deviations in parentheses, 95% credibility intervals in square brackets)*

	Single level	Two level, assembly	Two level, party	Cross-classified	Cross-classified + country dummies
Constant	2.10 (0.32)	2.07 (0.07)	2.18 (0.06)	2.11 (0.08)	2.53 (0.18)
	[2.05, 2.17]	[1.92, 2.21]	[2.05, 2.31]	[1.95, 2.26]	[2.18, 2.89]
Variance, MP level	1.95 (0.06)	1.67 (0.06)	1.71 (0.06)	1.63 (0.05)	1.63 (0.06)
	[1.83, 2.08]	[1.57,1.78]	[1.61, 1.83]	[1.44, 1.66]	[1.53, 1.74]
Variance, party level	—	—	0.27 (0.06)	0.06 (0.03)	0.06 (0.03)
			[0.17, 0.42]	[0.02, 0.13]	[0.02, 0.12]
Variance, assembly level	—	0.29 (0.06)	—	0.27 (0.06)	0.11 (0.04)
		[0.18, 0.44]		[0.16, 0.41]	[0.04–0.20]
ICC, party	—	—	0.14 (0.03)	0.03 (0.01)	0.03 (0.01)
			[0.08, 0.20]	[0.01, 0.06]	[0.00, 0.04]
ICC, assembly	—	0.15 (0.03)		0.13 (0.03)	0.06 (0.02)
		[0.10, 0.20]		[0.08, 0.20]	[0.01, 0.07]
Bayesian DIC	6657	6416	6483	6392	6386
N	1,898	1,898	1,898	1,898	1,898

TABLE 9.3 *Empty Bayesian models: media access (posterior mean, standard deviations in parentheses, 95% credibility intervals in square brackets)*

	Single level	Two level, assembly	Two level, party	Cross-classified	Cross-classified + country dummies
Constant	3.50 (0.02)	3.52 (0.05)	3.46 (0.05)	3.48 (0.05)	3.38 (0.12)
	[3.45, 3.55]	[3.43, 3.61]	[3.37, 3.55]	[3.38, 3.59]	[3.13, 3.61]
Variance, MP level	1.07 (0.03)	0.98 (0.03)	0.99 (0.03)	0.97 (0.03)	0.97 (0.03)
	[1.00, 1.15]	[0.92, 1.06]	[0.92, 1.05]	[0.90, 1.03]	[0.91, 1.05]
Variance, party level			0.09 (0.03)	0.04 (0.02)	0.02 (0.02)
			[0.05, 0.15]	[0.01, 0.10]	[0.00, 0.07]
Variance, assembly level		0.09 (0.03)		0.07 (0.02)	0.04 (0.02)
		[0.05, 0.15]		[0.03, 0.13]	[0.01, 0.08]
ICC, party			0.11 (0.03)	0.04 (0.02)	0.02 (0.02)
			[0.06, 0.17]	[0.01, 0.09]	[0.00, 0.07]
ICC, assembly		0.09 (0.02)		0.07 (0.02)	0.04 (0.02)
		[0.05, 0.13]		[0.03, 0.11]	[0.01, 0.08]
Bayesian DIC	5123	5019	5031	5007	5009
N	1,761	1,761	1,761	1,761	1,761

TABLE 9.4 *Explaining media reaction and media access (posterior mean, standard deviations in parentheses, 95% credibility intervals in square brackets. Changes in DIC with and without the variable in question in bold letters (a decline by more than 10 marked by *). Right-position, right-position—squared, and the country dummies are tested collectively)*

	Media reaction		Media access	
	MP variables only	Party and assembly variables added	MP variables only	Party and assembly variables added
Constant	2.55 (0.18)	2.43 (0.66)	3.42 (0.11)	2.83 (0.48)
	[2.20, 2.91]	[1.14, 3.74]	[3.21, 3.64]	[1.90, 3.76]
Female MP	−0.10 (0.07)	−0.10 (0.07)	−0.11 (0.06)	−0.13 (0.06)
	[−0.24, 0.04]	[−0.24, 0.05]	[−0.22, 0.01]	[−0.24, −0.01]
	0.4	0.2	1.6	2.6
Age MP	−0.02 (0.00)	−0.02 (0.00)	−0.01 (0.00)	−0.01 (0.00)
	[−0.02, −0.01]	[−0.03, −0.01]	[−0.01, −0.00]	[−0.01, −0.00]
	298.2*	296.8*	256.0*	257.2*
Experience MP	0.01 (0.01)	0.01 (0.01)	0.01 (0.00)	0.01 (0.00)
	[0.00, 0.02]	[0.00, 0.02]	[−0.00, 0.01]	[−0.00, 0.02]
	72.8*	69.3*	43.1*	43.3*
Elite MP	0.11 (0.10)	0.10 (0.10)	0.21 (0.08)	0.18 (0.08)
	[−0.09, 0.30]	[−0.09, 0.29]	[0.06, 0.35]	[0.03, 0.33]
	−0.7	−0.8	5.4	3.7
Generalist MP	0.14 (0.06)	0.14 (0.06)	0.08 (0.05)	0.08 (0.05)
	[0.01, 0.26]	[0.02, 0.27]	[−0.03, 0.18]	[−0.02, 0.19]
	71.0*	71.8*	54.6*	53.0*
Expansionist MP	0.02 (0.03)	0.01 (0.03)	−0.03 (0.02)	−0.03 (0.03)
	[−0.04, 0.08]	[−0.05, 0.07]	[−0.08 −0.01]	[−0.08, 0.02]
	105.0*	102.4*	91.8*	90.1*
Right-wing MP	0.01 (0.02)	−0.01 (0.02)	−0.02 (0.01)	−0.04 (0.02)
	[−0.02, 0.05]	[−0.05, 0.04]	[−0.04, 0.00]	[−0.07, −0.01]
	125.9*	125.6*	76.9*	74.9*
Right-wing MP^2	−0.01 (0.01)	−0.01 (0.01)	−0.01 (0.00)	−0.00 (0.00)
	[−0.02, −0.00]	[−0.02, −0.00)]	[−0.01, 0.00]	[−0.00, 0.00]
Incumbent party	—	−0.31 (0.08)	—	0.08 (0.06)
		[−0.47, −0.14]		[−0.04, 0.20]
		12.5*		−0.5
Party family (dummies)	—	66.9*	—	65.8*
Size assembly	—	0.0 (0.00)	—	0.00 (0.00)
		[−0.00, 0.00]		[-0.00, 0.00]
		−0.4		-0.8
Regional assembly	—	0.14 (0.22)	—	0.17 (0.13)
		[−0.31, 0.57]		[-0.09, 0.43]
		−1.01		-0.2
Country dummies	9.4	7.6	0.0	0.0
Variance, MP level	1.59 (0.06)	1.58 (0.06)	0.98 (0.04)	0.95 (0.04)
	[1.48, 1.71]	[1.47, 1.70]	[0.89, 1.02]	[0.88, 1.01]
Variance, assembly level	0.06 (0.03)	0.06 (0.04)	0.02 (0.01)	0.01 (0.01)
	[0.01, 0.14]	[0.01, −0.15]	[0.00, 0.05]	[0.00, 0.04]
Variance, party level	0.06 (0.03)	0.04 (0.03)	0.00 (0.01)	0.01 (0.01)
	[0.01, 0.13]	[0.01, 0.10]	[0.00, 0.04]	[0.00, 0.03]
Bayesian DIC	5639	5557	4382	4318

The second control variable, *age*, does generate consistent effects for both media reaction and media access. Younger MPs report that they look more to the media to inspire them than older MPs and they report higher success rates in getting coverage. Controlling for the other variables (including experience) the predicted media interactions decline by 1 (media reaction) to 2 (media access) per cent on average as the MPs get one year older.

As we can see from the table, more *experienced* MPs report stronger interaction with the media than their newer colleagues. One year of experience is expected to increase both media reaction and media access by roughly 1 per cent. This is entirely in line with our expectation.

The same applies to the agenda interactions of the *high profile* MPs (being party leaders, committee chairs, speakers, or mayors). We expected them to be more successful in getting into the media (access) but not to be particularly more reactive to media coverage. And this is what we find. The front-benchers do not appear particularly interested in media information (media reaction), but they do seem to have some persuasive powers over the gate-keepers in the media (media access). The expected increase in media success lies roughly between 3 and 33 per cent with a mean value of 18 per cent in the final analysis.

According to Table 9.4, MPs who are dealing with numerous issues—*generalists*—tend to be more interested in getting information from the media (media reaction) than single-issue MPs. That, too, is according to our expectation. The coefficient has a posterior mean of 0.14 in both models and a marginal posterior 95 per cent credibility interval between 0.1 and 0.26. Generalists also seem, again in line with our expectation, to be more successful in conveying their initiatives to the media. At 8 per cent in both models the difference is smaller.

As for MPs who are looking for new voters via acquiring new issues— we dubbed them *expansionists*—they appear strongly interested in information from the media (reaction). Being an expansionist increases the amount of reactivity with 1 or 2 per cent. We did not expect expansionism to have an effect on media access. Yet, we do find such an effect, and it is negative. Expansionists are less successful in persuading the media of the importance of their policy initiatives; they report on average 3 per cent less media access. This might indicate that MPs that need to enlarge their electorate are in a weaker political position. Perhaps they try to get their initiatives covered more indiscriminately which leads to more failures.

The *ideological* left–right position of an MP has an effect on his or her agenda interactions with the media as well. For media access, the evidence supports our expectation. We thought right-wing MPs would have less media access, and they do. In the elaborate model, a one-point shift to the right leads to a 4 per cent decrease in access. MPs at the far-right seem to struggle extra hard to get access to the media. Journalists and far-right MPs do not mingle. In terms of reactivity, we did not formulate any expectation about an ideology effect. Still, we see that, in the model with explanatory variables at higher levels, the effect of a right-wing position is negative. A one-point shift to the right on the eleven-point scale leads to 1 per cent fewer initiatives inspired by the media. That we control for squared ideology implies that the finding does not relate just to the extremity of the placement.

Turning to the party-level explanations, there is a strong tendency for opposition MPs to rely more on information from the media than government MPs. The effect is very substantial: MPs from the opposition report on average 31 per cent more media inspiration compared to government MPs. This finding supports earlier work, as well as our expectation, showing that there is a strong negative effect of incumbency on taking on media cues. The opposition uses the media, and the negative news in the media, as ammunition to tackle government.

Above we said that we would control for *party ideology*. We do so by using party family dummies. These show that party ideology, on top of MP ideology, affects media interaction. We did not expect to find such effects. Though not shown here, a more careful scrutiny of the dummy variables, shows that especially ethnic and regionalist parties stand out with larger values on both dependent variables. Ethnic and regionalist parties are more often inspired by the media and more often covered by the media.

On the assembly level, none of the two suggested characteristics receives support. We fail to find any visible effects of either the *size* or the type of the assembly (*regional* or national). It is not the case that smaller parliaments on average lead to more media reaction or more media access for individual members. And, regional MPs and national MPs report similar levels of agenda interactions with the media.

Finally, the variables on the lower levels of MP, party, and assembly soak up all *country* effects. While we still found considerable differences between the countries in Figure 9.2, inter-country variation no longer matters when all lower-level variables are taken into account; the country dummies do not yield effects. The initial country differences, hence, were due to composition effects and not to true differences between the countries.

9.7 CONCLUSION

This chapter has dealt with the agenda relationship between MPs and the media seen through the lens of the MPs themselves. We have studied how they describe their own and the media's role as agenda-setters. MPs provide both a short and long answer to the question 'Who is leading the parliamentary agenda interactions?' Their short answer, as reflected in Figure 9.1, simply is 'We do, not the media'. A high number of MPs deny any media reactivity whatsoever, even though many of them claim to succeed in presenting their own initiatives to the media. The longer answer, which we have focused on here, starts with 'It depends'. Our empirical analysis has identified divergences not only between MPs but also between parties, assemblies, and countries.

In accordance with most of the literature, we find that generalist MPs interact more with the media than specialist MPs; the young more than the old; and the experienced more than the inexperienced. The former get more *from* the media and they get more *in* the media. It is interesting to see that these three key predictors on the individual level—age, experience, and specialization—affect reactivity and access in the same way. Although the individual-level correlation between reaction and access is low, the data suggest the existence of two distinct types of MPs. Media savvy MPs who play according to the media rules, draw ideas from the media and are prominently present in the media, on the one hand. On the other hand, there are MPs who are isolated from the media: they ignore the media as a source of information and are ignored by the media in return. Apart from that, backbenchers, right-wing, and female MPs seem to have a harder time getting past the media gates. Expansionist MPs who look beyond single issues and their loyal group of voters, take more cues from the media but they feel less successful in gaining access to the media.

Moving to higher-level explanations, we find that parties make a difference. Our study strongly supports previous studies which find that government responsibility impairs media reaction. Much of the variation at the assembly level—just like the variation at the country level—tends to vaporize when taking into account variation at the MP level. Again, variation at the higher levels seems to be caused mainly by variation in composition at the lower levels.

Finally, what do our findings imply for the quality of representation? The evidence suggests that there are MPs who are at least a bit responsive to media cues. If we simply accept what MPs are saying, around one seventh of the things that happen in the fifteen countries' parliaments—or at least that what happens there as a consequence of private member initiatives—is related to the issues of the day. A good deal of MPs, though not always, regularly legislate and debate about current issues and search for a connection with the public debate outside of parliament. We are not claiming that trying to be responsive by following the media is always a good thing—it may also lead to shallow and populist policies—but some degree of overlap between what the people in the street talk about (which is what is in the media) and what happens in parliament is definitely healthy for democracy. But the best news sits probably at the other side of the equation. Unless MPs largely overestimate their own success, which is not entirely impossible, media are quite receptive to MPs' parliamentary action. About half of the things MPs personally undertake in parliament get some kind of media coverage. This is a remarkable finding. It implies that much action of legislators does get reported and conveyed to the public. It counters the many pessimistic accounts of the democratic quality and adequacy of media coverage. In contrast to most media critics' interpretations institutional politics still scores high on the media agenda.

NOTES

1. A supplementary analysis revealed problems with overdispersion in Poisson models. We know that the advantages of binomial regression models in single-level analyses are not directly transferrable to multilevel models (Rabe-Hesketh and Skrondal, 2012: 712). Negative binominal models, which can be used in single-level analyses in case of overdispersion, cannot be used automatically in a multilevel model.
2. In the analysis all the continuous variables are grand-mean centred.
3. Bayesian statistics assumes a prior distribution which describes information and uncertainty before considering the data. The posterior distribution expresses our new knowledge after having considered the information in the data. The updating, which occurs by means of Bayes' theorem, ensures that the posterior distribution is a combination of our initial belief contained in the prior and the new information provided by the data. An informative prior, that is, a peaked distribution with a small variance, will strongly influence the posterior. However, when the priors are vague and uninformative and sample size is large, the posterior will be dominated by the data. MLwiN, which is the statistical software we use here, assumes uninformative priors by default (see Brown 2012). In deriving the posterior we employ MCMC methods (more specifically the Gibbs sampler), which represent a class of algorithms for sampling from complex posterior distributions, approximating their true shape. The simulated distribution can then be used to produce point estimates, the latter called central credibility intervals. The intervals are determined from the 2.5th to the 97.5th percentile of the observed estimates. We also obtain standard deviations which can be interpreted as standard errors (Hox 2012: 277). To compare models and to guide the variable selection we use the Deviance Information Criterion (DIC), which is a generalization of the more familiar Akaike's Information Criterion (AIC). Finding the DIC in MCMC is trivial since it does not, in contrast to the AIC and BIC, require maximization over the parameter space. DIC reflects the trade-off between model fit and model complexity. Smaller values indicate better models. Apart from increasing the number of chains from 5,000 (after the burn-in) to 50,000, the settings are those used by MLwiN as default, including the burn-in-period (500 iterations) and the prior distributions. Starting values have been taken from preceding IGLS analyses. Finally, since an

accepted practice for how to use scaling weights in MLM models with more than two levels is not advanced yet, we follow the advice given by Carle (2009: 8) and fit the different models using unweighted data.

4. The correlation between the natural logarithms of these variables, which are used in the regression analysis below, is even lower: 0.05.

5. Note that, since the results in this case are not very strong as the 95 per cent interval is close to overlapping with zero, we have tried to specify the gender effect in terms of a varying slope to account for causal heterogeneity. This did not, however, improve model fit.

REFERENCES

Althaus, S. (2003), 'When News Norms Collide, Follow the Lead: New Evidence for Press Independence', *Political Communication*, 20: 381–414.

Altheide, D. and R. Snow (1979), *Media Logic*. Beverly Hills: Sage.

Brants, K., C. De Vreese, J. Möller et al. (2010), 'The Real Spiral of Cynicism? Symbiosis and Mistrust between Politicians and Journalists', *International Journal of Press/Politics*, 15 (1): 25–40.

Brown, W. J. (2012), *MCMC Estimation in MLwiN. Version 2.25*. Bristol: Centre for Multilevel Modelling, University of Bristol.

Carey, J. M. and M. S. Shugart (1995), 'Incentives to Cultivate a Personal Vote: A Rank Ordering of Electoral Formulas', *Electoral Studies*, 14 (4): 417–39.

Carle, A. C. (2009), 'Fitting Multilevel Models in Complex Survey Data with Design Weights: Recommendations', *BMC Medical Research Methodology*, 49 (9): 1–13.

Cook, T. (2005), *Governing with the News: The News Media as a Political Institution*. 2nd edn. Chicago: Chicago University Press.

De Swert, K. and S. Walgrave (2002), 'De kanseliersbonus in de Vlaamse pers: Een onderzoek naar regering en oppositie in drie Vlaamse kranten (1991–2000)', *Tijdschrift voor Sociologie*, 23, (3–4): 371–403.

Elmelund-Præstekær, C., D. Hopman, and A. S. Nørgaard (2011), 'Does Mediatization Change MP–media Interaction and MP Attitudes toward the Media? Evidence from a Longitudinal Study of Danish MPs', *Press/Politics*, 16: 382–403.

Entman, R. M. (2003), 'Cascading Activation: Contesting the White House's Frame after 9/11', *Political Communication*, 20 (4): 415–32.

Gelman, A. and J. Hill (2007), *Data Analysis Using Regression and Multilevel/Hierarchical Models*. Cambridge: Cambridge University Press.

Gidengil, E. and J. Everitt (2003), 'Talking Tough: Gender and Reported Speech in Campaign News Coverage', *Political Communication*, 20: 209–32.

Green-Pedersen, C. and R. Stubager (2010), 'The Political Conditionality of Mass Media Influence: When Do Parties Follow Mass Media Attention?' *British Journal of Political Science*, 40: 663–77.

Hamaker, E. and I. Klugist (2011), 'Bayesian Estimation of Multilevel Models', in *Handbook of Advanced Multilevel Analysis*. New York: Routledge.

Hox, J. (2012), *Multilevel Analysis: Techniques and Applications*. New York: Routledge.

Jackman, S. (2007), *Bayesian Analysis for the Social Sciences*. Chichester: Wiley.

Kingdon, J. W. (1984), *Agendas, Alternatives and Public Policies*. New York: Harper Collins.

Lunn, D., C. Jackson, N. Best et al. (2013), *The BUGS Book: A Practical Introduction to Bayesian Analysis*. Boca Raton: CRC Press.

Maurer, P. (2011), 'Explaining Perceived Media Influence in Politics: An Analysis of the Interplay of Context and Attitudes in Four European Democracies', *Publizistik*, 56: 27–50.

Midtbø, T. (2011), 'Explaining Media Attention for Norwegian MPs: A New Modelling Approach', *Scandinavian Political Studies*, 34 (3): 226–49.

Norris, P., J. Curtice, D. Sanders et al. (1999), *On Message: Communicating the Campaign*. London: Sage.

Rabe-Hesketh, S. and A. Skrondal (2012), *Multilevel and Longitudinal Modeling Using Stata, ii: Categorical Responses, Counts, and Survival*. College Station: Stata Press.

Sellers, P. (2010), *Cycles of Spin: Strategic Communication in the US Congress*. Cambridge: Cambridge University Press.

Sellers, P. J. and B. N. Schaffner (2007), 'Winning Coverage in the US Senate', *Political Communication*, 24: 377–91.

Soroka, S. (2002a), *Agenda-settting Dynamics in Canada*. Vancouver: UBC Press.

—— (2002b), 'Issue Attributes and Agenda-setting by Media, the Public, and Policymakers in Canada', *International Journal of Public Opinion Research*, 14 (3): 264–85.

—— (2006), 'Good News and Bad News: Asymmetric Responses to Economic Information', *Journal of Politics*, 68 (2): 372–85.

Strömback, J. (2008), 'Four Phases of Mediatization: An Analysis of the Mediatization of Politics', *International Journal of Press/Politics*, 13 (3): 228–46.

Tetlock, P. E. (2005), *Expert Political Judgment: How Good Is It? How Can We Know?* Princeton, NJ: Princeton University Press.

Thesen, G. (2011), *Attack and Defend: Explaining Party Responses to News*. Aarhus: Politica.

Tresch, A. (2009), 'Politicians in the Media. Determinants of Legislators' Presence and Prominence in Swiss Newspapers', *International Journal of Press/Politics*, 14 (1): 67–90.

Van Aelst, P., B. Maddens, J. Noppe et al. (2008), 'Politicians in the News: Media or Party Logic? Media Attention and Electoral Success in the Belgian Election Campaign of 2003', *European Journal of Communication*, 23 (2): 193–210.

—— A. Shehata, and A. Van Dalen (2010), 'Members of Parliament, Equal Competitors for Media Attention? An Analysis of Personal Contacts between MPs and Political Journalists in Five European Countries', *Political Communication*, 27 (3): 310–25.

—— and S. Walgrave (2011), 'Minimal or Massive? The Political Agenda-setting Power of the Mass Media according to Different Methods', *International Journal of Press/Politics*, 16 (3): 295–316.

Van Dalen, A. and P. Van Aelst (2012), 'Political Journalists: Covering Politics in the Democratic Corporatist Media System', in D. Weaver and L. Willnat (eds.), *The Global Journalist in the 21st Century*. New York: Routledge.

Van Dalen, A. and P. Van Aelst (2013), 'The Media as Political Agenda-setter in Comparative Perspective: Journalists Perceptions of Media Power in Eight West-European Countries', *West-European Politics*, 37 (1): 42–64.

Van Noije, L., J. Kleinnijenhuis, and D. Oegema (2008), 'Loss of Parliamentary Control Due to Mediatization and Europeanization: A Longitudinal and Cross-sectional Analysis of Agenda-building in the United Kingdom and the Netherlands', *British Journal of Political Science*, 38 (3): 455–78.

Viegenthart, R., H. Boomgaarden, and J. Van Spanje (2012), 'Anti-immigrant Party Support and Media Visibility: A Cross-party, Over-time Perspective', *Journal of Elections, Public Opinion and Parties*, 3: 315–58.

—— and S. Walgrave (2008), 'The Contingency of Intermedia Agenda-setting: A Longitudinal Study in Belgium', *Journalism and Mass Communication Quarterly*, 85 (4): 860–77.

—— (2011), 'Content Matters: The Dynamics of Parliamentary Questioning in Belgium and Denmark', *Comparative Political Studies*, 44 (8): 1031–59.

Walgrave, S. (2008), 'Again the Almighty Mass Media: A Subjective Assessment of the Media's Political Agenda-setting Power by Politicians and Journalists in Belgium', *Political Communication*, 25 (4): 445–59.

—— K. De Swert (2002), 'Does News Content Matter? The Contribution of the News Media in the Making of the Issues of the Vlaams Blok', *Ethical Perspectives*, 9 (4): 249–75.

—— S. Soroka, and M. Nuytemans (2008), 'The Mass Media's Political Agenda-setting Power: A Longitudinal Analysis of Media, Parliament and Government in Belgium (1993–2000)', *Comparative Political Studies*, 41 (6): 814–36.

Wolfsfeld, G. and T. Sheafer (2006), 'Competing Actors and the Construction of Political News: The Contest over Waves in Israel', *Political Communication*, 23 (3): 333–54.

Wood, D. and J. Peake (1998), 'The Dynamics of Foreign Policy Agenda-setting', *American Political Science Review*, 92 (1): 173–83.

Career Patterns in Multilevel Systems

Jean-Benoit Pilet, Filippo Tronconi, Pablo Oñate, and Luca Verzichelli

10.1 INTRODUCTION

Politicians are not different from any other professionals. Politics can be a passion, or a vocation, but for many of its practitioners it is also a job. Therefore, they do not see it as a temporary, short-term occupation. Politicians want to stay in politics, which means that they must make sure that they will be re-elected. And if they are ambitious (Schlesinger 1966), they want to rise up. They want to climb the ladder of political offices, eventually to its apex, whatever this apex could be for different individuals, in different countries and political systems.

That is why it is quite interesting to study the careers of politicians in established democracies (see Best and Cotta 2000; Cotta and Best 2007; Francis and Kenny 2000; Hibbing 1991; Matthews 1985; Moncrief and Thompson 1992). Within this field of research, a new topic of interest has recently developed: the organization of political careers across levels. In Europe in particular, state structures have been profoundly modified in recent decades by two concurring phenomena. Several countries have transformed their political institutions to create or to reinforce a regional level of governance: with quite a broad range of institutional arrangements, Spain, Belgium, Italy, the United Kingdom, and France are good examples of this trend. On the other hand and at the same time, the European integration and the direct election of the European Parliament has opened up new career possibilities for politicians. The direct consequence of these two changes is that most European countries can now be referred to as 'multilevel polities' (Marks and Hooghe 2001).

These evolutions are obviously very relevant for politicians' careers. Career patterns have been significantly modified (Borchert 2011; Borchert and Stolz 2011). The unidirectional career model according to which politicians climb step by step the ladder of politics from the local to the national level is no longer necessarily predominant. Other patterns have emerged in countries where state level and sub-state/regional level institutions co-exist. Some MPs still follow the unidirectional model, while others specialize in one level, either at the sub-state or the national level. Finally, there are also MPs hopping back and forth from one level to the other. This bi-directional pattern is particularly relevant within the EU context. The European scenario seems to be more and more important in political life, since broader skills in EU-related policies are needed for aspirant policymakers. However, the relative impact of the European parliament and the attractiveness of national (or sub-national) offices determine a high frequency of 'down-stream' steps from Europe to the national parliament. The limited importance of the European parliament as destination of a unidirectional and supra-national political career is also confirmed by attitudinal surveys: according to Hubé and Verzichelli (2012), the rate of national politicians who see a fully European perspective in their future is indeed rather limited.

This chapter is clearly positioned within this new field of research. We will look at political careers in legislatures, not taking into account politicians covering purely executive offices or other kinds of institutional appointments. Our first goal is to detect the dominant career patterns that can be observed among national and regional MPs in the multilevel countries covered in the PARTIREP survey (Austria, Belgium, France, Germany, Italy, Spain, and the United Kingdom). This first analysis can be an interesting complement to the significant body of recent publications dealing with changing patterns of political careers in multilevel systems (see, in particular, Stolz 2003; Borchert and Stolz 2011). Existing studies are mostly covering the US and Canadian cases, with a few extensions to some European countries (Germany, UK, Spain). With the PARTIREP data we can cover several countries in a comparative way.

But this chapter also wants to go beyond the mere identification of career trajectories of representative politicians across levels in European multilevel systems. As a matter of fact, these career patterns may have consequences on political representation. Members of parliament are meant to be representatives of the polity in which they have been elected. National MPs are representatives of the national state and are expected to serve its interests. Regional MPs are representatives of the region, and are expected to serve its interests. But when a politician moves throughout his/her career from one level to the other, sometimes several times, the question arises whether he or she is only considering the interest of the level at which he or she is elected? Having been at another level before might affect the choice made in this respect and members of parliament might carry with them the interest of the polity they were previously representing.

The answers to this question clearly depend on the theoretical perspective one adopts. From an institutionalist perspective, MPs' attitudes and behaviours are shaped by institutions. Therefore, what matters is for what institution the MP is elected, where he or she sits. Career trajectories have then no or little influence. Yet from a more sociological perspective, the answer would be different. MPs can in this perspective also be expected to be influenced by their past experiences. Socialization is then a key factor in shaping MPs attitudes and behaviours. As a consequence, career trajectories matter. MPs that have been previously serving as elected officials at another level might think and act differently from those who have always been active at the same level of government because they carry with them their past experiences.

Therefore, the second and more analytical goal of this chapter will be to explore this issue, to discuss the possible consequences of career trajectories on MPs attitudes and behaviours. This topic has already been covered in the US literature on political careers but has not be extended to multilevel career patterns (see Hibbing 1999 for a first review) and, particularly, to the European experiences. For assessing the impact of the careers on political representation, we will look at three elements: the MPs views on decentralization, the way in which they conceive their role in defending and promoting the territorial interests of the region or country they represent (the focus of representation), and their relations with MPs from other levels. We will evaluate whether these attitudes are more related to the assembly where the MP is sitting (according to an institutionalist perspective) or by career trajectories (according to the socialization perspective).

10.2 IDENTIFYING CAREER PATTERNS IN MULTILEVEL SYSTEMS

How politicians move throughout the different levels of a national institutional system over the time of their career is a topic that has been addressed for some years now. The scholars involved in such a discussion have, for a long time, identified what is often called the 'political ladder', a ladder that most politicians start climbing at the local level to move up, step by step, to the sub-national level and then to the national level. Moreover, within the same level, politicians also move steadily from more junior positions (backbencher, parliamentary leader, junior minister) to upper, more prestigious ones (frontbencher, member of the cabinet, leader of the executive). In order to disentangle such a complicated puzzle, different labels and concepts have been used by different scholars. Hibbing (1999) talks of a unidirectional career model, with all politicians looking in the same direction and trying to move (or to climb) towards it. Gaxie (1993) uses the metaphor of a pyramid. Squire (1988), on the other hand, stresses the differences between 'springboard legislatures', that are a stepping stone to other, more prestigious, positions, and 'career legislatures' in which most politicians stay for their whole career. But the basic idea has been the same in most of the analyses: politicians follow all the same pattern that pictures the hierarchy of power and prestige existing informally as well as formally between levels of power, as well as between institutions.

Yet, in recent years, comparative studies coordinated by Borchert and Stolz (2011) have questioned the validity of this unidirectional model of political careers. In several countries, layers of government have been added in the last decades. The hierarchy between them has been blurred by the professionalization of sub-national institutions, as well as by the creation of supranational elected institutions, like the European parliament. Trying to understand to what extent and how these changes may have affected career patterns, Stolz (2003) first analysed the proportion of members of national and regional parliaments in Belgium, Switzerland, Germany, the United States, Spain, Canada, Australia, Austria, and Italy that have been previously serving at another level. He clearly showed that the unidirectional career model heading towards the national level was not the only one that could be identified. In Canada, for instance, careers are distinct at the provincial and federal levels with little moves between the two. In newly regionalized entities with a strong identity like Scotland and Flanders, many politicians have left the national level to settle at the sub-state levels, and in others like Wallonia or the Spanish Autonomous Communities politicians were constantly 'hopping' from one level to another.[1] More recently, Stolz has, along with Borchert, coordinated a special issue of *Regional and Federal Studies* on career patterns in multilevel states (see Borchert and Stolz 2011). Comparing career patterns in Germany, Spain, the United Kingdom, the United States, Brazil, Austria, Australia, and Canada, they identified three career models: the unidirectional, the alternative, and the integrated models (Borchert 2011). The unidirectional model is the classical model of politicians moving steadily up the ladder, from the local to the sub-national and then to the national level. The alternative career model supposes the existence of two distinct political arenas with politicians making their career at one level only. Moves between levels are rather rare. Finally, in the integrated career model, politicians move easily from one level to the other. They travel from the regional to the national level back and forth following their ambition as well as the opportunities that are offered and that may vary over time. The various levels are conceived as part of an integrated political playing field.

This idea of co-existing career patterns is tested in this chapter for the seven multilevel systems covered by the PARTIREP survey (Austria, Belgium, France, Germany, Italy, Spain, and the United Kingdom). For each of them, we will in this chapter refer to the national/federal assemblies as 'national' and to the sub-national representative assemblies (Länder, autonomous communities, and so on) as 'regional' (see Table 10.1). In the British case, MPs elected from English constituencies have been filtered out from the dataset,

TABLE 10.1 *Description of the national and regional assemblies in the seven countries*

Country	National assembly	Regional entities
Austria	Nationalrat	Länder
Belgium	Chamber of representatives and Senate	Regions and communities
France	Assemblée nationale	Regions
Germany	Bundestag	Länder
Italy	Camera dei deputati and Senato	Regions
Spain	Congreso de los Diputados and Senado	Autonomous communities
UK*	House of Commons	Devolved assemblies in Wales, Scotland, and Northern Ireland

* In the UK, MPs elected in England have been excluded from all the analyses. For Spain, only members of Congreso de los Diputados were taken into account.

as they do not have any regional counterpart, differently from MPs elected in Scotland, Wales, and Northern Ireland.

The common denominator of all these regional entities lies in their directly elected assemblies. All regions also have an executive body somehow linked to the regional parliament by means of explicit or implicit confidence. Beyond this common trait, there are large differences in the size, institutional autonomy scope of governance and of these bodies. Belgium is probably the most advanced example of devolution of powers, and this is particularly true in the Flemish case, which decided to concentrate under a single institution the powers of the region and the linguistic community. French regions, on the other hand, are traditionally described as weak institutions, with limited fiscal autonomy and no legislative powers. There are also important variations within the status of individual sub-national institutions within each state (asymmetrical federalism), with some regions enjoying special—usually greater—authority compared to the others.

The PARTIREP survey includes biographical information on legislators in the countries covered, among which there is the indication of whether the parliamentarian has previously served at another level of power (always considering only offices in legislatures, leaving aside, therefore, appointed offices in the executives). On the basis of that information, we can confirm that we find different career trajectories (see Table 10.2). Interestingly enough, the majority of our respondents have only been active at one level. In our population, 32 per cent are national MPs who had only served at the national level. And another 56 per cent are regional legislators who have never been active at the upper level. It means that only 11.6 per cent of our respondents are MPs that have moved from one level to the other, regardless of the direction of their career moves.

For reasons of stinginess and consistency with the other chapters of the volume, we decided here to rely only on the data available in the survey. We

TABLE 10.2 *Types of careers in multilevel systems*

	No previous experience at the other level	Previous experience at the other level	Total	% of MPs with multilevel careers
National parliaments	380	93	473	19.7
Regional parliaments	659	43	702	6.1
Total	1,039	136	1,175	11.6

will therefore not build a detailed typology of representatives, since we have to differentiate between three main categories of MPs: the first category is composed of MPs who are active at just one level (with a sub-classification between pure regional and pure national representatives). The second group is composed of those who follow the traditional ladder of politics (national MPs with an experience of regional representative), and, the third group consists of those going down to the sub-national level (regional MPs who have previously been elected at national level). We have not collected additional data that could, for instance, help us to distinguish between legislators who have moved only once between levels, and those that are hopping from one level to the other on a regular basis.

A closer look at this distribution reveals a lot of variation among country representations (Table 10.3). The highest figure for level-hoppers (regional MPs) is to be found in Belgium (22 per cent). Actually, slightly less than half of regional MPs with a national background included in our sample have been interviewed in Belgium. Overall, however, the figures concerning the level-hoppers remain rather limited in all the countries (from 2 per cent of UK to 21 per cent of Belgium). Moreover, focusing on the minority of level-hoppers, the expected 'linear and unidirectional' career model (that is to say, from a regional to the national assembly) remains the most likely pattern of parliamentary hopping, since the grand mean (19.7 per cent) is more than three times higher than the mean of those who leave the national to enter the regional assembly. The difference would be much more evident if we excluded the Belgian case which, once again, looks particularly relevant in this respect. Belgium is indeed the only case showing a higher rate of hoppers from the national to the sub-national arena.

The highest rate of national MPs with a previous regional experience is to be found in France (42 per cent). One should note that no regional MPs have a national background in France and Germany, two countries with a completely different institutional setting. Almost no level crossing can be noted in the UK also: only one interviewee has passed from the national to the regional level, and there are no national MPs with regional experience. However, this does not surprise very much, since there are only two regional assemblies, and they are recently established, in the UK.

TABLE 10.3 *Types of career by country*

	Regional MPs			National MPs		
	No national experience	National experience	% of reg. MPs with nat. experience	No regional experience	Regional experience	% of nat. MPs with reg. experience
AUT	163	9	5.2	44	11	20.0
BEL	73	20	21.5	57	13	18.6
FRA	37	0	0.0	29	21	42.0
GER	145	0	0.0	107	23	17.7
ITA	79	3	3.7	36	9	20.0
SPA	118	10	7.8	88	16	15.4
UK	44	1	2.2	19	0	0.0
Total	659	43	6.1	380	93	19.7

Overall, we can make a distinction across countries where political careers at different territorial levels are clearly isolated from each other, and countries where they are relatively more integrated, meaning that moves from one level to the other are frequent, or at least conceivable. In our sample, only the UK fits the first type, while in all the other countries varying shares of MPs have taken office at a legislature at both levels. Within the group of integrated careers, a further distinction can be made, at least in theory, between (1) countries where the prevalent career pattern follows the traditional regional to national route, (2) countries where the opposite national to regional route is present, and (3) countries where career trajectories are equally distributed between the two directions. While we do not have here examples of the second type,[2] at least two countries (France and Germany), and possibly a two more (Austria and Italy) belong to the first group, while Belgium is the most unambiguous example of the third type, with Spain lying somewhere in-between.

10.3 CAREER PATTERNS AND MPS ATTITUDES AND ROLES

For understanding career choices and career patterns of politicians the central idea is that they define their career trajectories by taking into account which offices are available, how attractive these offices are, and how accessible they are to them (Borchert 2011). These three A's (availability, attractiveness, and accessibility) are first conditioned by the institutional context (Borchert 2011). In particular, the number of institutions at different levels defines the number of positions available. The relative power of each political entity determines the attractiveness of the different positions, for which the accessibility is also linked to a system of opportunities that can be regulated at a different territorial level. The degree of competition will be therefore directly proportional to the effective political power of the institutional entities.

Next to the institutions, two other elements have been shown to be important in explaining the changes of career patterns: political parties and the attitudes of legislators themselves. First of all, parties are central since they are the main gatekeepers of political careers (Cotta and Best 2007; Norris 1997). And, as demonstrated by Detterbeck, political parties in multilevel systems have been able to adapt to the multilayered architecture of the state and to organize efficiently the allocation of resources, including human resources, across levels (Detterbeck 2012, see also Fabre 2008). Parties have a direct capacity to influence the career of politicians across levels by either filtering the demands of those who would like to move to another level of power, or by forcing politicians to move to another level when it is in the best interest of the party. The capacity of parties to organize these moves across levels may vary from one country to another, depending in particular on their organizational strength, but the role of parties always remain crucial. In addition, individual politicians, though constrained by institutions and parties, have also their own ambitions and preferences that affect their career trajectories (see Herrick 2001). They may be willing to move to another level, or be reluctant to do so, because of their views on how the state should be organized. Legislators defending more autonomy for the region may, for example, be expected to be more likely to pursue ambitions to move to regional parliaments than MPs with more interest in federal/national politics.

These partisan and individual elements will not be taken into account in our analysis. The goal of this chapter is not to provide a (new) test of the factors driving career patterns in multilevel polities. Rather, we are interested in testing hypotheses about the link between types of career and attitudinal positions of representatives. We want to understand how career trajectories may be related to what legislators think (attitudes and beliefs) and to how they act (behaviours) in parliament and within the political system.

Surprisingly enough, the literature on these issues is not very well consolidated, especially outside the US. Therefore, a first way to address this topic is to go back to the traditional theories of representation, and more particularly of how the context in which legislators operate may be associated with how they conceive their role and function. The literature has widely acknowledged that the context in which legislators operate, and the events they are going through during their career affect how MPs see themselves and how they conceive their role of parliamentarians (Eulau and Wahlke 1978). In line with this approach, one can expect that career trajectories would also be elements that can be correlated to MPs' perceptions of themselves. We can examine whether moves across levels change the focus of representation of

MPs (Eulau and Karp 1977) and their relations to various principals. In particular, we are interested to see whether having been active at various levels of power makes a difference in who MPs claim to represent in terms of territory. In any political system MPs face a dilemma between representing the entire country or only their constituency (Fenno 1978). In multilevel systems, the representation of the sub-national entities adds up to that dilemma. On that basis, we will try to evaluate how MPs deal with these three foci of representation, and examine whether career moves across levels make a difference.

Another crucial dilemma every MP faces is the loyalty towards his or her party. This question has been addressed in the literature by examining how MPs would react when the position of their party differs from the position of the MP, or of his or her electorate (see Converse and Pierce 1979; Thomassen and Schmitt 1999). For us here the dilemma is when the position held by the national and by the regional parties differs. How do MPs react in such a situation? And do career patterns have an influence on their attitude? Logically, one would expect MPs to follow the position of the party at the level where he or she is. Yet, when one has moved, and would perhaps again move in the future across levels, the dilemma becomes even stronger.

Career trajectories are expected to make a difference in the attitudes of MPs, on their conception of their parliamentary role, as well as on their loyalty towards the different levels of power at which their party operate. Stemming from that, the next question is whether the presence of legislators with different career trajectories in multilevel countries has an influence on the institutions in which they serve, and more generally on the political system of the country itself. The underlying idea is that 'legislative institutions change along with the types of people attracted to serve in them' (Matthews 1985: 43). Borchert (2011) has argued that politicians who have crossed the boundaries between levels of government may have a positive impact on the functioning of the system. They are said to create links between layers of government, and thus to facilitate the functioning of the multilevel system. On the contrary, when the national and the sub-national levels are separate arenas, when careers are organized separately at each level, when two distinct political classes emerge, they cannot link across levels (Borchert 2011). MPs who have been elected at different levels throughout their career would then be expected to perform a function of vertical linkage in multilevel systems.

Our survey allows us a deeper exploration of one fundamental element of the idea of vertical linkage, which is the degree of continuity between service as a member of the national legislature and that of a member of regional assemblies. Logically we would expect MPs that have been previously active at another level of power to have maintained relationships with their former colleagues, and thus to have more contacts with them. The survey has asked members of national assemblies whether they have good contacts with members of regional parliaments, and to explain the purpose of these contacts.

The same question has been asked of members of regional parliaments regarding their relations with national MPs.

10.4 CAREER PATTERNS AND MPS ATTITUDES AND ROLES: EMPIRICAL TEST

The first element we would like to look at are attitudes of MPs towards the territorial organization of their country. In several European countries there is an ongoing discussion about the degree in which powers need to be (further) devolved to the sub-state level. We can expect members of regional parliaments to be more in favour of giving more powers to that level. Attitudes would then be determined by the level at which an MP is serving at this moment. Yet having served at another level might also have socialized MPs towards another attitude. In Figure10.1 we map the responses to the question whether all the powers in the country should be at the national or at the regional level, measured with a scale ranging from 0 (the regions) to 10 (the national state). The results are very straightforward: there are systematic differences between MPs belonging to different levels, regardless of their career type (mono-level or multilevel). That is consistent with the 'null hypothesis' arguing that the career does not impact on the attitudes of MPs. It is the current position and not the career history that shapes the view on the territorial organization of the country.

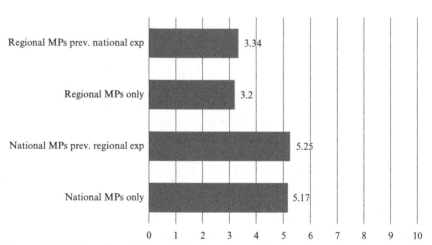

FIGURE 10.1 Views about the extent of regionalization (*)

(*). 0: more power to the regions—10: more power to the state. N = 1,058.

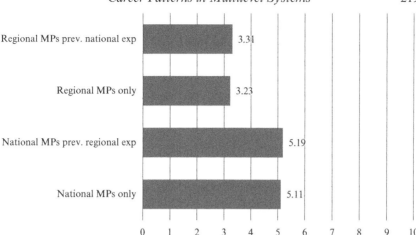

FIGURE 10.2 Views about the extent of regionalization among newly elected members of parliament (only MPs serving for their first term in this assembly) (*)

(*). 0: more power to the regions—10: more power to the state. N = 489.

We could argue that this happens because of a long socialization to the institutional environment in which the MPs work. If this is the case, we should find hints of a different pattern at least among *newbies*. That is to say, national MPs with a recent experience in regional assemblies should be more favourable to the issue of devolution. This is, however, not the case (see Figure 10.2). Once again, there is no significant difference in the preferences about distribution of powers within the group of newcomer national MPs.

The second element at which we look is the focus of representation. MPs in the survey were asked to rate how important it was to them to represent the collective interests of different territorial levels, among which is the regional one. Figure 10.3 reports the average results, along a scale ranging from 1 ('of no importance') to 7 ('of great importance'), comparing MPs again according to their career type. And here also the strongest differences are those between regional and national representatives, while differences within these groups are not substantial. In other words, where you are currently sitting is much more important than where you come from (that is, if you served in a different level before).

As we did in the previous analysis, we controlled for the 'socialization' variable, searching for possible differences in the perceptions and opinions of MPs at their first legislative term. Figure 10.4 shows, somewhat surprisingly, that regional MPs who have previously served in the national parliament are the most concerned about regional interests,[3] and national MPs with a previous experience as representatives at sub-national level are slightly more

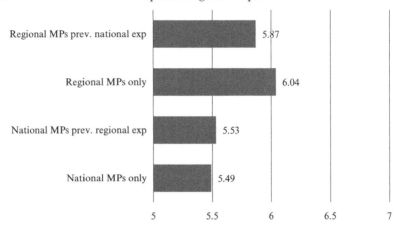

FIGURE 10.3 The importance of promoting the collective interests of the region (*)

(*). 1: of no importance—7: of great importance. N = 939.

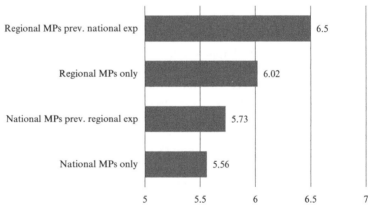

FIGURE 10.4 The importance of promoting the collective interests of the region (*) (newly elected MPs only)

(*). 1: of no importance—7: of great importance. Newly elected MPs only. N = 438.

concerned than regional MPs who only served at this level. These peculiarities notwithstanding, the overall pattern confirms our previous findings, that is, differences between levels of governments are sharper than differences between political career types.

Another interesting feature is the linkage between levels provided by contacts between members of different parliaments. The expectation is that national MPs who have served at the regional level have more contacts in regional parliaments, and use these contacts to coordinate policies of regional interest. The same should hold in the opposite direction for regional MPs

TABLE 10.4 *Contacts with regional/national MPs to coordinate regional and national policies*

	MPs from the same party %			MPs from other parties %		
	Yes	No	N	Yes	No	N
National MPs only	84.4	15.6	269	39.0	61.0	172
National MPs prev. regional exp	81.8	18.2	66	59.5	40.5	42
Regional MPs only	79.4	20.6	514	33.9	66.1	239
Regional MPs prev. national exp	71.9	28.1	32	39.1	60.9	23

with an experience at the national level. We have asked the MPs in the survey whether there are members of the national parliament or of regional parliaments with whom they have very good contacts, both within their own party and of other parties. And subsequently they were asked to indicate whether these contacts had been helpful for—among others—the coordination of national and regional policies. The figures in Table 10.4 give the percentages of MPs who say that they have contacts that have been useful for coordinating policies at two levels of governance. These contacts are relatively important, and appear to be very intense between members of the same political parties. Crossing both the level of governance and the party lines is less likely to happen, except for national MPs with a previous experience at the regional level. This is the only indication here that the career pattern can have an effect. Having been at the regional level seems to produce some inter-party relationships that can be used for building bridges between the levels.

So far we have not found much evidence for career patterns having an effect on the positions and attitudes of MPs, except indeed for the measure of contacts between national MPs and regional MPs that are more frequent for national MPs who have served at the regional level. Before summarizing and confirming these findings in a multivariate way, we also look at career perspectives (see Table 10.5). We asked the respondents in the survey what their expectations for their future positions were. We asked them: 'If it was up to you alone, where would you most like to be five years from now?' The answers confirm again that MPs are very much focused on the level at which they are currently serving. Only a minority of respondents imagine their future career in an assembly—or government—at a different level. However, among these, the traditional linear and unidirectional move from regional to national parliament seems to be the slightly more favoured option. Indeed, less than 10 per cent of national representatives see a regional office in their near future, while among regional MPs, fifteen have an ambition to be at the national level in five year's time. Regional MPs also mention more often a career position at a lower level, like the local municipalities of provinces, or simply see their career ending.

TABLE 10.5 *MPs' most preferred position for their future (in %)*

	National parliament	Regional parliament	National government	Regional government	Other*
National MPs only	66	4	17	5	8
National MPs prev. regional exp.	64	7	19	6	4
Regional MPs only	11	56	2	18	13
Regional MPs prev. national exp	13	46	3	10	28

* This category includes positions at the local level and retirement from public office.

The findings presented until now thus show that no clear difference is made by the types of careers MPs have on the attitudes, behaviours, and aspirations of members of regional and national parliaments in multilevel systems. These findings can be confirmed with a multivariate analysis, presented in Tables 10.6 and 10.7. We have used two dependent variables: the attitude on devolution of powers and the focus of representation (representing the interest of the region as a whole). For each analysis we have entered the type of parliament (regional or national) and the career pattern as independent variables. Both models also control for one party variable (belonging to the government or to the opposition), one systemic variable (the average degree of autonomy of the regions in the country of the MP), and one individual variable (seniority). The latter is measured as the year of first election to the parliament of which he or she is now a member.

The results shown in Table 10.6 for the preferences on the distribution of powers are consistent with our previous mono-variate analyses. Career patterns are not a viable explanation for different opinions on the extent of regional self-government. It is, on the contrary, the level of government at which an MP works that is the strong predictor of his or her views on decentralization. Regional MPs are, on average, more favourable to regional self-government than national MPs are, irrespective of their previous experience as representatives at the other level. Among the other control variables, seniority turns out to be non-significant, as well as the fact of sitting with the majority or with the opposition. The extent of regional policy powers is, however, a significant predictor of our dependent variable: the larger the scope of regional government, the higher the demand for more regional self-rule from MPs. This means that especially regional MPs in regions with a higher degree of autonomy are more in favour of even greater autonomy.

We have run a similar regression analysis on the territorial focus of representation, meaning the importance for MPs to concentrate on the promotion of the collective interests of the region from which they are elected (Table 10.7). The most important result, for the sake of the present discussion, is the fact

TABLE 10.6 *Predicting the views on the extent of decentralization (OLS unstandardized regression coefficients)*

	B	Std. Err.	Sig.
(Constant)	7.731	0.658	0.000
Career pattern (1 = multilevel)	0.143	0.259	0.553
Seniority (1 = newcomer)	0.007	0.161	0.965
Type of parliament (1 = regional MP)	-2.596	0.240	0.000
Ruling party (1 = yes)	-0.148	0.163	0.363
Extent of regional policy powers	-0.630	0.162	0.000

Dependent variable: extent of decentralization (0: more power to the regions—10: more power to the state). Rsq = 0.135. N = 1,057.

TABLE 10.7 *Predicting the views on the importance for the MP to represent the collective interests of the region (OLS unstandardized regression coefficients)*

	B	Std. Err.	Sig.
(Constant)	6.506	0.301	0.000
Career pattern (1 = multilevel)	0.008	0.118	0.944
Seniority (1 = newcomer)	0.123	0.078	0.115
Type of parliament (1 = regional MP)	0.165	0.112	0.141
Ruling party (1 = yes)	0.262	0.079	0.001
Extent of regional policy powers	-0.296	0.074	0.000

Dependent variable: importance of promoting the collective interests of the region (1: of no importance—7: of great importance). Rsq = 0.074. N = 938.

that having a single-level or a multilevel career pattern does not affect the dependent variable. This confirms some of the findings we have shown above, and it would basically mean that MPs, either at regional or at national level, first and foremost aim to represent the interests of the political territory of the assembly in which they are sitting (those of the region or those of the country). National MPs who have been previously elected at regional level are not paying more attention to regional interests, nor are regional MPs previously sitting in a national assembly more concerned with the national interest. Again, career socialization has no significant effect; what matters is where you are serving at the time of the survey.

10.4 CONCLUSION

This chapter focused on two research questions. We first explored different career patterns between legislatures in states where a regional level of government exists. Seven such countries are included in the analysis, adding up to 1,175 national and regional MPs. A recent stream of political science literature argues that regional parliaments are not necessarily conceived as springboards for national political careers. While this might be true for some specific contexts (see, for instance, Stolz 2011 on Scotland and Catalonia and Oñate 2013 for different regions in Spain), our findings support a more traditional view. To a large extent, regional and national legislative assemblies appear to be separate, alternative arenas with a limited number of exchanges between them. In our sample, about 88 per cent of MPs did not move from one level to the other. Among the remaining 12 per cent of level-hoppers, the traditional way 'up the ladder', from regional to national parliament is followed much more often than the opposite route: 18 per cent of national MPs have a regional background, while only 6 per cent of regional MPs have previously sat at national level.

At this stage, we can only try to put forward some tentative interpretations of these results. As we recalled in the initial pages of this chapter, career patterns have been explained as a combination of availability, accessibility, and attractiveness of offices (Borchert 2011). The question is therefore whether these three A's may account for the limited movement we observe across levels. First, availability does not seem to be the explanation of the relative impermeability of the different levels. Availability is obviously greater at regional level than at the national one. In all the countries covered in this chapter there are more seats available in regional than in national assemblies. Yet, we do not observe that it has an effect on career patterns by leading many national MPs to move to regional parliaments. Accessibility and attractiveness should then be considered more likely to shape individual career ambitions, and thus prevalent career patterns. And what we can derive from our data is that accessibility of both regional and national offices (i.e. their costs) is generally perceived as being lower than their attractiveness (i.e. the benefits one can get from reaching them). That is to say, the risks of running for office at a different level from the one in which the MP is currently sitting seem to be higher than the expected benefits in terms of career advancement. This calculus could be an explanation for the few moves we observe across levels. The general picture, however, should not hide considerable cross-country differences.

The second goal of this contribution focused on the consequences of different career patterns on the opinions and attitudes of elected representatives. In particular we analysed MPs' views on the extent of decentralization and their perception of the importance of the region as a focus of representation. Quite interestingly, the type of career (whether single- or multilevel) does not appear to shape in any way MPs' positions on these issues. In other words— and this is the most relevant finding of this chapter—the level of government where a MP is currently serving is more important than the previous trajectory of his or her political career. And this is true both for senior and newly elected representatives. This finding confirms what is observed in other chapters of this volume: institutions are central in understanding how elected representatives think and act. They seem to have stronger effects than other elements like, in the case of our chapter, the previous positions held by the legislator throughout his career. From a more theoretical point of view, that would confirm the relevance of an institutionalist approach over explanations related to a socialization effect. The attitudes of MPs in multilevel systems are better explained by the assembly in which they are elected than by their previous experiences at other levels of power.

NOTES

1. The concept of 'level-hopping' was first coined by Fiers (2001). See also Pilet, Fiers, and Steyvers (2007).
2. This does not mean, of course, that single regions within countries cannot represent significant deviation from the most common direction, as documented, for instance, by Stolz (2003) and Oñate (2013).
3. Although this result should be interpreted with caution, as only twelve valid cases are included in this category for this question.

REFERENCES

Berkman, M. (1994), 'State Legislators in Congress: Strategic Politicians, Professional Legislatures, and the Party Nexus', *American Journal of Political Science*, 38: 1025–55.

Best, H. and M. Cotta (eds.) (2000), *Parliamentary Representatives in Europe 1848–2000*. Oxford: Oxford University Press.

Borchert J. (2011) 'Individual Ambition and Institutional Opportunity: A Conceptual Approach to Political Careers in Multilevel Systems', *Regional and Federal Studies*, 21 (2): 117–40.

—— and K. Stolz (2011), 'Introduction: Political Careers in Multilevel Systems', *Regional and Federal Studies*, 21 (2): 107–15.

Converse, P. and R. Pierce (1979), 'Representative Roles and Legislative Behavior in France', *Legislative Studies Quarterly*, 4 (4): 525–62.

Cotta, M. and H. Best (eds.) (2007), *Democratic Representation in Europe*. Oxford: Oxford University Press.

Detterbeck, K. (2012), *Multi-Level Party Politics in Europe*. London: Palgrave MacMillan.

Eulau, H. and P. D. Karps (1977) 'The Puzzle of Representation: Specifying Components of Responsiveness', *Legislative Studies Quarterly*, 2 (3): 233–54.

226   *Representing the People*

—— and J. C. Wahlke (1978), *Legislative Bodies: Representative Government and Representation*. London: Sage.

Fabre, E. (2008), 'Party Organization in a Multi-level System: Party Organizational Change in Spain and the UK', *Regional & Federal Studies*, 18 (4): 309–29.

Fiers, S. (2001), 'Level-Hopping in a Multi-Level Political Landscape: Political Careers in Belgium and France', unpublished paper, ECPR Joint Sessions of Workshops, Grenoble.

Francis, W. and L. Kenny (2000), *Up the Political Ladder: Career Paths in US Politics*. Thousand Oaks, CA: Sage.

Gaxie, D. (1993), *La démocratie représentative*. Paris: Montchrestien.

Herrick, R. (2011), 'The Effects of Political Ambition on Legislative Behavior: A Replication', *Social Science Journal*, 38: 469–74.

Hibbing, J. (1991), *Congressional Careers*. Chapel Hill: University of North Carolina Press.

Hubé, N. and L. Verzichelli (2012), 'Ready to Run Europe? Perspectives of a Supranational Career among EU National Elites', in H. Best, G. Lengyel, and L. Verzichelli (eds.) *Europe of the Elites: A Study into the Europeanness of Europe's Economic and Political Elites*. Oxford: Oxford University Press, 43–66.

Marks, G. and L. Hooghe (2001) *Multi-level Governance and European Integration*. Oxford: Rowman and Littlefield.

Matthews, D. (1985), *Legislative Recruitment and Legislative Careers*, in G. Loewenberg, S. C. Patterson, and M. Jewell (eds.), *Handbook of Legislative Research*. Cambridge, MA: Harvard University Press.

Moncrief, G. and J. Thompson (eds.) (1992), *Changing Patterns in State Legislative Careers*. Ann Arbor: University of Michigan Press.

Norris, P. (1997), *Passages to Power: Legislative Recruitment in Advanced Democracies*. Cambridge: Cambridge University Press.

Oñate, P. (2013), 'Moving Up, Moving Down: The Parliamentary Elite in Spain: Political Arenas and Political Classes', in G. Lachapelle, W. Grant, and P. Oñate (eds.), *Handbook in New Regionalism and Multi-Level Governance*. New York: Routledge.

Pilet, J.-B., S. Fiers, and K. Steyvers (2007), 'Des élus multi-niveaux: Carrière politique et recrutement des élites en Belgique', in A. Faure, J.-P. Leresche, P. Muller et al. (eds.), *L'action publique à l'épreuve des changements d'échelle*, Paris: PUF, 114–24.

Schlesinger, J. (1966), *Ambition and Politics*. Chicago: Rand McNally.

Squire, P. (1988), 'Career Opportunities and Membership Stability in Legislatures', *Legislative Studies Quarterly*, 13: 65–82.

Stolz, J. (2003), 'Moving Up, Moving Down: Political Careers across Territorial Levels', *European Journal of Political Research*, 42 (2): 223–48.

Stolz, K. (2011), 'The Regionalization of Political Careers in Spain and the UK', *Regional and Federal Studies*, 21 (2): 223–43.

Schmitt, H. and J. Thomassen (eds.) (1999), *Political Representation and Legitimacy in the European Union*. Oxford: Oxford University Press.

The Institutional Constraints of Representation

Kris Deschouwer and Sam Depauw

11.1 THE DISCUSSION ON REPRESENTATION

The inspiration for the PARTIREP MP survey and for this book was the current discussion on the crisis of democratic political representation (see chapter 1). The general feeling is indeed that something is wrong. Central institutions of representative democracy, like parliaments and political parties, are not being trusted by the citizens. Parties who should structure the democratic dialogue face a volatile electorate and are losing members. Parties that criticize the functioning of representative democracy have successfully challenged the traditional governing parties. The latter face difficulties in delivering the promised policies to their voters because they also need to be responsive to other agents like international organizations, the European Union in particular (Mair 2009).

This rather gloomy picture about the health of representative democracy is well known. It obviously needs to be nuanced and qualified, but it is certainly the picture that is in the mind of many political commentators and political scientists. They point especially at the role played by political parties. Parties are indeed the central actors in today's democracy. Political parties select the candidates that run for election. Parties offer the potential voters a choice between different policy packages. Parties form governments and represent the country in the international forums. Modern democracy is party democracy. Parties are crucial, yet citizens do not like them.

It is against this background that candidates selected by parties need to seek election and re-election. One possible consequence of the increasingly bad press for political parties could then be attempts by candidates and by representatives to take some distance from their party and to stress their own personal convictions and track record more than that of the party. This is the process that is referred to as the 'personalization' of politics (Karvonen 2010; McAllister 2007; Colomer 2011). The concept covers a variety of meanings, but when it refers to the choices made by politicians, it does refer to the attempt to present oneself as being distinct from the party (van Holsteyn and Andeweg 2010). It actually suggests that candidates and representatives have the possibility to make their own choices, to decide what they want to say and what they want to do to increase their chances of being elected, rather than rely on the one-size-fits-all party label, party programme, party proposals, and party track record. This fits quite well into the recent developments and debates in the literature on representation. That literature has stressed the fact that representation is much more than its formal mechanism, that it is a complex and multi-faceted phenomenon. It has called attention to the creative and dynamic aspect of representation, where agent and principal and their interests are not given but are being created in the process of searching for the appropriate and legitimate linkage between the represented and the representatives (e.g. Mansbridge 2003; Saward 2006). It has expanded the scope of the research to non-elected representation and to the representation of animals and nature (Saward 2008; Eckersley 2011).

We have, however, limited our attention to representatives who have been elected according to the formal rules of parliamentary representation. We have tried to understand how they function in this world in which their activities are being questioned and criticized, in a world in which the centre of power is shifting, in a world where the trust and the loyalty of the voters is low. We have asked them how they perceive their role, how they define their focus and style of representation, how they seek and keep contact with their voters, how they campaign, how they use (or are used by) the media, how they interact with other members of parliament, whether they move between levels of government, and whether they vote according to the party line and why. Each chapter has focused on one or more of these topics. We have treated them as the dependent variables, because we wanted to see to what extent the choices made by members of parliament are choices indeed. We have interviewed MPs in fifteen countries and in seventy-three assemblies, which has allowed us to check in a very systematic way whether variation in modes of representation can be explained by the variation in institutions.

The findings of this project as reflected in the chapters of the book are fairly clear: representation by MPs depends on *where* they are.

Each chapter has offered country statistics for the variables under study. And for each of these the first conclusion was always that there was a strong variation between countries. Personal vote-seeking is the dominant campaign strategy in Ireland and Poland, while it is almost absent in Norway and in the Netherlands. Members of parliament in France and Italy have far fewer good contacts with colleagues from other parties than MPs in Switzerland or Portugal. Almost one third of the MPs in Belgium report that they go to the weddings of their constituents, while those in Switzerland or the UK hardly engage in that kind of activity. There are intense interactions between MPs and the media in the Netherlands, while these are fairly limited in France. These are just a few of the many examples of cross-country variation.

When institutional variables are entered into the models, the variation between countries turns into a variation between institutional rules and procedures. Representation differs between different electoral systems. Representation differs between unitary and federal-type states and between levels of government. And representation has a different meaning depending on the party to which a member of parliament belongs. Party, electoral system, and level of government are indeed the three most important sources of variation. In the following paragraphs we will recall and summarize the findings for them.

11.2 STILL THE PARTIES

Representation by elected politicians in parliamentary assemblies is representation by political parties. That is not only the normative expectation of the party democracy model; it is also an empirical fact. Political parties are the main actors and are the unit of action for individual MPs. Therefore it is and remains useful and meaningful to treat political parties as unitary actors when describing and analysing political representation and party government. One of the very important rules of the game for party democracy is the unified action of party members in parliament. Van Vonno et al. have shown in chapter 6 that if members of a party group normally vote in a coherent way, this is to a large extent the result of the fact that they believe that this is the way in which they should behave, even if they disagree with the party line. 'They did so voluntarily because they acknowledged the importance of party unity for parliamentary government. They accepted party unity as part of their role conceptions as elected representatives' (section 6.3.2). Individual MPs do find themselves in a difficult situation once in a while, when the requirement for party unity conflicts with their own opinion or with their willingness to keep some distance from the party line. The end result of the conflict—if conflict there is—is generally another familiar display of party unity.

It does matter, however, to which party an MP belongs. And here the distinction between governing and opposition parties appears to be important, a finding that is again very much in line with the expectations of a functioning party democracy. MPs of governing parties more often report a conflict between the party line and their own opinion. That is no surprise: governing parties—especially when the government is a coalition—need to be more pragmatic, need to accommodate each other, and need to comply with demands from agents other than their voters. Yet when parties are in government, they also display more unity.

Members of parliament know how the game is played. When they belong to a party they agree with the party line, and if they do not agree, they know that they have to accept the choices made by the party. At the very end of that chain lies the possibility of the party imposing discipline. Parties are after all the main selectorate of the candidates for the next election. And the larger the party control over the nomination process, the more MPs perceive their representation role as one defined by the party. The latter has also been nicely illustrated by Dudzińska et al. in chapter 2. The way in which parties select the candidates influences the focus of representation: 'The stronger the organizational power of the party organization over the selection and nomination process, the more parties are able to push MPs towards a party focus. If parties define the list order and if the voting rules do not allow voters to choose a particular person, a partisan focus of representation is more likely' (section 2.6).

The difference between belonging to a governing party and to an opposition party has appeared in several places in the book. Midtbø et al. for instance have found in chapter 9 that MPs of governing parties have less intense contacts with the media. That is another indicator of the way in which legislators understand and accept that the representational function is not an individual choice, but a role for which the script is written by the institutional context in which it has to be fulfilled. Their party is a very important part of that context. When that party belongs to a coalition government or to a minority government—so Jenny et al. have shown in chapter 7—the frequency of contacts with MPs from other parties is higher and the scope of them is broader.

The party government model not only implies that parties are unitary and united actors, it also assumes that the party line with which individual MPs have to comply is not merely a matter of short-term strategic positions like being in office or not. It actually mainly refers to longer-term choices that reflect the party ideology, the party's commitment to values and to the interests and identities of specific groups in society. Caramani et al. have focused on this in chapter 3. The development of political parties and the mobilization of voters along the lines that divide groups in society is the foundation of party democracy. The cleavage base of parties makes the dialogue between people and government meaningful and relatively predictable. Voters know what parties will do and parties know who their voters are and what their interests and demands are. The decline of group-based politics is therefore seen as one of the major developments that puts the model of party government and of partisan democratic representation under stress (Dalton et al. 1984; Franklin et al. 1992; Kriesi

1997). Analysing the way in which MPs reach out to their voters, Caramani et al. leave no doubt about their conclusion: 'Group-based strategies are still of major importance in political parties' endeavours for establishing responsiveness to societal concerns. This is the case notwithstanding the massive party de-alignment, the de-structuring of traditional cleavages and the emergence of the volatile voter' (section 3.5). Group-based politics has not disappeared. To the contrary: it is still there and it has reached out to new groups. While 'old' groups like class remain a very important focus of representation for members of parliament, new groups like age groups and women have been added to the repertoire. Caramani et al. add another argument to the statement that parties are and remain a prominent framework within which to organize political representation. When looking at group representation, they clearly find that parties of the left, that is, MPs belonging to parties on the left, are more inclined to represent groups, both old and new groups.

One of the central conclusions of this book, and a common thread throughout the chapters, is that parties shape the way in which members of parliament perceive and fulfil their representational role. That should actually not be a great surprise. The evidence about parties becoming less important in politics is evidence about the party on the ground (Katz and Mair 1995), about membership, about party identification among voters. Parties are, however, and more than ever the organizations that control government and that control the actions of the elected legislators in parliament. By looking at the parties in parliament, we have looked at the place where they remain the major players. The lack of trust in political parties suggests that although this major place is the logical consequence of the way in which democratic representation is organized—with parties participating in elections—it faces a real problem of legitimacy. We have measured and confirmed what is simply built into the institutions. 'Institutions induce the type of roles they are built for' (Dudzińska et al. section 2.6).

The lack of trust in and legitimacy of political parties might lead to a strategy in which the members of parliament and the candidates for election or re-election try to appeal to the voters by stressing their personal characteristics rather than that of the party. We do not have the data for showing an increase in that type of strategy. We have, however, found that the extent to which MPs prefer to stress their person above their party can be explained by—once again—the institutional setting in which they make their choices. It is in the first place the way in which MPs are elected that explains their degree of personal vote-seeking. The electoral system not only shapes the parties and the party system, it also shapes political representation. Thanks to the wide variety of electoral systems used in the seventy-three parliaments studied, this project has been able to confirm a number of patterns in this respect and to refine them.

11.3 THE ELECTORAL SYSTEM

Electoral institutions shape elected representatives' behaviour both in the district and in the legislative arena. Whatever further career goals representatives may have, they value re-election. Some are policy advocates; some look after the district; and others seek to climb the greasy pole (Searing, 1994). But first they seek re-election and their behaviour is shaped by the institutions that they compete under in order to be returned to parliament. On the one hand, elections serve to select representatives. On the other hand, the risk of being voted out next time makes representatives act in a particular manner (Mansbridge 2003, 2009). *Ceteris paribus*, elected representatives will do what they believe voters will reward and will refrain from doing what they will not. Central to the debate is the tension between collective accountability and accountability at the level of the individual elected representative (Carey 2009). Collective accountability operates through political parties and is frequently linked to PR electoral systems. Individual accountability, by contrast, suggests that elected representatives have more than one—competing—principal; in addition to the party they are accountable to the constituency (or some part thereof). That is, being responsive to this (sub) constituency might win them a personal vote that can make the difference between re-election and defeat at the polls (Carey and Shugart 1995). Individual accountability of this kind is frequently linked to single-seat districts but need not be.

Electoral institutions matter. They matter for the choices elected representatives make as to who are their principals and how they are responsive to them. Elected representatives, it seems, have some discretion in choosing who to represent but their choices are constrained by the electoral institutions (Saward 2010). Dudzínska et al. demonstrate in Chapter 2 that elected representatives favour the constituency more as the focus of representation under majoritarian than under PR electoral formulae. They do not primarily think of themselves as constituency delegates, however, but rather as trustees juggling the preferences of multiple principals. In PR systems elected representatives tend to focus less on the constituency and act less as a constituency delegate. They turn more to the party, but also to specific groups in society in high-magnitude constituencies. Group representation of old and new cleavages, Caramani et al. point out in chapter 3, grows more important with district population, which is highly correlated with how the electoral institutions define constituencies. A division of labour emerges in large constituencies among co-partisans representing different groups. In particular the representation of women benefits from PR electoral formulae, Erzeel et al. agree in chapter 4. Not only are there more women elected under PR than under majoritarian electoral formulae. They also act more on behalf of women in particular in preferential systems where they may benefit from women's preference votes.

There is frequently a tension between what is in the interest of the party and what is in the interest of the individual representative, when he or she faces competing principals (Carey 2009). More elected representatives prefer running a personal campaign, rather than a party campaign, under majoritarian rather than under PR electoral formulae, André et al. demonstrate in chapter 5. More importantly, running a personal campaign is more important in strong preferential systems than in non-preferential systems. Mixed-member systems generate mixed incentives based on whether representatives stood as candidates in the district and/or on the party list (rather than whether they were elected as district or list members) and fall somewhere between the two, as do weak preferential systems. This incentive to win a personal vote governs their behaviour both in the district and in the legislative arena. While representatives in preferential systems do not agree more often with the party line than in non-preferential systems, or feel more often they should defer to the party line even if they disagree, they do feel party discipline could be less strict in particular in high-magnitude constituencies—van Vonno et al. point out in chapter 6. There is a distinction, they argue, between the formal properties of electoral institutions and how elected representatives understand the incentives they generate. Representatives who actively cultivate a personal vote disagree more often with the party line; and when they disagree, they are less likely to defer to the party line out of loyalty. They do feel strongly that party discipline could be less strict when they are being responsive to their personal constituency. André et al. further demonstrate in chapter 7 that ballot structure affects representatives' constituency orientation. In preferential systems more are constituency members as district magnitude grows, but in non-preferential systems more are policy advocates as district magnitude grows.

Electoral institutions matter. But we are frequently less adamant as to why they matter—that is, about the causal mechanism underlying the empirical interrelations we observe (Shugart 2008). In elections constituents get to select the representatives that match their preferences and expectations. Particular electoral institutions may be related to constituency members, party delegates, or representatives of minority groups because that role corresponds to the cultural preferences and expectations shared by constituents and representatives alike (Saward 2010). More women for instance, Erzeel et al. suggest, are elected under PR than under majoritarian systems and they will take up women's interests more often. Or the risk of being voted out may generate incentives for representatives to take up the roles that they believe constituents will reward. Looking at elected representatives, rather than candidates, we cannot distinguish between selection and sanction models of representation (Mansbridge 2003, 2009). We cannot be sure that electoral institutions make representatives do what they otherwise would not have done or that they make them refrain from doing what otherwise they would have done (Przeworski 2004). The evidence that André et al. provide in chapter 7, however, tentatively suggests they might. The effect that electoral incentives have on representatives' constituency orientation is conditional on their beliefs about representation. Representatives who think of representation as translating constituents' preferences into public policy tend to look after constituents' interests irrespective of the electoral institutions they compete under. Electoral institutions that favour personal vote-seeking encourage in particular representatives who think of representation as winning citizen support for the policies they set.

11.4 THE MULTIPLE LEVELS

The countries selected for this research among members of parliament included eight multilevel states for which also members of sub-state parliaments were interviewed: Italy, Spain, Germany, Austria, Switzerland, Belgium, the UK, France, and Portugal. One of the important recent changes in the institutional architecture of politics has indeed been the creation, re-invention, or reinforcement of levels of political decision-making below the national state (Keating 2008). This revival of (attention for) regional politics has obvious consequences for the way in which the process of—partisan and electoral—political representation can be organized. This has been reflected in a large and still growing stream of research focusing on the different aspects of the representational process in federal or regionalized states where politics always involves in some way the interaction between different relevant levels of decision-making.

The research can be roughly classified into two major categories. In the first category is the analysis of elections and voting behaviour and more particularly the study of the meaning of regional elections as compared to statewide elections (Clark and Rohrschneider 2009; Jeffery and Hough 2009; Henderson and McEwen 2010). In the second category is the analysis of political parties. The way in which statewide parties organize and adapt to the multilevel setting, the way in which they respond to challenges of regionalist parties, and the way in which regionalist and regional parties behave and organize have been well researched (Detterbeck 2012; Detterbeck and Hepburn 2010; Deschouwer 2006; Libbrecht et al. 2009; Stefuriuc 2009; Meguid 2010). The way in which representatives and voters communicate with each other—the process of political representation itself—is more difficult to grasp and has remained under-researched (but see Brzinski, Lancaster, and Tuschhoff 1999a, 1999b).

That requires the representatives as the unit of analysis, and that is exactly where the PARTIREP MP survey has been able to gather new information. Is representing the people something that is being perceived, thought, and done differently depending on the level of government?

The answer given in many places in this book is positive. The type of political system—unitary or decentralized—and the level of government have been entered into the analytic models as independent variables that might explain the choices made by representatives. And controlling for the size of the parliaments, for the electoral formulae, and for the size of the districts, regional representatives appear to differ from statewide representatives in a number of ways.

The first finding is probably the most obvious. Members of regional parliaments have a stronger focus on smaller territories and on specific groups in society (see especially chapters 2, 3, and 10). While we control for the size of the assemblies and districts, this shows that regional parliaments are closer to the people and deal with issues other than the 'high politics' of the national state. Erzeel et al. have presented in chapter 4 a very strong effect of the level of government on the degree in which the interests of women are being represented. They expected this effect because many regional parliaments are relatively new parliaments where it is easier to be innovative and thus to include the interests of groups that were previously underrepresented or whose interests are not easily captured by partisan representation. Social movements—and especially the new social movements—might also find it easier to get access to the smaller regional parliaments than to the large statewide parliaments representing large populations in a large territory.

This closeness to the people is also illustrated by the analysis of constituency orientation in chapter 8. André et al. report that regional legislators are more likely to prioritize casework and project work at the constituency level compared to the national MPs. A possible explanation—so they state—is that regional parliaments have power over policies that affect more directly the citizens' day-to-day life, like social and cultural policies. And since members of regional parliaments have then a more limited ability to shape the big politics for their voters, it can be quite rewarding to look after their social and economic well-being.

When comparing between regional parliaments, they see that this inclination to provide services to the constituents is indeed related to the power of the sub-states. The regional legislators become less inclined to assume the representational role of constituency member when the extent of self-rule and shared rule is larger.

In multilevel states there is always one extra potential conflict: the question of whether the balance of power between the levels is right. Especially in the more recent federal-type states—but not only there—several of the sub-states demand an expansion of their autonomy. In chapter 10 Pilet et al.

have found a significant difference in the opinions of statewide and regional MPs in this respect. While members of the statewide parliaments defend the status quo, the members of the regional parliaments are in favour of a shift of power towards the regions. It is a difference of 2 points on a scale from 0 to 10. This raises interesting questions about the dynamics of multilevels states. There is a long and still open discussion about the extent to which a territorial re-organization of the state is a good strategy for accommodating regionalist demands (Anderson and Erk 2009). This is the so-called 'paradox of federalism'. On the one hand there is the argument in favour of devolution, in favour of granting territorial autonomy to groups who claim they have an identity that differs from the dominant culture of the state. Ignoring these demands will only make them stronger and accommodation can thus safeguard the territorial integrity of the state. The counterargument is that of the slippery slope. It says that granting autonomy to parts of the territory will give the identity claims a stronger legitimacy by institutionalizing the differences. Creating a separate political system, with an electoral competition, a parliament, and a government will then only reinforce the demands for autonomy. Especially regionalist parties would find a fertile ground in the new institutions of the sub-state (Brancati 2006). What Pilet et al. find, however, is that not only regionalist MPs defend the claims for more autonomy, but that on average all members of sub-state parliaments support more autonomy. It is evidence for the second argument in the discussion on the paradox of federalism: autonomy strengthens demands for even more autonomy.

It is certainly another piece of evidence for stating that the way in which members of parliament perceive their representational role is not very much a matter of personal choice, but to a large extent a function of the institutional setting in which the representation is being organized. Indeed, one of the strong conclusions of chapter 10 is that both the importance of the region as the focus for representation and the opinion on the balance of power in the state is determined by the level at which an MPs serves, and not influenced by the level where he or she might have served in an earlier phase of their career.

It confirms—if needed—once again the central conclusion of this book. We have analysed several aspects of representational roles, the many different ways in which MPs try to keep in touch with their voters, and the way in which they vote and behave in parliament. And for all these characteristics of political representation we have concluded that institutions matter. Modern democracy is organized as representative democracy. That representation is controlled by political parties who select candidates, run for election, and form governments. For members of parliament it matters to which party they belong. The electoral system by which the parties can elect candidates shapes the way in which they will behave if they seek re-election. And the level of government for which they have been elected strongly influences how they think and act. This form of political representation is today being questioned. Many wonder whether representation is doing what it should do and even whether it is at all able to shape democratic governance. For changing the way in which democratic representation is understood and put into practice by those elected to represent the people, the key factor is the institutional context in which parliamentary representation is deeply embedded.

REFERENCES

Brancati, D. (2006), 'Decentralization: Fuelling the Fire or Dampening the Flames of Ethnic Conflict and Secessionism?' *International Organization*, 60 (Summer 2006): 651–85.

Brzinski, J., T. Lancaster, and C. Tuschhoff (1999a), *Compounded Representation in Wetser European Federations*. London: Frank Cass.

—— (1999b), 'Federalism and Compounded Representation: Key Concepts and Project Overview', *Publius*, 29 (1): 1–18.

Carey, J. (2009), *Legislative Voting and Accountability*. New York: Cambridge University Press.

—— and M. S. Shugart (1995), 'Incentives to Cultivate a Personal Vote', *Electoral Studies*, 14 (4): 417–39.

Clark, N. and R. Rohrschneider. (2009), 'Second-order Elections versus First-order Thinking: How Voters Perceive the Representation Process in a Multi-layered System of Governance', *European Integration*, 31 (5): 645–64

Colomer, J. M. (ed.) (2011), *Personal Representation: The Neglected Dimension of Electoral Systems*. Colchester: ECPR Press.

Dalton, R., S. C. Flanagan, and P. A. Beck (eds.) (1984), *Electoral Changes in Advanced Industrial Democracies: Realignment or Dealignment?* Princeton, NJ: Princeton University Press.

Deschouwer, K. (2006), 'Political Parties as Multi-level Organizations', in R. Katz and W. Crotty (eds.), *Handbook of Party Politics*. London: Sage.

Detterbeck, K. (2012), *Multi-Level Party Politics in Western Europe*. London: Palgrave Macmillan.

—— and E. Hepburn (2010), 'Party Politics in Multi-level Systems: Party Responses to New Challenges in European Democracies', in J. Erk and W. Swenden, *New Directions in Federalism Studies*. London: Routledge, 106–25.

Eckersley, R. (2011), 'Representing Nature', in S. Alonso, J. Keane, and W. Merkel, *The Future of Representative Democracy*. Cambridge: Cambridge University Press, 236–57.

Erk, J. and L. Anderson (2009), 'The Paradox of Federalism: Does Self-Rule Accommodate or Exacerbate Ethnic Divisions?' *Regional and Federal Studies*, 19 (2): 191–202.

Franklin, M. N., T. T. Mackie, and H. Valen (eds.) (1992), *Electoral Change: Responses to Evolving Social and Attitudinal Structures in Western Countries*. Cambridge: Cambridge University Press.

Henderson, K. and N. McEwen. (2010), 'A Comparative Analysis of Voter Turnout in Regional Elections', *Electoral Studies*, 29 (3): 405–16.

Jeffery, C. and D. Hough (2009), 'Understanding Post-Devolution Elections in Scotland and Wales in Comparative Perspective', *Party Politics*, 15 (2): 219–40.

Karvonen, L. (2010), *The Personalization of Politics: A Study of Parliamentary Democracies*. London: ECPR Press.

Katz, R. and P. Mair (1995), 'Changing Models of Party Organisation and Party Democracy: The Emergence of the Cartel Party', *Party Politics*, 1 (1): 5–28.

Keating, M. (2008), 'Thirty Years of Territorial Politics', *West European Politics*, 31 (1–2): 60–81.

Kriesi, H. (1998), 'The Transformation of Cleavage Politics: The 1997 Stein Rokkan Lecture', *European Journal of Political Research*, 33: 165–85.

Libbrecht, L., B. Maddens, W. Swenden et al. (2009), 'Issue Salience in Regional Party Manifestos in Spain', *European Journal of Political Research*, 48 (1): 58–79.

Mair, P. (2009). 'Representative versus Responsible Government', working paper, Max-Planck Institute for the Sudy of Societies. Köln. Available at <http://www.mpifg.de/pu/workpap/wp09-8.pdf> accessed 11 December 2013.

Mansbridge, J. (2003) 'Rethinking Representation', *American Political Science Review*, 97: 515–28.

—— (2009), 'A "Selection Model" of Political Representation', *Journal of Political Philosophy* 17 (4): 369–98.

McAllister, I. (2007), 'The Personalization of Politics', in R. Dalton and H. D. Klingemann (eds.), *Oxford Handbook of Political Behavior*. Oxford: Oxford University Press.

Meguid, B. (2010), *Party Competition between Unequals: Strategies and Electoral Fortunes in Western Europe*. Cambridge: Cambridge University Press.

Przeworski, A. (2004). 'Institutions Matter?' *Government and Opposition*, 39 (4): 527–40.

Saward, M. (2006), 'The Representative Claim', *Contemporary Political Theory*, 5: 297–318.

—— (2008), 'Authorisation and Authenticity: Representation of the Unelected', *Journal of Political Philosophy*, 17 (1): 1–22.

—— (2010), *The Representative Claim*. Oxford: *Oxford University Press*.

Searing, D. (1994), *Westminster's World*. Cambridge, MA: Harvard University Press.

Stefuriuc, I. (2009), 'Government Coalitions in Multi-level Settings—Institutional Determinants and Party Strategy', *Regional and Federal Studies*, 19 (7): 1–12.

Van Holsteyn, J. and R. Andeweg (2010), 'Demoted Leaders and Exiled Candidates: Disentangling Party and Person in the Voter's Mind', *Electoral Studies*, 29 (4): 628–35.

Appendix

PARTIREP MP Survey Questionnaire

This is the 'master' version of the questionnaire in English. It was translated into all the languages needed for the MPs of the seventy-three parliaments. The wording of the questions was sometimes also slightly adapted to fit into the political institutions and political cultures of the different assemblies. There were also variations within language versions (e.g. the Dutch in Belgium and the Netherlands and the German in Germany, Austria, and Switzerland) to accommodate the different countries.

Another important differentiation was between levels of government. There were three—largely overlapping—versions of the questionnaire: one for MPs in statewide parliaments of unitary countries (NU), one for statewide parliaments in multilevel states (NM) and one for regional parliaments (RM). Each question mentions with these codes the level for which it was used.

We would like to start off with a number of questions about the workings of Parliament in general and the responsibilities of a Member of Parliament.

QUESTION 1. For each of the following tasks, how satisfied are you with [insert name of Parliament] and its members' performance?

NU NM RM

(*Please tick one box in each row*)

	very unsatisfied	fairly unsatisfied	rather satisfied	very satisfied
1. in scrutinizing the government	☐	☐	☐	☐
2. in representing the views and interests of the voters	☐	☐	☐	☐
3. in doing legislative work	☐	☐	☐	☐

QUESTION 2. The following question is about day-to-day practice in the [insert name of parliament]. Thinking of your fellow members of the [insert name of parliament], would you say that the following statements are true or false?

NU NM RM

	false	mostly false	neither	mostly true	true
1. members frequently question another member's sincerity and integrity in public	□	□	□	□	□
2. in private, it is not uncommon for women's competence to be questioned	□	□	□	□	□
3. members are mostly preoccupied with local issues	□	□	□	□	□
4. the parliamentary party spokesperson gets to determine the party's position on his/her topics	□	□	□	□	□
5. members frequently contact the media on a topic for which another member of that party is the party's spokesperson	□	□	□	□	□
6. usually confidential party discussions find their way to the media	□	□	□	□	□
7. members frequently take parliamentary initiatives without the parliamentary party's authorization	□	□	□	□	□

QUESTION 3. What do you yourself consider the most important task you fulfil as a Member of Parliament? And what do you think is your second most important task?

NU NM RM

(*Please mark the most important in the first column, the second most important in the second column*)

	1st choice	2nd choice
1. influencing government policy	□	□
2. providing assistance to individual voters in their dealings with public authorities	□	□
3. looking after the collective social and economic needs of the local area	□	□
4. liaising between members of the parliamentary party and the party leadership and managing Parliament's business	□	□

QUESTION 4. Some Members of Parliament specialize in one or two policy areas, while others prefer to speak on a wide range of issues from different policy areas? How would you define yourself?

NU NM RM

(*Please tick one box*)

I specialize in one or two policy areas	□
I try to keep up with a wide range of issues	□

QUESTION 5. How often, in the last year, would you say you have found yourself in the position that your party had one opinion on a vote in Parliament, and you personally had a different opinion?

NU NM RM

about once a month	about every three months	about once a year	(almost) never
□	□	□	□

QUESTION 6. And how should, in your opinion, a Member of Parliament vote in this situation?

NU NM RM

(*Please tick one box*)

MP should vote according to his/her own opinion	□
MP should vote according to his/her party's opinion	□

QUESTION 7. And, how should, in your opinion, a Member of Parliament vote if his/her own opinion on an issue does not correspond with the opinion of his/her voters?

NU NM RM

(*Please tick one box*)

MP should vote according to his/her own opinion	□
MP should vote according to the opinion of his/her voters	□

QUESTION 8. How should, in your opinion, a Member of Parliament vote if his/her voters have one opinion and his/her party takes a different position?

NU NM RM

(*Please tick one box*)

MP should vote according to the opinion of his/her voters	□
MP should vote according to his/her party's opinion	□

QUESTION 9. How should, in your opinion, a Member of the regional Parliament vote if his/her regional party has one opinion and his/her national party takes a different position?

RM

(*Please tick one box*)

MP should vote according to his/her regional party's opinion	□
MP should vote according to his/her national party's opinion	□

Next are a few, more general questions about voters' trust in politics and politicians.

QUESTION 10. It is often stated that voters have lost trust in politics and politicians. Listed below are a few statements that are very commonly heard in this regard. Regarding each of these commonly heard statements, could you indicate whether you personally agree or disagree?

NU NM RM

(*Please tick one box in each row—randomized order*)

	strongly disagree	disagree	neither	agree	strongly agree
1. the state no longer possesses the necessary instruments to solve society's most pressing needs	□	□	□	□	□
2. journalists' ways of covering politics mainly focus on soundbites and conflictual issues	□	□	□	□	□
3. too many citizens fail to see that their own interest is only one of many diverging interests in society	□	□	□	□	□
4. most citizens have no clear policy preferences	□	□	□	□	□
5. political parties are not offering really different options to the people	□	□	□	□	□
6. parties make too many promises on which they cannot deliver	□	□	□	□	□

7. most politicians are out of touch with people's concerns	☐	☐	☐	☐	☐
8. politicians let their own position on political issues be determined by the campaign advisers and the polls	☐	☐	☐	☐	☐
9. politicians are more concerned with the clash of persons than with the confrontation of ideas	☐	☐	☐	☐	☐
10. special interests have too much influence on public policies	☐	☐	☐	☐	☐

QUESTION 11. In recent years, different views on voters' distrust of politicians and political parties have inspired widely diverging suggestions for reform. Of each of the following directions that reform could take, could you indicate how desirable you consider them?

NU NM RM

(*Please tick one box in each row*)

	not at all desirable	not very desirable	fairly desirable	very desirable
1. to increase the number of referendums	☐	☐	☐	☐
2. to create more opportunities for citizens to set the political agenda	☐	☐	☐	☐

3. to have the selection of candidates decided on the basis of primaries in which all party members can take part	□	□	□	□
4. to delegate more decision-making to experts and independent agencies	□	□	□	□
5. to involve interest groups in society more often in decision-making	□	□	□	□
6. to increase the number of deliberative events, where groups of regular citizens debate and decide on a particular issue	□	□	□	□

Now we would like to turn your attention to the people you speak for and on whose behalf you act in Parliament.

QUESTION 12. How important is it to you, personally, to promote the views and interests of the following groups of people?

NU NM RM

(*Please tick one box in each row*)

	of no importance					of great importance	
	1	2	3	4	5	6	7
all the people who voted for you (by preference vote)	□	□	□	□	□	□	□

all the people who voted for your party	□	□	□	□	□	□	□
all the people in your constituency	□	□	□	□	□	□	□
your party	□	□	□	□	□	□	□
a specific group in society	□	□	□	□	□	□	□
all people in the country	□	□	□	□	□	□	□

For those answering '(1) of no importance' to a specific group in society, skip Question 13.

QUESTION 13. Thinking about various groups in society, how important is it to you, personally, to promote their views and interests?

NU NM RM

(*Please tick one box in each row*)

	of no importance					of great importance	
	1	2	3	4	5	6	7
1. young people	□	□	□	□	□	□	□
2. the elderly	□	□	□	□	□	□	□
3. employees	□	□	□	□	□	□	□
4. employers and self-employed	□	□	□	□	□	□	□
5. women	□	□	□	□	□	□	□
6. farmers and fishermen	□	□	□	□	□	□	□
7. ethnic minorities	□	□	□	□	□	□	□
8. a church or religious group	□	□	□	□	□	□	□
9. other	□	□	□	□	□	□	□

Which one?

QUESTION 14. Some interests are inextricably tied to territory, for instance, because the people who live near it, are employed by a large factory or frequently use a road. How important do *you*, personally, find it to promote collective interests like these of a particular local area, and what would that area be?

NU NM RM

[This question will differ from country to country]

So, how important do you personally find it to promote the collective interests of . . .

(*Please tick one box in each row*)

	of no importance					of great importance	
	1	2	3	4	5	6	7
1. your town	☐	☐	☐	☐	☐	☐	☐
2. your electoral canton	☐	☐	☐	☐	☐	☐	☐
3. your province	☐	☐	☐	☐	☐	☐	☐
4. another geographical area	☐	☐	☐	☐	☐	☐	☐

Which one?

The next few questions will focus on how you keep in touch with the people you represent.

QUESTION 15. Mentioned below are some of the many different things that Members of Parliament do to keep in touch with constituents. For each one, do you actually do it *outside election campaign periods*, might you do it, or would you never?

NU NM RM

(*Please tick one box in each row—randomized order*)

	Actually do it					
	at least once a week	at least once a fortnight	at least once a month	at least every three months	might do it	would never
1. attending (or sending out letters on the occasion of) weddings, wedding anniversaries, and funerals in your local area	□	□	□	□	□	□
2. meeting with (small parties of) constituents in their private home to talk about their wants and needs	□	□	□	□	□	□
3. giving lectures and speaking at debate nights	□	□	□	□	□	□
4. sending out a personal newsletter and direct mailing	□	□	□	□	□	□
5. holding surgeries	□	□	□	□	□	□
6. advertising your constituency work services (e.g. in newspaper ads or by visiting neighbourhoods)	□	□	□	□	□	□

7. publicizing your successes in attracting business and obtaining government grants for the local area	☐	☐	☐	☐	☐	☐
8. meeting local businesses and action groups	☐	☐	☐	☐	☐	☐
9. featuring in the local media	☐	☐	☐	☐	☐	☐
10. other	☐	☐	☐	☐	☐	☐

(please specify)

QUESTION 16. In a typical month, how many *working hours* (incl. at public events and meetings) would you say you spend in your constituency?

NU NM RM

number of working hours per month

QUESTION 17. Roughly what proportion of this time is taken up by attending local community functions and social events in the constituency?

NU NM RM

%

QUESTION 18. How many requests for help (letters, e-mails, phone calls, visits) in dealing with public authorities do you receive in an average week? And how many inquiries from individual citizens relating primarily to policy matters do you receive per week?

NU NM RM

	number of requests per week
requests for help in dealing with public authorities	
policy-related requests	

QUESTION 19. How many hours per week would you say you, personally, spend dealing with these requests for help in dealing with public authorities?

NU NM RM

_____

_____

QUESTION 20. What do you think would happen, if you were to reduce the efforts you make in assisting voters in their dealings with public authorities?

NU NM RM

(*Please tick one box in each row*)

	strongly disagree	disagree	neither	agree	strongly agree
1. I would lose a significant number of votes as a result	□	□	□	□	□
2. I could well face a serious challenge in the candidate selection process as a result	□	□	□	□	□
3. I would lose touch with the problems voters face in their daily lives as a result	□	□	□	□	□

QUESTION 21. To retain their seat in Parliament, Members of Parliament often face hard choices. How would you choose to allocate your limited resources? Would you choose to spend more effort and money on achieving the goal on the left-hand side, would you choose to spend more effort and money on the goal on the right-hand side, or would the allocation of resources to both goals be about equal?

NU NM RM

(*Please tick one box in each row*)

	1	2	3	4	5	
1. on a personal campaign	☐	☐	☐	☐	☐	on a party campaign
2. to mobilize the party faithful	☐	☐	☐	☐	☐	to persuade floating voters and supporters of the other parties
3. to retain the support from the groups in society that have supported you in the past	☐	☐	☐	☐	☐	to seek out groups in society that haven't supported you in the past
4. to be considered a leader by voters	☐	☐	☐	☐	☐	to be considered by voters as one of them
5. to obtain the national party leadership's support	☐	☐	☐	☐	☐	to obtain the local party's support

Now we would like to ask you a few questions about the people and organizations you meet, and consult with.

QUESTION 22. In your role as a Member of Parliament, how often in the last year have you had contact with the following groups, persons, or organizations?

NU NM RM

(*Please tick one box in each row*)

	at least once a week	at least once a month	at least every three months	at least once a year	(almost) no contact
1. youth organizations	☐	☐	☐	☐	☐
2. organizations for the elderly	☐	☐	☐	☐	☐
3. workers' organizations and trade unions	☐	☐	☐	☐	☐
4. employers' organizations	☐	☐	☐	☐	☐
5. women's organizations	☐	☐	☐	☐	☐
6. farmers' organizations	☐	☐	☐	☐	☐
7. organizations of ethnic minorities	☐	☐	☐	☐	☐
8. churches or religious organizations	☐	☐	☐	☐	☐
9. environmental organizations	☐	☐	☐	☐	☐
10. journalists	☐	☐	☐	☐	☐

QUESTION 23. Parliaments are often said to be institutions that allow building bridges to *other* parties and some MPs indeed do have very good contacts also with MPs from other parties. What is the case with you? Are there other parties which include MPs with whom you have good contacts?

NU NM RM

I don't have very good contacts with MPs from other parties.	□		
I have such contacts with MPs from the following parliamentary party or parliamentary parties (please write in parliamentary party name)	. . . (Party)	. . . (Party)	. . . (Party)

For each of the contacts you mentioned, have they been helpful politically?

(*Please answer for each party separately in the column below the parliamentary party name*)

(*Multiple answers are possible*)

1. No, contacts have a purely private nature	□	□	□
2. Yes, for doing something for my local area	□	□	□
3. Yes, for understanding internal affairs of the other party	□	□	□
4. Yes, for sending informal messages to the other party	□	□	□
5. Yes, to ensure fair play between the parties	□	□	□
6. Yes, to seed ideas within the other party	□	□	□
7. Yes, to get concessions in inter-party negotiations	□	□	□
8. Yes, to start joint initiatives in parliament	□	□	□
9. Yes, to create a coalition government with another party	□	□	□
10. Yes, when in opposition, to get information about government policy	□	□	□
11. Yes, for promoting women's interests	□	□	□

QUESTION 24. And if you think of Members of the national Parliament. Are there Members of the national Parliament—in your party and of other parties—with whom you have very good contacts?

RM

I don't have very good contacts with Members of the national Parliament	□		
I have such contacts with Members of the national Parliament from the following parliamentary party or parliamentary parties (please write in parliamentary party name)	in my own party	. . . (Party)	. . . (Party)

For each of the contacts you mentioned, have they been helpful politically?

(*Please answer for each party separately in the column below the parliamentary party name*)

(*Multiple answers are possible*)

1. No, contacts have a purely private nature	□	□	□
2. Yes, for doing something for my local area	□	□	□
3. Yes, to coordinate national and regional policy	□	□	□
4. Yes, to pass on individual voters' requests for help that are related to the national level	□	□	□
5. Yes, to undertake joint initiatives and actions	□	□	□
6. Yes, to improve relations between the regions	□	□	□
7. Yes, for promoting women's interests	□	□	□

QUESTION 24. And if you think of Members of the regional Parliament. Are there Members of the regional Parliament—in your party and of other parties—with whom you have very good contacts?

NM

I don't have very good contacts with Members of the regional Parliament	□		
I have such contacts with Members of the regional Parliament from the following parliamentary party or parliamentary parties (please write in parliamentary party name)	in my own party	. . . (Party)	. . . (Party)

For each of the contacts you mentioned, have they been helpful politically?

(*Please answer for each party separately in the column below the parliamentary party name*)

(*Multiple answers are possible*)

1. No, contacts have a purely private nature	□	□	□
2. Yes, for doing something for my local area	□	□	□
3. Yes, to coordinate national and regional policy	□	□	□
4. Yes, to pass on individual voters' requests for help that are related to the regional level	□	□	□
5. Yes, to undertake joint initiatives and actions	□	□	□
6. Yes, to improve relations between the regions	□	□	□
7. Yes, for promoting women's interests	□	□	□

Next are a few questions about the initiatives you took in Parliament and what prompted you to act.

QUESTION 25. Of the initiatives (e.g. bills, written and oral questions) which you personally raised in Parliament in the last year, roughly what proportions of these did you respectively *derive from* the media, from interest groups, from within the party, from meeting with individual citizens, and from your personal experience? Could you please give a rough estimate in percentages?

NU NM RM

1. the media	%
2. interest and action groups	%
3. within the party (e.g. leadership, research centre)	%
4. meeting with individual citizens	%
5. personal experience	%
6. other	%

(Please specify)

QUESTION 26. Thinking of these initiatives, how often have you or a spokesperson informed the media about them? A rough estimate in percentages is sufficient.

NU NM RM

(out of the total of initiatives raised)	%

QUESTION 27. And how often have these initiatives that you raised actually been covered by the media? Again, a rough estimate in percentages is sufficient.

NU NM RM

(out of the total of initiatives raised)	%

QUESTION 28. There are many opinions on how citizens can most effectively influence decisions in society. Can you indicate for each of the following actions how effective you think they are, 1 being not at all effective and 7 being very effective?

NU NM RM

	not at all effective					very effective	
	1	2	3	4	5	6	7
1. boycott certain products	□	□	□	□	□	□	□
2. vote in elections	□	□	□	□	□	□	□
3. participate in public demonstrations	□	□	□	□	□	□	□
4. participate in illegal protest activities	□	□	□	□	□	□	□
5. work in a political party	□	□	□	□	□	□	□
6. contact politicians by mail	□	□	□	□	□	□	□
7. contact politicians by e-mail	□	□	□	□	□	□	□
8. sign a petition	□	□	□	□	□	□	□
9. feature in the media	□	□	□	□	□	□	□
10. work in voluntary organizations	□	□	□	□	□	□	□
11. join an Internet political forum or discussion group	□	□	□	□	□	□	□

QUESTION 29. How often do you speak at the meetings of your parliamentary party group?

NU NM RM

(almost) at every meeting	at least once a month	at least every three months	at least once a year	(almost) never
□	□	□	□	□

QUESTION 30. And how often would you say you speak at the meetings of your parliamentary party group to signal a situation in society that you consider disadvantageous for women?

NU NM RM

(almost) at every meeting	at least once a month	at least every three months	at least once a year	(almost) never
□	□	□	□	□

QUESTION 31. And how often would you say you yourself bring a proposal to your parliamentary party group to resolve such a situation in society that you consider disadvantageous for women?

NU NM RM

(almost) at every meeting	at least once a month	at least every three months	at least once a year	(almost) never
□	□	□	□	□

QUESTION 32. Generally speaking, what is your opinion about party discipline in your parliamentary party? Should it be more strict than it is now, should it remain as it is, or should it be less strict than it is now?

NU NM RM

	should be more strict	should remain as it is	should be less strict
party discipline	□	□	□

QUESTION 33. More specifically, what is your opinion about party discipline in your parliamentary party group when it comes to the following aspects?

NU NM RM

	should be more strict	should remain as it is	should be less strict
1. keeping internal party discussions confidential	□	□	□
2. taking political initiatives only with the parliamentary party's authorization	□	□	□
3. sticking to parliamentary party line in votes	□	□	□

QUESTION 34. Members of Parliament face tough choices everyday in their job. Presented below are a few of those choices you may face. For each of them, we would like to ask you for your opinion as to which choice a Member of Parliament should make.

NU NM RM

(If you agree completely with the statement on the left-hand side please indicate 1. If you agree completely with the position on the right-hand side please indicate 5)

	1	2	3	4	5	
1. politicians should translate the political views of citizens into policy as accurate as possible	□	□	□	□	□	politicians should seek support from the voters for the political views of one's party
2. in elections, politicians should account to the voters for their actions in the past	□	□	□	□	□	in elections, politicians should put their plans for the future to the voters
3. the most important policy questions should be put to the voters in a referendum	□	□	□	□	□	the representatives of the people should have the final word in all decisions
4. a Member of Parliament should hold to the party platform against competing interests	□	□	□	□	□	a Member of Parliament should compromise with competing interests

The next question is about democracy in general.

QUESTION 35. There are different opinions about what makes a country a democracy. How important would you say it is in a democracy?

NU NM RM

(Please tick one box in each row)

	not at all important	not very important	fairly important	very important
1. that the majority of the population does not override the concerns of any significant minority	□	□	□	□

2. that the same political party does not remain in power for a long period of time	□	□	□	□
3. that the state manages to solve society's problems—even if its actions sometimes cause protests	□	□	□	□
4. that the representatives of the people have the final word in all decisions	□	□	□	□
5. that organized groups in society are consulted on policy when they are concerned	□	□	□	□
6. that the electoral system allows voters, and not the party leaders, to decide who will sit in Parliament	□	□	□	□
7. that the most important policy questions are put to the voters in a referendum	□	□	□	□
8. that people be given ample opportunities to participate in public decision-making	□	□	□	□

QUESTION 36. For each of the following divisions in society, how important is it that the various groups corresponding with them are present in Parliament in proportion to their number in the population?

NU NM RM

(*Tick one box in each row*)

	not at all important	not very important	fairly important	very important
1. gender	☐	☐	☐	☐
2. age	☐	☐	☐	☐
3. region	☐	☐	☐	☐
4. social class	☐	☐	☐	☐
5. ethnic origin	☐	☐	☐	☐
6. religion	☐	☐	☐	☐
7. language (or culture) NM RM	☐	☐	☐	☐
8. other(please specify)	☐	☐	☐	☐

Now we would like to turn to your opinion about a number of topical issues.

QUESTION 37. In politics, people sometimes talk of left and right. Using the following scale, where 0 means left and 10 means right where would you place...

NU NM RM

	Left									Right	
1. your own views?	0	1	2	3	4	5	6	7	8	9	10
	☐	☐	☐	☐	☐	☐	☐	☐	☐	☐	☐
2. your party? NU	0	1	2	3	4	5	6	7	8	9	10
	☐	☐	☐	☐	☐	☐	☐	☐	☐	☐	☐
3. your regional party? NM RM	0	1	2	3	4	5	6	7	8	9	10
	☐	☐	☐	☐	☐	☐	☐	☐	☐	☐	☐
4. your national party? NM RM	0	1	2	3	4	5	6	7	8	9	10
	☐	☐	☐	☐	☐	☐	☐	☐	☐	☐	☐

5. the electorate at large NM NU	0	1	2	3	4	5	6	7	8	9	10
	□	□	□	□	□	□	□	□	□	□	□

6. the electorate at large in your region RM [Only in Belgium]	0	1	2	3	4	5	6	7	8	9	10
	□	□	□	□	□	□	□	□	□	□	□

QUESTION 38. There is always some discussion about the proper division of powers between the regional and national levels of government. Some think that more powers should go to [insert region]. Others think that more powers should go to [insert country]. Where would you place...

NM RM

	more powers to [region]			good as it is ↓			more powers to [country]		
1. your own views?	0	1	2	3	4	5	6	7	8	9	10
	□	□	□	□	□	□	□	□	□	□	□
2. your regional party?	0	1	2	3	4	5	6	7	8	9	10
	□	□	□	□	□	□	□	□	□	□	□
3. your national party?	0	1	2	3	4	5	6	7	8	9	10
	□	□	□	□	□	□	□	□	□	□	□

QUESTION 39. Some say European integration should be pushed further. Others say it already has gone too far. Where would you place your own views?

NU NM RM [Not in Norway and Israel]

has already gone too far						should be pushed further				
0	1	2	3	4	5	6	7	8	9	10
□	□	□	□	□	□	□	□	□	□	□

QUESTION 40. People hold different views on political issues. What do you think of the following?

NU NM RM

(*Tick one box in each row—randomized order*)

	strongly disagree	disagree	neither	agree	strongly agree
1. larger income differences are needed as incentives for individual effort	☐	☐	☐	☐	☐
2. government should play a smaller role in the management of the economy	☐	☐	☐	☐	☐
3. people who break the law should be given stiffer sentences	☐	☐	☐	☐	☐
4. immigrants should be required to adapt to the customs of our country	☐	☐	☐	☐	☐
5. government should make sure that films and magazines uphold moral standards	☐	☐	☐	☐	☐

QUESTION 41. And how about the following statements about women and men in society, what do you think?

NU NM RM

(*Tick one box in each row—randomized order*)

	strongly disagree	disagree	neither	agree	strongly agree
1. on the whole, women and men enjoy real equality today	☐	☐	☐	☐	☐

2. government should ensure that women and men have equal opportunities	☐	☐	☐	☐	☐
3. affirmative action is a legitimate measure to address the under-representation of women in politics	☐	☐	☐	☐	☐
4. women's organizations are no longer necessary today	☐	☐	☐	☐	☐

The final few questions are about your intentions for the future.

QUESTION 42. If you were to decide to stand at the next national elections, how confident do you feel that you would be renominated by your party?

NU

If you were to decide to stand at the next federal elections, how confident do you feel that you would be renominated by your party?

NM

If you were to decide to stand at the next regional elections, how confident do you feel that you would be renominated by your party?

RM

I would surely win the reselection contest	I would probably win the reselection contest	It could go either way	I would probably lose the reselection contest	I would surely lose the reselection contest
☐	☐	☐	☐	☐

QUESTION 43. If you were to decide to stand at the next national elections, how confident do you feel you would be re-elected?

NU

QUESTION 43. If you were to decide to stand at the next federal elections, how confident do you feel you would be re-elected?

NM

QUESTION 43. If you were to decide to stand at the next regional elections, how confident do you feel you would be re-elected?

RM

I would surely be elected	I would probably be elected	It could go either way	I would probably not be elected	I would surely not be elected
☐	☐	☐	☐	☐

QUESTION 44. Do you intend to stand in the next national elections?

NU

QUESTION 44. Do you intend to stand in the next federal elections?

NM

QUESTION 44. Do you intend to stand in the next regional elections?

RM

(In mixed-member systems)

1. district candidate	☐
2. list candidate	☐
3. both district and list	☐
4. not decided yet	☐
5. no	☐

(In all other systems)

1. yes	☐
2. not decided yet	☐
3. no	☐

QUESTION 45. If it was up to you alone, where would you most like to be five years from now?

NM RM

(*Multiple answers are possible*)

A member of the national Parliament	☐	A member of the regional Parliament	☐
A member of the national government	☐	A member of the regional government	☐
A member of the European Parliament	☐	Provincial governor	☐
Mayor	☐	Other (please specify)	☐
Retired from public life	☐		

QUESTION 45. If it was up to you alone, where would you most like to be five years from now?

NU

(*Multiple answers are possible*)

A member of Parliament	☐
A member of the government	☐
A member of the European Parliament	☐
Mayor	☐
Provincial governor	☐
Retired from public life	☐
Other (please specify)	☐

Index